LOST IN THE LAND OF OZ

Kiss Sleeping Beauty Good-Bye

LOST
IN THE
LAND OF OZ

Befriending Your Inner Orphan and Heading for Home

Madonna Kolbenschlag

1817
Harper & Row, Publishers, San Francisco

New York, Grand Rapids, Philadelphia, St. Louis
London, Singapore, Sydney, Tokyo, Toronto

FIRST HARPER & ROW PAPERBACK EDITION PUBLISHED IN 1990.

Library of Congress Cataloging-in-Publication Data
Kolbenschlag, Madonna, 1935–
    Lost in the land of Oz : befriending your inner orphan and heading
for home / Madonna Kolbenschlag.–1st Harper & Row paperback ed.
        p.   cm.
    Includes bibliographical references.
    ISBN 0–06–250495–9
    1. United States–Moral conditions.   2. Community.   3. Alienation
(Social psychology) in literature.   4. Self.   5. Social values.
I. Title.
[HN90.M6K65   1990]
307–dc20   90–4205
                                                              CIP
    ISBN 0-06-250495-9 (pbk.)

90 91 92 93 94 MCN 10 9 8 7 6 5 4 3 2 1

To the very special women and men
who have been my faithful companions
on the journey home,
and
to Gaia,
my sister, Earth

This earth is my sister;
I love her daily grace, her silent daring
and how loved I am—
how we admire this strength in each other,
all that we have lost, all that we have suffered,
all that we know;
we are stunned by this beauty,
and I do not forget:
what she is to me,
what I am to her.

Susan Griffin

Acknowledgments

Looking back, I realize this book was a decade in the making, shaped out of the events and experiences of the challenging, surprising years of the 1980s.

It would not exist if not for the women and men who have shared their stories with me along the way – in living and loving together, in the work and projects and causes we have shared, in the myth workshops and retreats I have conducted, and in the painful crises that sometimes caused their paths to cross mine. Their stories have helped me to interpret my own; their friendship has given me strength, insight, and inspiration.

I am especially grateful to my editor, Rebecca Laird, who first recognized that I had a story to tell, and to the many other Harper & Row associates who have been so helpful and affirming. A special word of thanks is due to my first reader, Mary Rehmann, whose responses to drafts kept me true to myself, and to all my friends whose support and caring helped me to survive the long months of birthing this book.

Contents

Introduction

This is a book about surviving as a spiritual orphan.

Most of us discover, as life goes on, that we are ophaned in many ways: by our family of origin, by the gender, class, and culture in which we are socialized, by systems and institutions, sometimes by our work, by traditional belief structures, and by those who are closest to us. We spend a good deal of time and energy in denying, compensating for, silencing and bribing our inner orphan. This book is about knowing and accepting that inner orphan and giving it the power to make our lives and our world creative, harmonious, and whole.

We discover our inner orphan through the myths we live by. Myths are the most powerful forces in the universe. We can be imprisoned by them, crippled by them; we can also be liberated and empowered by them. Myths tell us truths about our own experience; they mirror our personal story. But they are also revelations of a larger story that is evolving: the story of the earth-community and all its creatures, the Gaia.

Myths are timeless, boundaryless. This is a book that allows myths to play before our consciousness, like dolphins in the sea of time. It is written from the point of view of a North American woman, but it speaks through the medium of myth for many others. America itself was a myth long before it was a place, a people. It was imagined as a New World, a new beginning where orphans and refugees could build a new way of belonging to each other and to the world. Likewise the future of the world will be mythologized out of the shards of the past, long before it becomes a reality. America was and is a great laboratory for social experiment. Pieces of our story have a way of becoming part of the story of people everywhere.

For some people today the most urgent questions concern hunger and homelessness, staying alive. These are truly the abandoned ones of the earth. But many of us who are more privileged also experience a sense of abandonment and aloneness. Why?

The most urgent question for the contemporary person is not freedom or fulfillment, or the future. Ultimately, the only real question is, What does my life mean? How does it make sense? Is there a larger story, a universal myth that is unfolding and that I am living? These questions are essentially spiritual, religious questions. The answers will not be found in the usual self-help or how-to books. There are no sages or gurus, no therapists or "channels" to lead us step-by-step to our own sense of meaning, to our own gift to Gaia. And yet, there is no way we can make the journey alone. We can only go in the company of other spiritual orphans, other pilgrims.

My book, then, may seem like a contradiction, a paradox. It is a map of a journey, designed to be pondered in private; but it is also a map that can only be understood when it is shared with others. Indeed, the meaning of this book can only be interpreted by the echoes it calls forth from your own story, your own depths. Perhaps you have nothing to lose by reading it except your illusions and your aloneness. Orphans have a way of finding each other.

LOST IN THE LAND OF OZ

The Children
of Macha

Myths are like deep, ancient wells from which fresh, pure streams flow. Their constancy and persistence contradict the myriad changes that may take place in the surrounding landscape over time. In certain myths there is a truth about human experience that survives all the mutations and transformations of different eras of civilization. The waters that flow from these subterranean depths send waves of insight upward, through the tangled roots of history and the immediacy of the events in our own lives.

Once, on a visit to Northern Ireland, I stumbled across one of those ancient wells—a story that seemed to provide springs of illumination. It heightened my awareness of the singularity of our contemporary experience; namely, that what we experience in common is becoming much more significant than the unique experience of the individual. The web of life that connects us is drawing us closer together, even as we feel more and more alone. We begin to see that our personal difficulties, struggles and inadequacies are woven into a context of shared human condition that is radically flawed. The past is a gift, but it is also a curse. What may have advanced human existence in earlier times, can become—in a later era—a prescription for catastrophe.

The Celtic myth of Macha is really a cluster of tales that have survived from ancient times, a metaphor richly multivalent in its resonance with our society and the ways in which power is exercised. Originally rooted in the mythology of the mother-goddess, three dominant roles are apparent in the later fusions of the myth: Macha, the warrior and challenger to male domination; Macha, the embodiment of sexual and maternal energy; Macha, the agrarian protectress and deity. A modern laminated version of the story might go like this:

Once Ireland was ruled by three kings, who reigned alternately, each for seven years. One of the kings died, leaving a daughter, Macha, to succeed him. But when her turn came to reign, the other two kings refused to entrust royal power to a woman. She triumphed over them in battle and they were driven from the kingdom. Later after the death of one of the conquered kings, his five sons tried to claim the kingdom from Macha. She disguised herself as a leper and lured each of the five brothers into a trap, each one thinking he would take her by force and rape her. She bound each one up by turns and then brought them as her servants to her kingdom, where they assisted her in building the future capital.

Another time, Macha disguised herself as a poor peasant woman and took a young widower to be her lover and spouse. They both desired a child and she soon became pregnant. Her husband was in the habit of boasting about her prowess, and once in the presence of the Ulster court bragged about this pregnant woman who could run faster than the king's horses. The court was insulted and demanded that he prove his claim. He, not suspecting that she was more than mortal, insisted that she compete with the king's horses in a race—in spite of her plea to wait until after the birth, so as not to endanger the child. Nevertheless she accompanied her husband to the court, reluctant, but deciding "to test their hearts even as they proposed to test her legs." When no one stepped forward to cry "Stop!" she girt herself up for the race and a few minutes later flew across the finish line before the horses were barely at the halfway mark. Then, as quickly as she had run, she brought forth a set of twins. She stood before the now frightened men of Ulster with her newborn babes at her breast. She cursed the men for their cold hearts and pride, and warned them that misery and suffering as painful as the labor of childbirth would be their punishment for nine times nine generations. (Some versions of the story say that Macha died after uttering her prophetic curse. Most versions simply say she took her twins and left the land of Ulster forever.)[1]

The Celtic myth of Macha is an awesome metaphor for the wound in our contemporary civilization: a divided consciousness that abuses power and breeds all sorts of social ills, while denying the life-giving "feminine" experience and values in human society. This wound in our consciousness, in our culture, has made orphans of us all.

The myth connects with our own inner sense of disconnection and desolateness that we often repress, as well as with our own perception of contemporary events. Which of us cannot say that our trust in human goodwill and integrity was not shaken by the investigation of the Shuttle disaster, by the seamy revelations of Watergate and Contragate? And is it not easy to see in the story of Macha and her children the Soweto woman and her family, harrassed and evicted by police in the middle of the night; the Ukranian mother and her children fleeing the Chernobyl disaster; the Salvadoran refugees huddled in a camp in a strange land; the divorced single parent, struggling to work, support, and raise her children in a society that is hostile to her in the role of provider? Which of us has not been touched in some way by the AIDS epidemic, or stunned into a new awareness that personal acts have universal reverberations? We are each only a small cell in the larger living organism of our shared humanity and cosmos.

When I read this tale to an audience in Northern Ireland some years ago, they were overcome with a sense of catastrophe and guilt. It would be the same in any place where violence has been the result of the denial of our own humanity and the failure to attend to our own wholeness as a people. We all live under the threat of this curse – of a random, fateful violence that hangs over civilization like an unpaid bill.

The children of Macha are all around us. We ourselves, no matter what privileges we enjoy, are not untouched by the prevailing reality of our world – loss, abandonment, suffering, powerlessness. Here in the story of Macha is a glimpse of the root causes of our wounded world: an offense against life itself, the abuse of the maternity of creation and of the deepest caregiving, nurturing instincts in ourselves. Our own personal pursuit of happiness and fulfillment must be read against the backdrop of this larger reality.

1.

THE ABANDONED SELF

There are few things more anguished and desperate than the look on a small child's face when she has just discovered that she is lost in the cavernous aisles of a department store or a supermarket. The caretaking parent has suddenly vanished, and the child is overwhelmed with feelings of abandonment, confusion, and panic. The child may begin to cry for help in her desperation, or she may simply hide and no one will be aware of her crisis.

The "lostness" of the child, and the feelings that identify that experience, are characteristic of the human condition today. Perhaps it has always been so, but now the lostness seems more universal, more apocalyptic, and at the same time more spiritually wounding. The development of technology, the velocity of communication, the impersonal nature of public policies, the mobility of populations, the cumulative monopolies of resources and power, the changing family and corporate structures – all that we know as "modernity"– have disrupted human bonds and connections in unexpected ways and left us vulnerable. Like the small child in the department store, we are surrounded by people, processes, and products over which we have no control and from which we cannot draw strength and nourishment because we are "lost," orphaned.

Our participation in the contemporary world is intensified and accelerated by the media and by growing political and economic interdependence everywhere. Our proximity to so many and so much increases our sense of estrangement, and at the same time, our longing for kinship and familiar connections.

Perhaps we have thought of ourselves as individuals who had some degree of influence over what happens to us. Now we find ourselves caught up in the collective fate of a people and a planet. Our own anonymity and vulnerability make us as fearful of the economy as of random violence.

We look around us, hoping to find peers, companions in our confusion. Where is Everyman, the spiritual pilgrim who can tell us where the pitfalls are, how to avoid the ditch and personal disaster? In a thunderous avalanche of demographics the answer comes back: don't look in the usual place for someone to identify with. All that has changed. Everyman today is a woman, with children, uprooted from her home, making her way alone in a chaotic social environment. Her origins, her resources, her future, and her destination, are uncertain. This woman is all of us – the "have-nots" of the world, the unemployed, the homeless, the disenfranchised. Even the privileged ones – the professionals, the colonels, the elites – experience the radical abandonment and disconnection of our times. Who has not seen them struggling to anesthetize their feelings of loneliness and impotence with indulgence in affluence, celebrity, or power?

The face that stares at us from behind the barbed wire of a camp in Honduras, or from a crowded tenement room in Chicago, or from the window of a condo in Washington, D.C. is the face of our times. It is the face of the refugee, or one fleeing oppression, poverty, hunger; or perhaps fleeing oneself, and the responsibility to and for others that is the deepest expression of the human spirit.

What a contrast the image of the refugee presents when compared with the traditional image of the hero. So many of our expectations of life, of each other and of ourselves are shaped and colored by these hero-images. We draw our constellation of hero-myths from many sources today. The names of the epic heroes of the ancient myths are not as familiar to young imaginations today, but their progeny live on in Captain Kirk, Rambo, and Lee Iacocca. Our heroes are our ego archetypes, and they rush in to fill the smallest vacuum in the personal and collective psyche.

In the ancient myths the hero left his homeland in order to pursue a great cause or seek his fortune, to go in search of the Grail, perform heroic tasks, or explore the unknown. He usually returned matured and burnished by his adventures, tested by trials, ready to assume his privileged, imperial role in the feudal society. With the rise of democracy and mercantilism, a new hero appeared on the scene – the foundling. The hero was an orphan who eventually discovered his true identity as a royal person, who perhaps had been cheated out of his birthright; the heroine was an individual who, because of her virtue, "merited" improvement in her status. In the outcome of the story, the hero or heroine was integrated into a higher class and culture. We think of those fictional archetypes of Tom

Jones, Pamela, Jane Eyre, Oliver Twist. Life for these characters was a search to recover or discover what was rightfully theirs: identity, privilege, belonging to a higher class. (For women, this usually meant "marrying well"–hopefully a prince!)

In the New World, this archetypal hero story was often translated into parables of success, like the Horatio Alger stories and all of their descendants. Again the hero was a homeless, orphaned boy (less frequently an Orphan Annie). There was no "royal claim" for the hero, but hard work and frugal virtues permitted him to "merit" opportunity and success. The self-reliant "royal ego" entitled him to certain rewards.

Another popular transformation of this figure was the Western hero, often a kind of "Lone Ranger" who wandered about bringing order out of chaos and avenging villainy with swift justice. As with the "success hero," self-reliance was his trademark. Sometimes he remained a loner and an outsider; often as not, he settled down, married, and became a founding landowner or marshal of a new town in the West.

These legendary voyages, journeys, and "rises" have been models for human existence for centuries, but the patterns and motives they represent are now proving inadequate. Since the dawning of the nuclear age after World War II, we have witnessed the disintegration of the dominant infrastructure of creed, code, caste, and class that has characterized Western culture. Plurality, deep divisions, and individual options reign unchecked by the moderating forces of the extended family, religious or ethnic tradition, or the neighborhood school. We have entered the era of the "deregulated family" and the marketization of "human potential." The social fabric that insured systematic transmission of values has been torn to shreds. One obvious effect of this mythic vacuum is a vulnerability that makes us all more susceptible to the resurgence of old archetypes and stereotypes.

Inevitably the individual's understanding of herself and her social world has been distorted by events and dissipated by changing social conditions. Contemporary social arrangements seem blurred, indefinite in the atmosphere of radical autonomy which has flourished in modern Western cultures. Robert Jay Lifton tried to capture the cultural paradigm in his image of the "Protean man"– an individual who could only survive in the new era by acquiring a "polymorphous versatility" and an "uncommitted mobility," an amoebalike capacity for repeatedly willing the death and rebirth of the self.[1] It was a metaphor that seemed to make sense of the new social reality: of "fatherlessness" and the death of the superego, of the threat of unpredictable and uncontrollable human catastrophes that war and nuclear technologies had presaged, of the intrusion of the Third World and the underclasses into the protected enclaves of the privileged.

Lifton's protean metaphor described a symptomatic response – unfortunately it did not provide an adequate paradigm for behavior. It mirrored, but did not model an adaptive response to the new social reality, which has grown more urgent in its demand for a new infrastructure to replace the old.

And so we live in an acute stage of social fragmentation brought on by the myth of individualism and the rapid advance of technology and communications. The overwhelming reality is that "we are alone" and "there is no safety." We feel disconnected, unsupported, and unprotected.

It is precisely this new social reality that generates nostalgia for "the good old days." The fear of the future is directly related to the regressive politics of recent years: radical conservatism; libertarianism; vigilantism; the obsession with privacy, "national security," and domestic sovereignty. The "self-reliance" philosophy has been converted from the early American spirit of enterprise to a militant, fortressed isolationism. It should not be surprising that the new social reality spawns urban vigilantes and international Rambos. Collectively and personally we still look in the rearview mirror for our heroes, our default models for behavior. Indeed men and women today seem to be caught in between metaphors, bereft of paradigms for new ways of relating in and to a complex world.

Because symbols and metaphors are the fundamental architecture of our social arrangements they are slow to change. Indeed it is easier to change ideas and doctrines in others' minds than it is to change their myths and symbols. The heart of the myth and symbol is metaphor, and without metaphor, change is impossible. Metaphor draws the imagination into a new logic that reveals the way to a new reality.[2]

We know from our own experience, whether it is on the personal or social level, that we cope with overwhelming realities by inventing a new metaphor. For example, in order to deal with the enormity of the mass exterminations of World War II we invented the metaphor of the "holocaust" and "psychic numbing." Or, in a personal crisis such as divorce, we invent an analogy that somehow captures the pain at the same time that it reconciles us to the process – as with the image of an amputated "phantom" limb.

Scientists as well as poets and musicians speak of the metaphor as the catalyst for solving a problem, inventing a formula, or composing a symphony. Philosopher Susanne Langer has said that it is impossible to approach an unsolved problem except through the door of metaphor. Only metaphor can break through logical impossibilities, can bridge the gap between the empirical and the intuitive, between what the facts indicate and what our values and desires dictate. Metaphor gives coherence to our experience. Those who cannot give meaning to their experience through metaphor are prone to despair and breakdown.

Contemporary medicine uses metaphors to assist the body in healing itself. Moreover, metaphors shape our reality by shaping our worldview as well as our inner environment. One has only to consider the impact of such metaphors as "the survival of the fittest" and "the domino theory" to know how powerful and how easily translated metaphors are. If images and metaphors are powerful enough to restructure consciousness and physiological processes, then they are powerful enough to create social change. This is precisely the challenge of personal and social transformation: how to change the metaphors, and thus, the myths, that we live by.[3]

Whether rich or poor, privileged or underprivileged, if we have grown up in a developed society we have been saturated with expectations. From the moment we are born, our surroundings begin to tell us what we need (or should desire), what will fulfill our needs or desires, what we should expect of things, of people, of institutions, of society, of life, of ourselves. We become creatures of gargantuan expectations and an inflated false ego that must be fed.

It will not be many years until we sense the disparity between our expectations and our experience. Broken relationships, failed ambitions, or the inadequacy of our families will bring home the cruel truth. More often than not, the disparity will be experienced as a low-grade depression or a nebulous anxiety that nags us from deep in our spirit. We soon discover that the channel between our expectations and our deep feelings is clogged with pain. We know, for example, that we deserve to be loved and cared for, but we experience abandonment. We know that we need to have a sense of connectedness and belonging, but we experience loneliness and rootlessness. We know that social institutions like the Church, the corporation, the local schools, exist to enable human flourishing, but we experience deprivation within them.

Psychologist Edward Edinger has described how metaphoric symbols seep into the ego, which absorbs them and acts them out unconsciously or projects them onto the external environment. This may be harmless enough unless that individual happens to be an Adolf Hitler under the influence of a Napoleonic or Wagnerian archetype. In the mature consciousness, a kind of conscious dialogue between the ego and the emerging symbols becomes possible. The metaphor then performs its proper function as releaser and transformer of psychic energy with the full participation of the conscious understanding.[4]

If we look upon metaphors as images that acquire meaning through analogy with human existence, then at one pole of consciousness is the metaphor for the self, and at the other, the metaphor for God. In respect to the self-image, it is my contention that we are alienated from one of the most powerful metaphors, a symbolic ego archetype that mediates our experience—*the archetype of the orphan*—and that, in order to recover personal wholeness and political equilibrium, we must learn to "befriend" the orphan in each of us.

Perhaps this partially explains the astounding popularity of the musical production of Victor Hugo's *Les Misérables* for over six years. Audiences in Paris, London, and the U.S. are hypnotized and deeply touched by this story of heroic altruism, hope, and despair. From the moment that the orphan girl Cosette appears on stage, we enter into the feelings of Jean Valjean, struggling to honor a trust, to befriend and care for this "lost one"—and to befriend and redeem the orphan in himself and in society in the process. His nemesis, Javert, remains immune to the orphan as well as his own "lostness," and when the law—the "code"—fails to support his expectations, he despairs and commits suicide. Indeed, it is interesting to examine the central figures in our popular stage musicals of the last forty years and note the number of orphans that have absorbed our attention. This powerful archetype seems to be breaking through our consciousness in many art forms, and certainly in the form of biography (e.g., Eileen Simpson's *Orphans*, and Gail Sheehy's *Spirit of Survival*).

The orphan archetype is powerful because it breaks through our defenses: the denial of our pain, the refusal to acknowledge our true condition, and the inability to own our "shadow" that we project onto others. *The orphan is a metaphor for our deepest, most fundamental reality: experiences of attachment and abandonment, of expectation and deprivation, of loss and failure and of loneliness.*

We have noted that the orphan archetype is illustrated in numerous fantasy heroes of our own Anglo-American culture. But the roots of the type are much more ancient, from the Sumerians to biblical figures like Moses, Ruth, and Esther; from a pantheon of Greek gods and heroes to the

Syrian queen Semiramis; from the founder of Rome, Romulus, to the English king Arthur and the knight Tristan. There are analogues in the oriental and pre-Columbian mythologies. All of these figures shared the fate of being separated from their mothers and raised by others, deprived in some way of normal familial ties.

The orphan often suffers a profound sense of worthlessness, and at the same time a sense of being someone unique and precious. Alchemists had a curious affinity with this aspect of the orphan image. They often referred to the gem known as the lapis philosophorum ("philosopher's stone") as the "orphan stone." According to Jungian analyst Rose-Emily Rothenberg, "This stone represents the totality, or the 'one'; it corresponds to the psychological idea of the Self. . . . In one text it was known as the homeless orphan who is slain at the beginning of the process of alchemical transformation."[5] The mythology of the stone suggests an analogous biblical image that appears in both the Old and New Testaments: "The stone which the builders rejected has become the cornerstone" (Psalm 118:22; cf. 1 Peter 2:7). Scriptural exegetes have long seen this image as a symbol of the Christ and the grace of redemption, even as the alchemical orphan stone became a symbol of individuation and transformation.[6]

Like the stone that is both precious and worthless, *the orphan is an empowering metaphor because it is a self-image born of mourning.* "Development is a lifelong series of necessary losses and subsequent gains. . . . We become a mourning and adapting self, finding at every stage opportunities for creative transformations."[7] The image of the orphan can, like a stone dropped into the quiet pool of memory, stir an endless series of ripples that ricochet against the shores of our true self, a subtle current that pushes us on in the spiritual journey.

My earliest memory is an experience of being orphaned. I am standing up clutching the rail of an unfamiliar crib, anguished and crying. My parents told me later that when I was two and a half years old we went away on an extended visit to another city. My first night alone in strange surroundings was traumatic—it left an indelible groove in my infant memory. Some years later I had another experience of orphanhood, a sudden fantasy that I might actually be an orphan and didn't really belong to my parents. Now, looking back, I wonder what triggered that childhood fantasy. Had I been rejected? Was I feeling "different" from other kids, from my parents' expectations? At the time I remember looking in the mirror and realizing that I looked far too much like my parents for the fantasy to be entertained seriously.

Another time a classmate of mine who had become a good friend invited me to her house for the first time. She was very rich and lived on a huge estate, with servants and all the trappings of the affluent life. I remember the anguish of feeling "poor," of being an outsider. And I remember the feeling of loneliness, abandonment, and fear that I experienced once when I was terribly ill and confined to a hospital in a strange city. For days I had no visitors, no family, no friends. I felt lost and forgotten, that no one really cared that I existed.

Life was eventually to provide me with a generous supply of losses, catastrophes, and displacements. While the experiences were all different, they elicited the same feelings. Gradually I have learned how important it is to get in touch with these losses and befriend them – the deaths, the separations, the divorces, the failures and displacements, the handicaps and illnesses, the uprootings and transplantings. These experiences leave grooves in the soul that require healing and leaving. If we do not grieve our losses, befriend our inner orphan, we may find ourselves in a permanent state of not knowing:

- that we are lovable, loving, and loved
- that we are capable and competent
- that we belong, that we are connected
- that we can contribute, take part in shaping our world
- that we have a future
- that we can grow, be transformed
- that life has meaning.

The myth of the orphan and our experiences of being "orphaned" connect with a deep, subconscious level of our experience where the fundamental "mother lode" of our feelings originates. We begin life in a symbiotic relationship with another being, our mother, who is the source of our first experiences of pleasure, pain, security, power, and fear. All of life becomes a struggle to recover that primitive oneness of the womb and at the same time a struggle to become a separate being. We exchange that first "holding environment" for many others in a lifetime – relationships, families, institutions. These are environments in which a living organism can grow and which can, finally, be safely transcended. But even as we evolve, that original mother lode of feeling remains and becomes the parent-medium in our search for identity and intimacy. Indeed, it is the ground of a lifelong psychological amniocentesis by which we assess the quality of our holding environments, their capacity to nourish and buoy up our life project.[8]

We are all too familiar with the effects of the actual experience of being orphaned in that crucial period when the mother-child bond is formed. The deprivation of nurturance and parenting in infancy plants seeds of apathy, anger, violence, and autism. These defense mechanisms cover the effects of rejection: a deep sense of unworthiness and guilt, the fear of abandonment, self-pity, and the pull toward death. But the "motherless child" can surface in all of us – even in someone who had a "happy childhood" and enjoyed the nurturing presence of two parents.

Every parent transmits something of her "unmastered past" to her child. A mother or father can only react, respond empathically to the extent that they are free from the shadow of their own childhood. The mother's own infancy and childhood may have been deprived. Not only is the actual physical presence of a parent important, but of greater importance is the parent's availability. If the child's communication – preverbal or nonverbal, tactile or emotional – cannot reach the mother because she herself was deprived, the child will close down, repress its own distress and need. When a woman has to suppress all her own needs, they rise from the depth of her unconscious and seek gratification through her child. . . . "She herself was narcissistically deprived, dependent on a specific echo from the child that was so essential to her, for she herself [is] a child in search of an object that could be available to her."[9]

The child experiences a primordial sense of abandonment and desertion that burrows deep into the psyche while on the surface it adapts and accommodates the parent's absence. Even as adults, these deprived children will believe they had a happy childhood, with understanding parents (at least one); they have no conception of their true needs and the inadequacy of their first holding environment. This is a common underlying symptom in adult men and women who seek therapy for some other reason. The consequences of this early adaptation are critical. One consequence will be the impossibility of experiencing feelings of one's own, such as anger, loneliness, anxiety, either in childhood or adulthood. Another is often the adoption of a masked self – the true self remains immured in a state of noncommunication. A third consequence will most likely be the formation of a dependency syndrome, such as alcoholism or relational addiction.

The "orphaned" person carries the burden of these unmet needs and early deprivations into adult life. He or she will cling desperately to any person who is likely to fill the void. "He will hold on to whatever object, person or form of behavior that, to him, represents security (sex, money, etc.) until he finds the object no longer carries the same meaning for him, i.e., it no longer carries the projection of the mother. At this point, the orphan might simply discard the object of the projection or turn away, often harboring hostile feelings toward the one that did not fulfill his needs or expectations."[10]

Because the "orphaned" person feels a sense of worthiness only vicariously through the presence of another person, the need for attachment becomes vital and constant. If a mutual dependency develops, they both may become engaged in unconscious controlling behavior motives to keep each other in a symbiotic bond. Neither can leave this bond of union until the contents of their involvement can be made conscious. Sheer suffocation, abuse, or transference of feeling may cause one of the partners in the dependent relationship to attempt to sever the bond. Rothenberg describes the ensuing scenario: "This sets into motion one of the most obsessive of all the orphan's complexes, the fear of being left. This includes the ever present concern about the possibility of being left out and conversely, the need to be included constantly." The orphan has an immense fear of being left or abandoned, especially by a person who has carried the weight of the lost parent for him. "He will go to untold lengths to prevent this from happening. The fear may be quite pervasive in his life. He might even leave the other person first, in spite of his desire to stay in the relationship, just to avoid the repeated experience of being left."[11] Thus until the orphan becomes conscious of her fundamental, perhaps preconscious, deprivation and its behavioral consequences, she may constellate her original fate of being left over and over again.

Paradoxically, the orphan often exhibits a deep sense of inferiority, unworthiness, and at the same time a sense of superiority, of specialness – perhaps a feeling of being especially chosen by God or fate. This dual complex is frequently manifested, on the one hand, in symptoms of depression, and on the other hand, of grandiosity. The truly orphaned personality does not know or love his true self. He does everything to make others love him in the way he once, as a child, so urgently needed to be loved. But whatever could not be experienced at the right time in the past can never be recovered later on. As the narrator of *Unknown Woman* came to understand, "We each get only one chance to have a mother."[12]

The orphaned personality denies this reality and lives as though the lost mothering could be salvaged – "the grandiose person through the illusion of achievement, and the depressive through his constant fear of losing the self-object. Neither of them can accept the truth that this loss or this unavailability has already happened in the past, and that no effort whatsoever can ever change this fact."[13]

Thus the great imperative of life is *to encounter our own orphan self, to consciously work through our fate. Only then can we be free enough to truly love. Only then can the orphan reflexes be transformed into deep wells of creativity.*

Paul Tournier, in his book *Creative Suffering*, has elaborated on the link between deprivation and creativity. He notes the extraordinary number of orphans who have emerged in history as political leaders. Tournier draws upon the work of Dr. Andre Haynal, author of an essay on deprivation and orphanhood. Haynal writes, "I am convinced that there is a relationship between the processes of bereavement, loss, deprivation, and creativity. One cannot but be impressed by the high proportion of orphans one finds among creative artists."[14] Is it possible that dereliction is a prerequisite for grace and competence? History does not provide statistical proof, since for every one hundred famous persons who were orphans, there are probably one million who have been handicapped for life by deprivation in childhood. But the question persists. Is there something—as with the orphan stone—"both worthless and precious" about being an orphan, about suffering attachment deprivation?

We may find some insight into this question from the experience of survivors. Among those who qualify as orphans are a few hundred elderly Americans who are survivors of the "orphan trains" which transported neglected and abandoned kids from the congested East to new families and new lives in the Heartland and the West. The trains were operated by the New York Children's Aid Society and other welfare agencies from 1854 to 1929. The project was aimed at giving deprived children a new start in new surroundings. When the trains chugged into a prairie town the farm families and townspeople would "inspect the shipment" and make their choices. One survivor remembers that he and his brother were so poor they were dressed in gunnysacks and shared a single pair of boots when they arrived. While many of the orphans were rescued from literally scavenging the streets for food, many of them were subsequently abused and exploited as farm laborers. Nevertheless a 1910 survey concluded that 87 percent of the chidren sent to country homes had "done well," and had grown up to be resourceful, hard-working, civic-minded citizens. All of the survivors interviewed for a 1985 study had a number of qualities in common: they were fatalistic, strongly committed to family, very self-reliant, and many felt that they were in some way "cho-sen" or "gifted" by the accidents of their existence.[15] Perhaps this confirms Tournier's thesis that "the decisive factor in making deprivation bear fruit is love."[16]

If the orphans and hoboes stirred the imagination of the nineteenth century, another kind of survivor haunts the consciousness of the twentieth – those who have survived a nuclear blast, or the demonic hor-ror of the holocaust, famine and drought, disappearance and torture, those buried alive in gulags and prisons, the dispossessed and displaced masses in refugee camps. It is the refugee, especially, that is the invention of contemporary terror – the refugee is rendered undesirable, unwanted overnight. Homeless, without resources, without citizenship, the refugee is the ultimate consequence of selfishness, scarcity, and oppression. Today millions are herded into camps; they are the disposable waste of international politics – and there are no orphan trains for them. The refu-gee is a new species of human being, the most radically orphaned of all creatures. To be transported out of your home on a government truck one morning and put down in an uninhabited place is to be asked to build not only your own shelter but your whole life over again, from scratch.

Yet, even in this most devastating desolation, the resilience of the orphan surfaces. When I visited refugee camps in Central America I dis-covered that the displaced person seems to experience her situation in three phases. First, there is shock: a numbness born of despair and isola-tion. In the next phase, as the sense of shared fate prevails, cooperative structures begin to emerge in the camp. The people seem to transcend the notion of merely coping and acquire a sense of building for the future. Finally, as in El Salvador, some reach a consciousness that empowers them – in spite of the risk and the threats – to return to their abandoned homesites, to rebuild their lives upon their roots. The miracle of resettle-ment is an exodus reversed. From where do they draw their strength? How well I remember the look on one campesino's face when I asked him, "How do you keep going?" (He had lost his land and his country, his wife and children had been killed, his brothers had been tortured and mur-dered.) His reply to my question was simply, "Those who are not called upon to struggle are forgotten by God." Again that sense that in some strange way he had been "chosen," graced to undergo this suffering – he drew strength from that realization. But what of those who endure situa-tions in which there is no hope, in which there is unrelenting terror and misery? How does the human spirit survive?

Certainly one answer, that emerges from the experience of survivors of oppression and terror is the phenomenon of the *self-in-solidarity*. In the face of absolute tyranny, and the obliteration of self-determination and the ordinary sources of self-worth and hope, the sense of shared fate carries an amazing strength for individuation as well as for survival: "our story is my story." The self that appropriates the story of the shared history is empowered to transcend oppression and limitation. I may be no one, unable to accomplish anything, but because "our story is my story," *I am*.

Gail Sheehy documents some answers to the question of how the human spirit survives in her books *Pathfinders* and *Spirit of Survival*. In *Pathfinders* she records the common denominator in the lives of some of the most successful and satisfied adults she interviewed: most of them had endured a very traumatic period in childhood or adolescence, having endured extreme poverty or the loss of a parent through abandonment, divorce, sudden death, alcoholism, or mental illness. The deprivations seem to have enhanced their personal resilience, and they performed well beyond their years and normative expectations. Many of them, it should be noted, found a nurturing presence in the person of a mentor or model.

The refugees of the "killing fields" of Cambodia present an even more dramatic instance of survival. In telling the story of her own adopted daughter in *Spirit of Survival*, Sheehy observes:

The Cambodian children now resettled in the United States offer a fascinating study in the resilience of the human personality. All were coerced into cooperating with the forces of evil in order to survive. Either sole survivors or fugitives from families marked for death, they were raised for four years in a climate of terror and emotional apathy. Here were children separated from all normal sources of love and guidance and exposed to the most malevolent in men and women. Most were at a stage – latency – when moral development is not yet proactive, only reactive to reward and punishment, and the overriding wish at that stage is to please figures of authority. The children of Pol Pot were rewarded if they could live with horror and show no pain and compassion.

The question they bring with them is compelling: Given a recovery period in a society that offers them safety and caring and choices, might they even surpass in achievement many American children cushioned by privilege? These young survivors have much to teach us about the victorious personality.[17]

Among the qualities Sheehy observes in these extraordinary children, she notes how the very experience of knowing one has survived what seemed insurmountable provides a kind of "shield of perceived invulnerability" against future disasters in adult life. A sense of grace and luck increases their resilience and power. Each narrow escape, each instance of being in the right place at the right time, avoiding detection, seeing the bomb drop or the mine explode just behind or in front, each risk taken builds the survivor's strength and belief in herself. As Sheehy's daughter expressed it, "The more that happened to me, the more special I felt." This shield of invulnerability is often linked with a conviction that the survivor has a special work to do in the world, a special purpose to fulfill. Life has been granted to them over and over again. As one survivor put it, "It was no longer even mine: I was living, in a way, by proxy."[18]

Sheehy asks, "For children betrayed by virtually all they have been taught to trust, what can be the root of hope?" She discovered that survivors of extremity develop an extraordinary self-trust and detachment, which allows the survivor to build up a psychological immunity to long-term distress. The ability to maintain a secret inner life is paramount as well as the ability to maintain an extraordinary tolerance for ambiguity and paradox.

The orphan is a self that is born of mourning, and – if it survives – it is a tough, resilient, resourceful self. The source of that strength is represented in many ways throughout the history of the orphan hero. One of the constant themes in the orphan mythology is the intervention of, or recovery of the lost mothering-spirit in the form of magical presences or mentoring figures.

"Cinderella" offers a classic paradigm in which the orphan is tested by trials before she can merit a rescue and elevation – through marriage to the prince – to a better life. Throughout Cinderella's ordeal, the spirit of her dead mother – in the form of helpful turtle doves (or in some versions, a fairy godmother) – intervenes. Each time Cinderella confronts a crisis she retreats to her mother's grave beneath the hazel tree and pleads for her help. Each time help is granted. The mother's emissaries – the doves – also help the prince to identify his "true bride" and even carry out a final act of retribution for the abuse to Cinderella when they pluck out the eyes of the cruel stepsisters.

In "Hansel and Gretel," the children of an abusive mother are able to exorcise her evil spirit in the form of the witch and find their way back to their home and holding environment, now rid of the mean and cruel spirit which drove them out into the forest. Again, when they encounter an insurmountable obstacle in the form of a great body of water that they cannot cross, a helpful animal, a white duck, appears and ferries them across. In general, the absence of the "good mother" is so consistent a theme in the classic fairy tales that the nurturing, supportive, mothering spirit seems to be transferred to nature or to other figures – animals, dwarfs, magical creatures, or fairy godmothers.

The modern fantasy tale retains much of the ethos of the traditional fairy tale, but creates a broader spectrum of character and cultural context. Perhaps the most representative modern fairy tale of the North American culture is L. Frank Baum's *The Wizard of Oz* and the whole series of Oz adventures which succeeded his 1900 classic. In the entire Oz canon, "good mothers" are generally dead or otherwise unavailable; "bad mothers" in the form of surrogate or wicked witches seem to abound. In the Oz books, as in traditional fairy tales, mothers are generally more malevolent than fathers when they do appear. In no other American children's books, even Horatio Alger's, do there seem to be so many orphans. No human Oz protagonist ever has both parents at once. In *The Wizard of Oz* Dorothy's orphan status and the desolation of Kansas, her holding environment, is clearly established in the first paragraphs of the story:

When Aunt Em came there to live she was a young pretty wife. The sun and wind had changed her, too. They had taken the sparkle from her eyes and left them a sober grey; they had taken the red from her cheeks and lips, and they were grey also. She was thin and gaunt, and never smiled, now. When Dorothy, who was an orphan, first came to her, Aunt Em had been so startled by the child's laughter that she would scream and press her hand upon her heart whenever Dorothy's merry voice reached her ears; and she still looked at the little girl with wonder that she could find anything to laugh at.

Uncle Henry never laughed. He worked hard from morning till night and did not know what joy was. He was grey also, from his long beard to his rough boots, and he looked stern and solemn, and rarely spoke.

It was Toto that made Dorothy laugh, and saved her from growing as grey as her other surroundings.[19]

As is often the case with an author's first book, *The Wizard of Oz* is exceptionally endowed with an intuitive representation of both psychological and cultural myth – it has a power of metaphor and symbol that derives from unconscious rather than conscious design. Indeed, it is an extraordinary metaphor for transformation, and Dorothy is the classic archetype of the spiritual orphan.

Over the years I have discovered that Dorothy is one of the imaginary characters of childhood that both men and women have identified with the most. In the work that I have done with women, in the process of working through their own personal myth structure, I have been amazed at the number of times the Dorothy-script surfaces in the consciousness – sometimes in the dreams – of women in transition or undergoing a major transformation in self-image. In the therapy sessions I have conducted with women, a new paradigm emerges that helps women make sense of the shifting sands of their lives: the image of the spiritual orphan, the one who "learns by leaving and going where she has to go," for whom there are no role models and few mentors, who feels alientated from most of the systems created by the dominant male culture. In describing the "Life Stages of the Spiritual Orphan," I have combined many of the insights of Carol Pearson and Katherine Pope with the analysis they offer in their book on *The Female Hero*.[20]

LIFE STAGES OF THE SPIRITUAL ORPHAN

EXIT FROM THE GARDEN: Flight or escape from the garden of security, dependency, innocence. The hero comes to realize the people she had previously seen as guides (parents, spouses, spiritual authorities) are really her captors. She becomes a spiritual orphan. She slays dragons. The grey, confining landscape suddenly becomes a landscape of unlimited possibility, rich and full of adventure. Dorothy's house – symbol of female confinement – is destroyed by the cyclone. She can never return to the same home. The home collapses on the wicked witch, killing the first "dragon," negative female energy and self-hatred. Dorothy's act of leaving home and the destruction of the witch releases the Munchkins from their bondage. Dorothy is a liberator.

DISCOVERY OF INNER AUTHORITY: The spiritual orphan meets a spiritual mentor-mother who assists her on the way. (The Good Witch of the North gives Dorothy the magic shoes.) Orphan heroes usually have a major encounter in this stage with a seducer-rescuer-father figure (the Wizard). They also meet helpful companions (Dorothy meets three male companions who embody aspects of her own autonomy that she must develop, a spirituality of courage, wisdom, compassion). But the journey is Dorothy's; her companions grow because she grows. She slays the dragons and rescues them (inverting the traditional fairy tales). In the encounter with the symbol of patriarchy (the Wizard), she discovers he is a "humbug," a fake. She demythologizes the father-savior-lover, who she thought would solve all her problems. Her anger becomes a positive force, not self-destructive. (She is outraged at the burning of the Scarecrow and throws water at the Wicked Witch, dissolving her.) In a fit of rage she calls the Wizard a "bad man." But he is not evil; he simply cannot measure up to her expectations and projections: "I'm really a very good man, but a very bad Wizard." The spiritual orphan purges her own illusions.

REINTEGRATION OF THE FEMININE: The spiritual orphan meets a female figure (Good Witch of the South) who convinces her that she has the power within herself to solve her problem, to get where she wants to go. Dorothy clicks her heels together and says, "Take me home to Aunt Em!" She returns to Kansas to find not greyness and sterility but new life, fertility, and the love of her parents. Above all she finds a new relationship to Aunt Em, symbol of her lost mothering. (Aunt Em no longer looks horrified at Dorothy, pressing her hand to her heart. She embraces Dorothy, covers her with kisses.) Dorothy's transformation of her self resonates in the cosmos: the world to which she returns is transformed.

While these insights have come primarily from women, I believe this reading of the myth of Oz offers a paradigm for human transformation. Moreover, the key element in the transforming myth is the reintegration and empowerment of the authentic feminine self, the reunion with the spirit of the "lost mother" and the "lost sister," the revaluation of what is female-identified in the culture, the reconnection with earthliness and sexuality, with the Earth as mother and sister of all creatures, with the feminine in God.

From the reflections offered by women who have identified Dorothy as a kind of ego archetype, it is clear that they identify with the quality of self-trust that characterizes the survivor personality. There is also a strong cultural resonance with the values of self-reliance and mastering one's environment. (We will say more about this in the next chapter.) In contrast to the old fairy tale heroines, Dorothy rescues herself and her companions. She does not depend on "snaring" a prince or reconciliation with a father-figure in order to improve her situation. This is a classic New World hero—there is always a sense in the narrative that Dorothy will be resourceful enough to triumph over adversity. Her three male companions, in search of intelligence, courage, and compassion, are metaphors of the "survivor" qualities that Dorothy herself develops. Born from the imagination of L. Frank Baum in 1900, Dorothy is very much a child of the twentieth century.

We identify with Dorothy as an ego archetype because we believe in the New World values she represents: self-trust, self-reliance, the capacity to eventually master a hostile environment, the resourcefulness to get home, to reconnect with roots, and family. But there is much in our contemporary experience that has changed the meaning of being orphaned in the traditional sense. Again, the image of the refugee comes to mind – the one who can never go home again, who may never be able to reconstruct home or roots again, the one who may wander forever. Today there are many who are orphaned in a much more radical sense than we could ever imagine – the victims of economic catastrophe, of famine and repression and genocide. In a sense, perhaps, these lost ones have always existed. The difference is that today we are aware that they exist within a proximity of minutes or hours.

The orphan today is one who experiences a profound powerlessness to influence his or her fate, the one who is engulfed by sweeping social tidal waves that were previously unknown. The values of self-reliance, resourcefulness, and the ability to master one's environment are often canceled by these new and overwhelming realities. It seems as if hard work, good will, and pluck aren't enough in the kind of world we live in now.

Whether near or far from our own lives, we all know these new "orphans." Close to home, we all know someone like Rebecca.[21] Rebecca could have been your ordinary middle-class neighbor – until one day she had to take out a restraining order to exclude her abusive husband from the family apartment. Deprived of her husband's earnings, she went on welfare with her two children, aged three years and eighteen months; at the same time she applied to go to a school for skills training. She could not pay the rent out of her welfare check. Emergency assistance was eventually terminated; she and her children were evicted. She did find a part-time job in a bank, but her welfare payments and food stamps were reduced as a result. In order to work she has to pay $90 per week for child care, which is about half of what she earns.

Should we be surprised that Rebecca feels trapped and abandoned? She feels little identification with the self-reliant heroes of the myths. Rebecca is orphaned, not only from the ordinary supports of family and spouse, but from the very social systems that were originally set up to help her out of the trap. Rebecca has fallen into despair and powerlessness from which escape seems impossible.

The profound and absolute sense of abandonment experienced by oppressed people is compounded by the sense of being abandoned by the entire world, even by a provident Creator. The anguish, loneliness, and despair are as deep as humans can experience. This is what it means to be orphaned in the ultimate sense of the word – thrown away, erased even from memory.

And we who have witnessed these events in our own time, we who have seen abandonment in our own cities and neighborhoods, we who have experienced it in our own lives, perhaps in our own relationships – have we recognized our own face in the mirror? Have we seen the orphan in ourselves? We avoid looking in the mirror, into the depths of our own experience. Our social milieu colludes with us in an elaborate conspiracy of denial.

Anxiety ought to be the pain-reflex that leads us to insight. But our consumer society anesthetizes it with an unlimited supply of antidotes. There are many hiding places where we can escape the reality of death and suffering, of loneliness, of separations and the loss of nurturance. We can hide in our compulsion to live the good life, in collecting and consuming money, cars, and people. We can hide in a career or a role, in the pursuit of celebrity or in dependency. We can hide in any one of a thousand addictions, or behind an armor-plated need for control. An "I'm OK, You're OK" society cooperates in the delusion by convincing us we can escape the feeling of brokenness and incompleteness that surfaces when our anxiety analgesics wear off. Everywhere we can reach out and grasp the seductive promise of immortality, fullness, and indestructibility.

Sooner or later, we are dragged – kicking and screaming, whining and whimpering – to a realization: that fidelity to life, and the pursuit of the true self, requires the courage to allow one's anxiety to emerge into consciousness instead of repressing it and replacing it with some form of idolatry. In the next chapters we will explore some of the ways in which culture, gender, roles, relationships, and religion function as repressants – and what fidelity to our true possibilities may require.

Yes, anxiety is the mirror that reflects our true condition – the fragmentation and chaos of the world around us, and the fundamental incompleteness of our own being. The encounter with the lost ones of the world – with refugees, prisoners, the homeless, the untouchables, the victims of catastrophe – is no less threatening than the encounter with the abandoned orphan within each of us. Thus, whether it is in the primal scream of the descent into the self or the cry of outrage, grief, and mourning – the prophetic *za'ak* – recognizing and befriending the orphan within are essential to wholeness, newness, and completion. Indeed the befriending of our anxiety is the prologue to spiritual transformation. The dark night and the empty tomb surround the center of Light: "The nearer we come to the center, the more we leave the images behind, the more are our fears turned into anxiety. And anxiety, if we face it, is turned into awe."[22]

The myth of the spiritual orphan can be a healing metaphor, for it presents us with a social and psychological reality in which anything and everything can be at risk. The old myth of the imperial self and the self-reliant hero—the autonomous personality—cannot survive in the new situation, except where control creates the illusion of survival. Those who tomorrow may have no birthright, no home, no parents, no motherland, no father-God of necessity must live in the context of connection, out of a consciousness of their interdependence. We have to learn to parent each other and give sanctuary, to open our door to the stranger, to create new "holding environments" in place of the lost mothering center of our civilization.

In spite of the illusion that partners, family, clan, nation, or church project in my life, my reality is that I am needy, love-starved, lonely, frightened of what may happen; I am bereft of models and mentors, detached from my history and roots, longing for connection. Only when I have accepted the reality of my orphan self, can I begin to really live.

Although the words and the nuances of language and culture may differ, all the prophets and teachers of the great religious traditions of the world offer reassurance and a promise of a "holding environment" as we see in John 14:18, "I shall not leave you orphans." But Jesus of Nazareth has perhaps been only partially understood. The spirit that remains with us is of one who left us a way of living *and* of dying, it is the bequest of one who came to terms with abandonment in his last breath: "My God, my God, why have you forsaken me?" (Matt. 27:46).

The Snow Queen

here was once a wicked magician who invented a very sinister mirror—everything good and beautiful, when reflected in it, shriveled up to almost nothing; and those things that were ugly and mean were magnified, appearing ten times worse than before. The magician was delighted with his clever invention, and others who came to his school of magic eagerly carried off the mirror so that they too could see the world "as it really was," at least according to the wicked magician. In the course of this heavy use, the mirror fell from their hands and broke into millions, billions, trillions of pieces. And then it caused even greater unhappiness than before, because fragments of it, scarcely as large as a grain of sand, would fly about in the air and sometimes get into people's eyes, causing them to view everything in a distorted way or giving them eyes only for what was perverted and corrupt. Some fragments lodged like splinters in people's hearts, and they became cold and hard like ice. Other fragments were made into spectacles and caused a great deal of mischief and misery.

In a certain large city, where there was not enough room for all the people to have a garden of their own, there lived two poor children, a boy and a girl named Kay and Gerda, whose parents lived in adjacent houses. A large wooden garden box adjoined the houses and a beautiful rose-tree and herbs grew in each box. It was here where the little boy and girl passed many delightful hours and became best friends. In the winter, the snow fell and covered the garden box and flowerpots and they could not meet as easily. One winter night the boy Kay saw a strange lady dressed in white who seemed to emerge out of a falling snowflake. She was fair, but cold, and her eyes had a look of unrest. The lady in icy white beckoned to him. Spring came soon after and Kay forgot the lady as he resumed the joys of sharing with Gerda.

One day while they were together Kay experienced a sharp pain in his heart, and at the same time, something very small flew into his eye. (Kay had been struck by splinters from the magic mirror.) Soon Gerda noticed the change in him. He grew critical and sarcastic; he could no longer see the beauty in simple things, but saw only ugliness. His heart grew cold like a lump of ice. He mocked Gerda because she could feel sympathy and weep tears. Even the games he played and the pastimes he enjoyed changed. His rational curiosity seemed to replace his appreciation of the splendor of creation – he analyzed snowflakes under his microscope instead of smelling the flowers. One day he went out to race with the other boys on his sled. He was, as they say, abducted by the Snow Queen who lured him to her horse-driven sleigh. As they flew across the country-side and the blizzard raged, Kay grew frightened. He would have repeated the Our Father but he could remember nothing but the multiplication tables.

The Snow Queen carried him off to her palace. She was so beautiful and so intelligent that he soon forgot little Gerda and all his loved ones left behind. He did his best to please the Snow Queen with his skill in fractions, square miles, and other rational feats. In time, the vast, empty corridors of the Snow Queen's palace were so cold that Kay grew quite blue. But he did not observe it, for the Snow Queen had kissed away the shrinking feeling he used to experience; and his heart was like a lump of ice. Kay busied himself with icy chips and fragments, making them into figures – his "ice-puzzle of reason." Kay struggled with the most difficult puzzle of all – for the Snow Queen promised him that when he succeeded in forming the word "Immortality" she would give him the whole world and a new pair of skates besides. But he could never do it.

Gerda wept for Kay and longed for his return. The other boys said he surely must be dead. But Gerda was in the habit of talking to her other friends, the birds and flowers, the rivers and streams, the sunshine. They gave her many hints that Kay was not dead and gone. Early one morning she set off to ask more questions about her lost playmate, and thus began Gerda's long journey through many adventures to find Kay. She met a helpful raven who was sure he had seen Kay in a nearby castle. Gerda showed much courage in entering the castle by night. It was not Kay, but the young man and his betrothed turned out to be a helpful prince and princess. Later when she was seized by robbers she was befriended and released by a young robber maiden who wished to help Gerda find her friend Kay. She directed her, with the help of a reindeer to two wise women, one in Lapland and one in Finland, where the Snow Queen's palace was.

The reindeer asked the Finn woman if she would give Gerda some magic to overcome the spell of the splinters in Kay's eye and heart – the spell of the Snow Queen. The wise woman replied, "I can give Gerda no power so great as that which she already possesses. Seest thou not how strong she is? Seest thou not that both men and animals must serve her – a poor girl wandering barefoot through the world? Her power is greater than ours; it proceeds from her heart." By the time she arrived at the Snow Queen's palace, the reindeer could go no farther, and Gerda had lost her shoes and gloves. She stood alone, freezing, in that ice-cold, barren region.

Gerda braved the elements and the grim, forboding palace to find Kay. He did not respond to her at first, but when she sang a favorite song they had often shared, he began to weep. The splinter fell from his eye with his tears, and the splinter in his heart dissolved. They took each other by the hand and left the palace, and as they walked on, the winds were hushed and the sun burst forth from behind the clouds. Wherever they went it was spring, with its bright flowers and green leaves.[1]

As a child I was enchanted and haunted by Andersen's characters of the Snow Queen and the Ice Maiden (another of Andersen's fairy tales). They seemed to me the saddest of all creatures, and their power – to make things freeze up – seemed the most wicked and frightening of all. Later, as a woman, I discovered the secret of the poignancy of so many Andersen tales. Andersen searched his whole life for the feminine counterpart of himself and never found a soul that answered his own need. The author of "The Ugly Duckling" grasped intuitively the reality of the orphan self, the wounded child in himself.

Like many of Andersen's stories, "The Snow Queen" is psychobiographical. Kay represents the author's own longing for a feminine spirit, a lover to transport him out of his brilliant but artificial inner world, someone to help him befriend mortality and earthliness.[2] But the story is also filled with archetypes and soars beyond the personal to the universal: Kay can be seen as a character-type of the flawed development of the male personality, unable to free the feminine in himself, unable to rescue himself. So he is dependent on "redemption" and parasitic transference from woman. (Jung would probably take a more romantic view, interpreting this as a positive phenomenon, a projection of the "Anima.")

At a more symbolic and allegorical level, the tale takes on a cultural relevance to the splintering, fragmenting effect of the rational-technological spirit, which freezes up feeling in our cultural psyche. In Kay, we experience the death of the feminine in us all. And with Gerda, we risk the journey into the frozen Arctic only by leaving everything behind. All the trappings of the false self must be sacrificed. In this sense, perhaps, Kay is our past; Gerda, our longing for a different future.

2.

A NATION OF ORPHANS

In December of 1980 I moved to Washington D.C., from a small university town in northern Indiana. I was blown there by one of those academic cyclones that occasionally disturb the quiet, reasoned routine of scholars and plant them in a whole new universe. Indeed, I felt much like Dorothy in *The Wizard of Oz*, fresh from the grey somnolence of Kansas, suddenly dazzled by the brilliance and energy of the Emerald City of Oz. Dorothy and her friends were given tinted glasses to soften the glare; I had to develop my own filters for processing the frenetic pace, the dance of power, and the puppetry of politics that I found there. As a congressional aide for several years, I was to learn in a most intimate way the truth about the Land of Oz and its minions.

There was much about the first half of the 1980s that was reminiscent of the 1890s, the years just before L. Frank Baum wrote and published *The Wizard of Oz*. I arrived in Washington when the Midwest and Northeast were experiencing the deepest recession in years. It was all reminiscent of the terrible depression of 1893 with its massive unemployment; high interest rates; record numbers of foreclosures, bankruptcies and bank failures; epidemic of mergers and trust takeovers; and raging debates on monetary policy. The federal government, which had enjoyed a surplus in 1890, was running a deficit of $70 million by 1894—an astronomical sum by nineteenth-century standards. James Coxey's army of "broken veterans of industry," the unemployed, marched on Washington. A disenchanted public pressed their representatives to support bills for public works projects designed to provide more jobs. While presidents preached the Monroe Doctrine and made preparations to invade Latin America, most Americans were concerned about the loss of employment or of their family farm.

With the Democratic party in disarray and the Republicans hostage to big business interests, a third political force—chiefly allied with laborers and farmers – emerged. They called themselves "populists." The great champion of the populists, William Jennings Bryan, lost the election of 1896 – the year of the "Silver Crusade"– by a relatively narrow margin. If the elections of the 1980s have been dominated by the Political Action Committees, lobbies, and single-interest groups, the 1890s were dominated by Mark Hanna, who shook down the banks, the railroads, and the insurance corporations for enormous contributions for his candidate, William McKinley. Bryan received more votes than had ever before been cast for a presidential candidate, but McKinley won. It was later described as a fight conducted by trained, experienced, and organized forces, dominated by the influence of money, the power of the press, and the prestige of the power moguls. Between 1896 and 1900 the depression receded and the war with Spain – our invasions of Cuba and the Philippines – focused the attention of the world on the United States. Shades of the 1980s!

Baum published *The Wonderful Wizard of Oz* in 1900. Originally an Easterner, his sojourn in the West exposed him to the stark realities of life on the plains. In 1891 he moved to Chicago, just in time to be engaged and intrigued by the populist movement. As an experienced journalist and writer, his observations and ironic perceptions surfaced as a subtheme in his imaginative children's stories. Some commentators believe the parallels and the political analogies in *The Wizard of Oz* are so dramatic that it has the force of symbolic allegory. Henry Littlefield offers the following analysis:

Dorothy, blown out of a drab, colorless Kansas by a cyclone, is Baum's populist hero, struggling against drought, locusts, and inflation. In the original story, Dorothy's magic shoes are not red, as Judy Garland's were, but silver, suggesting the free silver policy which populists saw as one remedy for the tyranny of the gold standard. It is clear from a careful analysis of the story that Dorothy's three companions are also symbolic: the Tin Woodman represents the laborer, "rusted out" by mechanization and "frozen" in unemployment; the Scarecrow represents the farmer, whom the prestigious editor William Allen White accused of "ignorance, irrationality and general muddleheadedness"; and the Cowardly Lion represents the charismatic leader, William Jennings Bryan himself, a pacifist and an anti-imperialist. Likewise, the witches of East and West, and North and South, have their respective associations – Baum located social evil mostly in the East and West. (It is interesting to note that Dorothy destroys the Wicked Witch of the West by dousing her with water, which the drought-ridden farmers desperately needed and which – if wisely managed – could "save" them from their plight.)[1]

Dorothy and her friends decide to seek the help of the Wizard of the Emerald City. Each comes with a specific agenda: the Tin Woodman needs a "heart" (renewed vitality); the Scarecrow, "brains" (strategies that work); the Cowardly Lion, "courage" (a winning program and political style); and Dorothy wants to get back to Kansas. The Emerald City and the Wizard are, of course, caricatures of the nation's capital, the president and his administration. It is in the chapters dealing with the Wizard that Baum's irony seems to be most consciously drawn and acute.

The Wizard's reputation for success in dealing with his suppliant-constituents is, of course, a charade. To each seeker he assumes a different shape, telling each one how to find his or her heart's desire, i.e., what they most want to hear. Dorothy eventually unmasks the charlatan, revealing that the great Wizard is really nothing more than a little, bald-headed old man who uses "smoke and mirrors" to gain his political ends. Baum's portrayal of the president as a former circus balloonist, whose skills were limited to ventriloquism and "going up in a balloon on circus day, so as to draw a crowd," was a scathing comment on the American criteria for leadership.

In the denouement of the story, Baum's populists discover that the solutions to their problems lie within themselves, that looking to the awesome power of the Wizard is a delusion. They begin to discover that they are not powerless. Dorothy finds out how to return herself to Kansas. The "silver shoes" drop off somewhere over the desert and are never seen again. Dorothy has discovered the "humbug" of too great expectations of leadership and the foolishness of seeking outside herself and her peers for help.

One evening in March 1987, I was reminded of Dorothy and the Wizard when President Reagan went on national television to admit his incompetence in the Iran arms affair. I was no longer the naive innocent that had come to Washington at the beginning of the Reagan era in late 1980. I had been deeply affected and changed by the events, intrigues, and manipulations of power in those years. I had shuddered at the close-ups I had of our foreign policy, economic policies, and derailment of civil rights legislation. As with Baum's classic, beneath the fairy tale I had discovered ignorance, deception, and the demonic. I felt orphaned in the midst of the Emerald City.

The periodic purgations that the tangled web of national politics inevitably produces should cause us to wonder what it is in our cultural consciousness that leaves us so vulnerable to unchecked privateering and corruption. Is it our "tough freedom," the absence of social controls, that leaves us easy prey to charlatans and fools? Is it that the mindless engine of profit and consumption so absorbs our attention that we don't see what track we may be on? Or is it something deeper, more elemental? And perhaps the ultimate questions are, What does this have to do with me, and why should I care?

Like Baum we like to think that we can live out our "story," our personal ambitions, with some degree of autonomy, privacy, and purpose, that the culture in which we play out our script is really only a backdrop, a stage set for the dream of our life. This is an innocent assumption. As with Baum, we can set out to make our lives a fairy tale, but we will end, willynilly, with a political allegory in which we are inextricably involved. Below and beyond our personal project lie the bog and fossil beasts, the deep structures of our culture – the myths that still shape our behavior and set limits to our being, myths that often enable and fuel our energies, and often as not, cripple or misdirect them.

We come into this world securely anchored in this cradle that is our culture, unaware of the limitations and possibilities that have already been tentatively determined by the environment in which we will grow and be nourished.

More than any other society in modern times, our New World culture is a civilization of "fatherless ones." Politically, our culture was born out of a conscious rejection of the tyrannical patriarchs of the Old World, out of the ethos of religious dissent, and out of the search for a social space where caste, class, and old codes could not dwarf human capacity. Most of us are descended from willing or unwilling immigrants to the New World, blown here by the cyclones of history. We have all collected folklore about our own family's exodus from oppression, famine, or poverty.

Anthropologists have noted the value North American culture places on early independence and the parental behavior that encourages self-reliance in the infant. Adolescent rebellion is celebrated and sustained well beyond the norm that prevails in other cultures. Perhaps we come by our orphan psyche because the primordial act that gave birth to our nation was the rebellious act of separation from the British crown, the father-king. The American Revolution was in many ways the fulfillment of the Enlightenment, the displacement of monarchs and surrogate deities by the common man, the individual. The reasoning conscience replaced the superego of feudalism; the consent of the governed replaced political dependency and cultural heteronomy as a universal social aspiration. But in this process of shedding the collective superego, the individual ego assumed a heavy burden.

The emergence of a nation of "United States" and the American ethos from which it was born arrived on the doorstep of history as a foundling of sorts, but this experiment in self-governance was not without roots and a legacy from the past. The displacement of the divine right of kings and theocratic absolutism left our founding fathers vulnerable to even more powerful spirits.

More than any other previous culture ours was born from a constellation of highly developed, rationalized myths about what the culture would be.[2] Our nation was spawned out of a mythology that was enhanced and promulgated in print rather than through an oral, genealogical transmission, disseminated rather than generated. It was the first cross-cultural mass daydream of a New Man and a New World. The dream and the experience of the New World have created the fundamental myths of our culture. I believe there are two: first the imperative of continuous *self-creation* (the result of fatherlessness and the death of the cultural superego), and second, the necessity of self-creation and *empowerment through the power of will* (hence, through force and violence).

I call this the "orphan complex"–the one abandoned by history or cast upon the shore of a wilderness must create a world, and himself in the process. Neither identity nor security is a "given" for the orphan.

The myth that drew the first European explorers to the shores of the Western hemisphere was the myth of the New World, a dream that fused all the earlier utopian fantasies of Arcadia, the New Atlantis, the fabled Islands of the West, the Garden in the Wilderness. Always it was the expectation of a place where everything could begin again, a free space where the promise of unlimited resources stirred the imagination and will, where humanity would be unspoiled by the corrupt traditions and oppressions of the Old World, a land of innocence, a mystical "Virginia." So the idea of "America" became a very abstract, platonic notion. Is it any wonder that we were destined to be creatures with great expectations? For each of us, reality has been filtered through that platonic aura. The famous epilogue of F. Scott Fitzgerald's novel *The Great Gatsby* captures the aura perfectly:

Gatsby believed in the green light, the orgiastic future that year by year recedes before us. It eluded us then, but that's no matter–tomorrow we will run faster, stretch out our arms farther. . . . And one fine morning– – –

So we beat on, boats against the current, born back ceaselessly into the past.[3]

The Puritans spiritualized the myth of the New World as an "errand into the wilderness," a new exodus into the Promised Land, the building of a City on the Hill. If they conceived of the transcendent purpose of the new people in a new land, the Puritans also brought a context of concreteness to the emerging worldview. Like the pioneers of the West and the settlers of the Heartland they faced the overwhelming reality of confrontation with untamed nature and with "savage" Indians.

The early dissenters were orphaned in several ways. Not only were they "fatherless" and bereft of the class, creed, and code myths—the cultural *superego* that the Old World had provided—they had also repressed the cultural *id*: the drives, the appetites, the energies of the sexual and the sinister. The Puritan world was dualistic, almost Manichaean, and decidedly hostile to pluralism. (Was this a case where the oppressed eventually took on the mind of their old oppressors?) In a psychological sense the shadow of the repressed id needed an object. Witches (also associated with natural impulses and sinister powers) provided an occasional instance; but the overwhelming experience of the wilderness and the strangers occupying it offered an even better object for the projection. The terrors of the unknown "out there" were exaggerated by the terrors of the unknown within—the "Indians" became the object of the projected id.

By contrast, the North American Indian cultures, for the most part, tended to value the free exercise of natural impulses. The Indian practices of sexual freedom for the unmarried and their custom of allowing both consenting partners to dissolve a marriage horrified the early colonists.[4] (This, like other "savage" practices, was largely an adaptation to the precariousness of survival in a wilderness that was respected and left untrammeled.)

If we can judge by journals, narratives, sermons, and other evidence of the period, a phenomenon occurred in the cultural-political dimension that is analogous to the psychological defense mechanism known as "splitting." Common in infants and schizophrenics, the insecure or threatened personality splits the significant objects in its environment into "good" and "bad." It is a delusion which functions as a control mechanism when the personality is unable to cope with overwhelming reality, complexity, ambiguity, and change. And so our earliest cultural ancestors "split" their New World into the "powers of darkness" and the "powers of light." The powers of darkness were associated with the "savage" Indians and with a whole constellation of human capacities that for centuries had been associated with "inferior" beings: feelings and emotions, sexual impulses, the body, unspoiled nature, birth and death, female-identified experiences, and–above all–dark skin. The powers of light, of course, were associated with the complementary constellation: reason and abstract thought, asceticism and the postponement of gratification, order and "civilization," the search for immortality, male-identified, "superior" experiences, and–of course–light skin.

The split in consciousness was as old as the Greeks and the Gnostics, but was given a special intensity by the inevitable encounters in the wilderness between an indigenous people and the white intruders. "Tales of strife between native Americans and interlopers, between dark races and light, became the basis of our mythology and the Indian fighter/hunter emerged as the first of our national heroes. . . . The story of the evolution of an American mythology is, in large measure, the story of our too-slow awakening to the significance of the American Indian in the universal scheme of things generally and in our American world particularly."[5]

Thus our collective memory of the Native Americans would always connect us with the land and the forests and waters in their natural, unexploited state, with the "dark forces of the blood," and the threat of uncontrolled chaos and strange ways. The hero-self in the New World, unencumbered with the past, was left unconnected and unprotected, thrown into an untamed environment. His own self-creation was bound up with the projection of the stranger as an enemy. With no language, no history, no values in common (or so it seemed), the right of the interlopers could only prevail by force. Violence was justified as a kind of "exorcism," a purging of "savage" elements from a land that was destined to be *ours*, not *theirs*. Only through force of will, and ultimately by physical and psychological force, could the orphan-hero tame the powers of darkness.

We have underestimated the persistence of this phenomenon in our culture, even in our politics. And we underestimate the extent to which it has influenced our own unconscious responses and choices. As psychohistorian James Glass observes,

It should not be assumed that splitting is a characteristic only of withdrawn or asocial schizophrenics. Unyielding conceptions of good and bad appear consistently in the political universe. It is not unusual to find in political life a Manichaean split between absolute good and absolute evil, nor is it unusual to find such splits in ethical systems that are held together by rigid positions and arguments. Such readings of politics may derive from internal, psychodynamic structures projected in language as ideological or religious dogma, as the isolation of a racial or ethnic group as the bearer of a historical evil, or as the imposition of tyrannical laws. Entire societies, dominated by schizoid psychological structures, may be split and driven into extraordinary political actions.[6]

Thus the slavery question and our national history of racism should come as no surprise. Nor should we be surprised that with the closing of the frontier and the final "pacification" of the Indian population in the 1890s, the national psyche sought another dark-skinned object for the projection of the myth: Teddy Roosevelt took his Rough Riders to Cuba, and we invaded the Philippines in the last years of the nineteenth century. In 1905 U.S. troops landed in Honduras for the first of five times during the twenty years that followed. In 1908 U.S. troops landed in Panama for the first of what would be four times within the next decade. In 1912 the U.S. Marines began twenty years of repeated occupations in Nicaragua. Should we be surprised that high-ranking government officials in the 1980s speak of the "Evil Empire" and draft policies accordingly? We have lived through too many cycles of "Yellow Perils," "Aryan Nations," and "Red Scares" not to see that the myth is very much alive.

Working in Washington in the 1980s was in many ways a study in the recycling of the myth. Particularly in the development of our relations with Nicaragua over the past century we can see the compulsive nature of this phenomenon. I once asked a high-ranking government official at a White House briefing why it was that we believed in a policy of "constructive engagement" with the South African government, but not with Nicaragua. The official stumbled through an absurd rationalization. The real answer to the question, of course, lies in understanding the power of the myth.

The orphaned spirits of the first settlers in the New World had no models, no ego archetypes that fit their circumstances. They had embarked on the journey of continuous self-creation without benefit of mythic heroes to blaze the trail ahead. Their siege psychology generated only two possible responses: passive submission or violent retribution. As they pushed the frontier westward and penetrated the wilderness beyond the mountains, the prototypes of the orphan-hero emerged. The American Revolution itself provided a clue to the kind of ego archetype that would measure up to the extraordinary demands of the new society. In the catalytic event of the Boston Tea Party in 1773 the American rebels adopted Indian dress in executing their raid; and the militia at Concord, Lexington, and countless other places on the Freedom Trail were said to have fought the regulars "in the Indian manner." The Whiskey Rebels of 1794 even adopted

Indian war paint at their meetings and redressed their grievances in a mock "Indian Treaty" in which they used the Indian as a symbol of their independence, courage, and defiance of authority in their faithfulness to principle. Thus the Indian, both hated and admired, paradoxically became a model for the hero of the New World.

The hunter-hero/frontiersman had to learn from and imitate the Indian in order to survive and "tame" the wilderness and its minions. The stoic virtues and nature-knowledge of the Native Americans passed by osmosis to those who sought to conquer them. It was John Filson, a schoolmaster turned surveyor and land speculator, who offered the first real portrait of the new hero. In a postscript to his "real estate handbook," *The Discovery, Settlement, and Present State of Kentucke* of 1784, he described the adventures of one "Daniel Boone." Copied by imitators and plagiarists, appearing in countless reincarnations and versions under other names in both literature and the popular arts as "the man who made the wilderness safe for democracy,"[7] the Boone legend constituted the first nationally viable statement of a hero-myth for the frontier.

Daniel Boone was the ancestor of the Leatherstocking myth and the Deerslayer figure in the next century: the idealized half-Indian, half-white, the friend and protector of the weak and vulnerable and the avenger of justice – chief among those in need of a protector and avenger being the chaste white woman, after whom the dark-skinned races surely lusted. Kit Carson and the "mountain man" of the West were more rough-hewn versions of the same myth, classic archetypes of the self-created, self-willed, self-reliant hero. Snippets from the early descriptions of these figures set the mold for the American "hero." They were

strange, fearless, and adamantine men, renouncing society, casting off fear, and all the common impulses and affections of our nature . . . finding in their own ingenuity, their knife, their gun and traps, all the divinity, of which their stern nature and condition taught them the necessity . . . that became almost as inaccessible to passions and wants, and as sufficient to themselves, as the trees, or the rocks with which they were conversant.[8]

In the twentieth century these figures acquire more than the edge or advantage of Indianlike skills and knowledge. The myth is translated into social and political models as well as into popular culture. For example, the elite Army Ranger Corps owes its inspiration and ethos to the tradition of the Indian fighters (and imitators) who were led by Major General Robert Rogers of the pre-American Revolution Colonial Army. Boone and

Carson, the Rangers and the Rough Riders, the Lone Ranger, Captain Kirk, and Rambo are all cast from the same myth.

Since the earliest years of our Republic, a variety of social philosophers and cultural analysts have attempted to explain our national character. Crèvecoeur spoke of the American's instinct to pursue "self-interest." De Tocqueville observed "democratic individualism," and feared that because "each man is forever thrown back on himself alone, there is danger that he may be shut up in the solitude of his own heart." The classic writers of America – Melville, Hawthorne, Faulkner – focused on the perils of "the shut-up heart." Later David Riesman painted the American as one lost in "the lonely crowd." More recently Christopher Lasch anatomized *The Culture of Narcissism* and Robert Bellah revealed our *Habits of the Heart*. Tom Wolfe captured the acute stage of a cultural paradigm when he announced "The Me Decade."

Has the myth of self-creation – the unique inheritance of the children of the New World forged in successive chapters of wilderness, frontier, free land, industrial expansion, capitalism, free trade, nationalism, manifest destiny and imperialism – doomed us to a self-destructive narcissism? Has it left us vulnerable to autism and detached autonomy in our lifestyle? Has it made us think of self-interest as the center of the commonwealth, the U.S. as the center of global political order, and humans as the center and crown of the biosphere? Have we become a "nuclear" people, that is, a people known by our common isolation, self-reliance, and perceived autonomy?

The delusion of Narcissus has been a popular preoccupation of art, literature, and social science in the Western culture. The temptation of Narcissus is the unwillingness or inability to be-in-relation, to "connect." Narcissus can only relate to, love that which is a projection of himself. He cannot truly see the actual other and therefore cannot receive into himself the uniqueness, the giftedness or the brokenness of the other. The pathology of Narcissus has three aspects. The first is the tendency to "objectify" the other, which denies personhood, and allows the objectifier to reduce the other to a useful or useless thing. The objectifier either uses others, seeks to deny or annihilate their existence, or is simply numb to their reality. In the second aspect the nuclear person is encapsulated in himself, absorbed only by projected feelings (sentimental or romantic love), or by things (social autism). The third aspect is a characteristic self-rejection and the parasitism of the internal saboteur. As in the myth, Narcissus reaches out, pleads with the image in the pool not to reject him, but it does. The lover is inaccessible to himself.

Thus the failure of the democratic orphan-hero to connect with his partner in the wilderness, the Indian, and his repressed love/hate for his archetypal other was to have inescapable consequences for generations of Americans. Instead of the crucible of being-in-relation, the new man assumes the burden of self-creation alone. We have popularized the myth of the "self-made man" in the image of a self-sufficient, competitive, tough, pragmatic, and resourceful entrepreneur. As Bellah and colleagues have noted in *Habits of the Heart*, we are a nation of "managers" and "therapists": for the therapist in the inner world of the self, as for the manager in the external milieu, the emphasis is on "what works," on results. The means, executed in the "tough freedom" of the new culture, inevitably leave us alone and private, unprotected and unconnected. Free to "create" ourselves, we are trapped in a "culture of separation."

The self-project becomes adversarial, an unrelenting combat. In this struggle intelligence is crucial, but *will* is the supreme necessity. The urgency of "control" is acted out in the public and private sphere. Control is substituted for relationship. The wilderness must be tamed, the Indian eliminated or contained, the black man enslaved, women confined to their place. It is important to understand how the archetype of the initial rejection is translated through history, transferred to new objects with the passing of time and the onset of new experiences.

Parenthetically, it is interesting to note that the Indian is always associated with everything that is *not* white, male, of European origin, and superior. The Indian, no matter how admired, is identified with the "feminine" constellation of value. This is a crucial division for a patriarchal society, and the macho tendency of the New World was clear and uncomplicated from the beginning. Kenelm Burridge observes:

The personality of the occidental was long ago transformed by a breaking with the ancestral customs and the removal to the heaven of a universalized paternal authority . . . . The colonial arrangement particularly suited a European psychological style . . . . [C]olonial life is simply a substitute to those who are still obscurely drawn to a world without women . . . who have failed to adapt infantile images to society.[9]

Thus the orphan consciousness, unredeemed, has an obvious affinity for excluding and denigrating the "feminine" as childish and inferior.

As a case in point, an illuminating study by Fred Pike traces the association of the Indian stereotype with the Latin American cultures.[10] After its discovery by Europeans the territory subsequently to become the

United States was often represented as an Indian princess. (Later when the Indians were doomed to become a vanishing race, the Indian princess was replaced by a new symbol: Uncle Sam.) Andrew Jackson's epithets for the "red men" were the classic stereotypes later applied to the black slaves: Indians were like "children," lacking in intelligence, industry, and moral habits, incapable of self-government.

As the pacification of the Native Americans gradually closed the frontier, the stereotype resurfaced. In 1874, on the Centennial Stock Certificates issued by the U.S. government, Latin America was represented with the image of two Indian maidens. As the century drew to a close the Indian-Latin American association was reinforced by the Hispanic opposition to our manifest destiny of expanding our borders and colonial interests. As Pike notes, "It was a natural step from Cherokee to Mexican, or from the Plains Indian to swarthy 'Greasers.' Indians and Hispanics seemed linked in a diabolical alliance of barbarians to impede the course of culture and righteousness."[11]

The mythology waxed: Theodore Roosevelt believed we had the same civilizing duty toward Filipinos as toward Apaches. McKinley thought it was necessary to "civilize" and "Christianize" the Philippines. An American general reported from Puerto Rico that the vast horde of mixed-blood islanders were "no more fit to take part in self-government than our reservation Indians." Woodrow Wilson exhorted the citizens of Mexico, Central America, and the Caribbean republics to substitute individualistic, capitalistic cultures for the "primitive" cultures in which they lived. He sent U.S. troops to occupy Nicaragua. John F. Kennedy invaded Cuba, fortress of the archetypal untrustworthy Latino, Fidel Castro. Ronald Reagan invaded Grenada and sent mercenaries to Nicaragua. The consciousness persists.

The demonizing language of public policy which has been so characteristic of our history with the Indians, Latin Americans, and "others" who fall victim to similar projections, reveals another disabling characteristic of the self-made, self-created man. When the human will exhausts the limits of its power to create, when frantic efforts at mastery and control reach their limits of effectiveness, when our human willfulness is frustrated and our expectations dashed, we often invent a Satanic projection, an "Evil Empire." As one philosopher argues, Satan is a projection of the exhausted sense of human autonomy and omnipotence. Those who must find all their resources within themselves will despair, then project.[12] The contemporary politics of the Neo-Right are a dramatic illustration of our cultural vulnerability to a frustrated self-reliance that has to invent devils it can blame.

It will be obvious that one of the risks of the self-creation mythology is paranoia. The nuclear, narcissistic self is threatened on all sides. This attitude is mirrored in paranoid –"nuclear"– politics where violence is not caused by the American way of life but by the insistence that the superiority of this way of life be accepted by billions of underdogs. Paranoid politics is marked by alternating cycles of feelings of powerlessness and grandiosity; more and more reality is gradually ceded to delusion. This perhaps explains the tendency of American politics to attract and shape actors like Gordon Liddy and Oliver North.

If, as some psychologists maintain, "paranoia is a special kind of distortion of autonomy,"[13] our historic failure to connect with the archetypal "other" is the crucial event in our nuclear situation. In public and in private, we are victims of delusion. "The core of delusion lies in its hostility to any embodied relation; the world is held within."[14] This hostility to embodied relation, to the "actual other" has, as we have noted, a special relevance to the development of the myths that shape the American consciousness. But it is a universal problem, and has its unique characteristics in many cultures. The acceptance of the "actual other" is the key to social harmony, even as it is the sine qua non of personal development: I can only become uniquely and wholly myself by responding to what is not myself.[15]

What kind of a world do nuclear people create? What is the condition of our social relations today? In an era when worldwide mobility and communication are forcing us into greater proximity and interdependence, we find ourselves overwhelmed with alienation, wars, repression, violence – often between those who are of the same family or nationality, or who must share work and subsistence in the same living space. We are haunted by the unspeakable acts of our times: genocide, torture, random violence, decimation or starvation of innocent populations, pollution and destruction of our environment, policies that treat human beings as cannon fodder and "collateral damage." The *refusal to relate* is the sin of our times: the refusal to recognize and respect another's existence; the refusal to speak, to negotiate; the refusal to confront; the refusal to touch one another and cherish the flesh of the "other." As Carter Heyward has said eloquently in her book *The Redemption of God*, "Evil is the result of our unwillingness to bear passion – that is, to suffer an active sense of power in relation . . . . Evil is the image of our fearful dispassion."[16] The most dramatic manifestation of sin and suffering in the world today is our radical nonrelation. Our consequent paranoia, our desperate goals of national and personal "security," spawn all manner of domestic and geopolitical aberrations.

The "fatherlessness" of the first-generation American is real; the burden of self-creation in a new milieu, without roots and resources can be overwhelming. But other supports often remain in place: a close-knit family, religious faith, a sense of values and moral boundaries, and above all, the promise of a better life yet to be fulfilled. It is in the third to fifth generations that the orphan complex really takes hold. By this time the family has become more "nuclear"–members are split off from one another by work, education, the generation gap. The practice of religious faith may have declined or disappeared; rituals that once united the family have lapsed. Affluence–or poverty–has made the family susceptible to fragmentation and separation; upward mobility may have caused many dislocations and uprootings. The bombardment of influences and gratifications from outside the family has transformed priorities and personalities. The canopy of shared values has been eroded.

The orphan generation has arrived at a more fundamental state of "fatherlessness." As Bellah et al. frame the task in *Habits of the Heart*, "The self is defined by its ability to choose its own values."[17] In the absence of a shared canopy of values and of agreed-upon criteria for right and wrong, for the process of discernment itself, the right act becomes simply the one that yields the most exciting challenge or the most good feeling for the self. The myth of self-creation is reduced to the pursuit of personal wants and inner impulses and the need above all to feel that "I'm OK." The authors of *Habits of the Heart* ask, "What kind of world is inhabited by this self, perpetually in progress, yet without any fixed moral end?"[18]

The orphan self is an improvisational self, free of most of the constraints of a cultural superego: religious practice and strict moral codes, inherited ideas and values, geographic and ethnic roots. Even when some individuals enjoy the support of these mediating structures the culture in which they are immersed impresses its message explicitly and subliminally: the only myth that is left is the myth of self-creation, which is often translated into the pursuit of success.

Ivan Illich once observed that in a consumer society there are two kinds of slaves: the prisoners of addiction and the prisoners of envy. "To be somebody" is the overriding compulsion of the orphan generation. The cost is high in terms of anxiety, stress, and fear. This fear and poverty of support mechanisms are the key to the vulnerability of the orphan consciousness. There are some who would insist that the dominant experience of our culture is not that of a holding environment but of an abyss of addiction – a social environment that has itself become addictive because of our desperate need to alleviate our anxieties and stresses, placate our expectations, assuage our lack of connection.[19]

It is common to associate the problems of substance abuse and other forms of addiction with the underclass, with sociopaths, with "problem" personalities, or with those who are exploiters or otherwise alienated from society. Then one day a photograph appears on the front page of a national newspaper and we are taken aback: fifteen Wall Street stockbrokers, still dressed in business suits, handcuffed, being led off by Federal agents as suspected drug dealers or inside traders.

Roland Delattre has described our social environment as "the culture of procurement,"[20] a term that carries nuances of both acquisition and prostitution. The "culture of procurement" is a culture of addictive acquisition in which the dominant two-thirds of American society participates. This dominant culture – the culture of brokers and doctors, of politicians and lawyers, of managers and therapists – nourishes and rewards addictive behavior and attitudes. Delattre notes that this dominant behavior is not just a respite from stress and anxiety, a refuge from the fear of failure: "it has also become one of the most likely conditions and ingredients of socially and culturally defined success in the dominant sectors of American society."[21] The level of stress, loneliness, and emotional denial endured by those who rise or want to rise in the corporate culture makes some pattern of addictive dependence a virtual condition of success.

Addiction is the inheritance of a nation of orphans, of personalities driven by the myth of self-creation. Some believe it finds quintessential expression in the military-industrial complex and the compulsive procurement of what is bigger, better, or newer, or what promises more "control" over perceived threats in the geopolitical environment. Star Wars is one of the most recent examples of the addictive dynamics; already scientists and Pentagon experts are predicting the technology that will be needed next – one fortunate "fix" generates another.

Some of the characteristic syndromes of addiction as experienced on the personal level are emerging in our culture as a collective phenomenon. For example, the swings between powerlessness and grandiosity in typical addicts resemble what Frances Fitzgerald describes in observing U.S. leaders: "a defensive churlishness combined with adolescent self-promotion" in policy decisions and political behavior. She describes a pattern of political thinking that indulges in fears of Armageddon on the one hand and a kind of megalomaniacal expectation of the final solution, deal, or weapon that will insure "victory for our side" on the other.[22] Meanwhile, real needs and crises are ignored. Another aspect of addictive behavior is the loss of moral and ethical boundaries and the distinction between private and public responsibilities. As the perpetrators of Contragate or the Wall Street inside traders clearly show, we seem to be losing our sense of right and wrong, our sense of just proportion in our public behavior. Addicts indulge a compulsion to make ends justify any means.

Addicts require immediate satisfaction; and the traditional asceticism of capitalism – delay of gratification – has long since disappeared in the latter-day descendants of immigrants. The acceptance of the current norm of "deferred payment" has produced a society that compulsively lives beyond its means, even when it comes to federal budgets and the balance of trade. The greatest consumer nation in the world has recently become the world's greatest debtor nation.

Another characteristic that people driven by self-creation exhibit is the necessity to experiment with ways of producing a self. The psyche is converted to a product, and "Everyman is an independent contractor."[23] It should not be surprising then, that the American culture has produced the most prodigious literature of self-help that the world has ever seen, or that human potential movements are often spawned and flourish in our society.

In the absence of a clearly defined, sustained, and sustaining canopy of values and holding environment, what does the orphan substitute? If not addiction, perhaps an even more fierce attachment to the myth that defines our self-creation and the power of willing and doing: the American Dream. It is surely one of the most repeated cliches in our language, yet it means different things to different people. We all claim it; we assume that we believe in it. But what is it? Is it success? Is it wealth? Is it happiness? Or, as Snoopy says, is it "having a roof over your head and no overhead"? The American Dream is the ultimate myth of the New World.

The American Dream is above all the dream of being Someone, of standing out in the crowd, of living a life that has meaning in the eyes of others. Success and approval in a nation of orphans inevitably has to be ratified by publicity. Much of our experience as Americans makes us crave celebrity. We fantasize about being a "star" and we consume those who are: athletes, astronauts, rock musicians, politicians, even popes. We are hooked on the dream of celebrity. Whether you are Lee Iacocca or J. R. Ewing, or the doctor who invented the mechanical heart, or Mother Teresa, or Madonna—you want to stand for something, achieve something, fulfill a mission, leave your mark on the world. The orphan desperately seeks some form of symbolic immortality, the ultimate approval. Celebrity means something that I can accomplish on my own, that is uniquely mine, that makes me stand out. Some people amass wealth and power to get that recognition. Some amass information; some write books. Some do good deeds.

The drive for celebrity is the thread of commonality that links disparate and diverse personalities: a Lee Iacocca, or an Oliver North, a Christiaan Barnard, or a Shirley MacLaine, a presidential assassin, or a serial killer. Lee Iacocca's best-selling autobiography is a classic in the long tradition of American self-creation that began with Benjamin Franklin's *Autobiography*; in fact it celebrates many of the same virtues and attitudes, the asceticism of the American Dream. Iacocca speaks of himself with the same innocence and resourcefulness as a modern Daniel Boone, pursuing his American Dream in the corporate wilderness and making America safe for profit and production along the way. But merely being a millionaire and having the sense of achievement that comes with rescuing a major corporation from extinction is not enough. His parable of self-creation also requires celebrity—hence, the flirting with politics (the reward of large egos) and his widely publicized autobiography.[24]

He is the quintessential first generation cultural orphan: parents who passed through Ellis Island, a close-knit, devout family life, a father who struggled to run his own business, a mother who worked so her kids could afford lunch, children who saw education as their way up the ladder of success. Iacocca was a hustling, eager, ambitious overachiever for whom automobiles were the way to the Dream. He is a workaholic and, as he admits, one whom the Depression turned into a materialist. He is above all, a hero whom adversity has made better and even more successful.

Ironically, perhaps even appropriately, the villain of his story and the source of most of the adversity in his life is a third generation orphan, Henry Ford II. If Iacocca's perspective can be trusted, Ford is a classic study in the decline of the bourgeois. Isolated, passively aggressive, and paranoid, Ford has no notion of how to get money, he is simply bent on protecting what he has inherited from contamination by strangers, especially "wops" (the acronym once attached to certain ethnic immigrant groups meaning "without passports"). Like his wife (a companion and friend of Imelda Marcos, formerly of the Philippines), Ford is addicted to the lifestyle that his wealth brings. His machinations and dictatorial control are rooted in fear and anxiety; his chronic paranoia and insecurity wreak havoc and deception. He is orphaned from his own capabilities, from his own self. If Iacocca paints himself as the naive orphan impelled by the myth of continuous self-creation and the power of will, Ford is portrayed – in Iacocca's account – as the corrupt and degenerated image of the same impulse, tainted with the passage of time.

Iacocca gives us very few glimpses of the self beyond the corporate wizard in his autobiography. There are only fleeting references to his family life, but among them are one or two admissions that his wife's early death may have been due at least in part to the pressures and stress of the years at Ford and the struggle with Chrysler. It is ironic that a man whose life suppressed so much of the feminine side of culture, that bruised the women in his life, should end his story with a paean to Lady Liberty. Iacocca's involvement in the restoration of Ellis Island and the Statue of Liberty was more than just another expression of his drive for celebrity. It is perhaps, more than any other visual image in our culture, the one closest to the heart of a first-generation orphan. The Statue of Liberty announced the promise of America to his immigrant parents. He associates his own roots and basic values with the passage through Ellis Island:

> Those seventeen million people who passed through the gates of Ellis Island had a lot of babies. They gave America a hundred million descendants, which means that close to half of our country has its roots there. And roots are what this country is yearning for. People are aching to return to basic values. Hard work, the dignity of labor, the fight for what's right – these are the things the Statue of Liberty and Ellis Island stand for.[25]

The Statue of Liberty is the closest thing to an ancient goddess of life that we possess in the New World. Above all it is symbolic of *acceptance*, of a holding environment which – like a mother – will protect the orphans and the survivors of tyranny and poverty, a refuge for strangers where they can begin again, where new life and hopes can flourish. Emma Lazarus's poem, inscribed on the Statue of Liberty, appropriately celebrates the goddess of life as "the Mother of 'Exiles":

THE NEW COLOSSUS

Not like the brazen giant of Greek fame,
With conquering limbs astride from land to land;
Here at our sea-washed, sunset gates shall stand
A mighty woman with a torch, whose flame
Is the imprisoned lightning, and her name
Mother of Exiles. From her beacon-hand
Glows world-wide welcome; her mild eyes command
The air-bridged harbor that twin cities frame.
"Keep, ancient lands, your storied pomp!" cries she
With silent lips. "Give me your tired, your poor,
Your huddled masses yearning to breathe free,
The wretched refuse of your teeming shore.
Send these, the homeless, tempest-tost to me,
I lift my lamp beside the golden door!"[26]

How ironic it is that today so many should experience our country not as a place of acceptance but as a culture of *denial* – denial that is expressed spiritually in our nuclear, paranoid, and addictive habits; denial that is expressed in our rejection of the "actual other," the stranger who seeks a new home on our shores; denial that is expressed in our public policies that care more for missiles than for our children; denial that is, in fact, the repression of the feminine in ourselves.

The signs of our hostility to the "other" – especially the one who threatens our lifestyle – are everywhere. Aliens are welcome only when we need them, and not for very long. Instead of being the "melting pot," we have split into an aggregate of small, protected enclaves guarded by single-interest politics. The neglected or unwanted child is treated in the same way as the refugee: "Stay out of sight or you will be sent away." "Don't cost us anything or you will be eliminated." The symbolism of the Statue of Liberty is an ironic counterpoint to the spirit of the times.

Our first birth is into a nation of orphans, a "fatherless" tribe. Where are the "mothers"? Where is that nurturing, life-giving presence brooding over our national life? As we approach our third century as a nation, we must ask at what cost our orphanhood, our free space, our self-creation, have been bought. Can we get back to Kansas? Can we be reunited with the "lost mother"? Can earth, and the land we love, have a second birth?

The Frog Princess

ost of us have heard of the Frog Prince. The phrase stirs a vague memory of a story in which a princess kisses a frog and releases him from a magic spell. (The truth is, in some of the original versions of the fairy tale, the princess smashes the impertinent, intrusive frog against the wall – and her rejection releases him from the spell!)[1] There is another story, a Russian fairy tale about a Frog Princess that is less known:

Once upon a time there was a king who had three sons. Each son was instructed to make a bow and shoot an arrow. Wherever the arrow landed, each would find his bride. The first two sons were successful: one found a duke's daughter where his arrow landed and the other found a merchant's daughter. When the third son finally released his arrow, it landed in a swamp. When he went to retrieve his arrow, he was greeted by a frog.

The young man fretted and wept, wondering how he could live with a frog. Nevertheless, he took her to wife, as he had been commanded. In time, the king demanded that the three brides make him gifts and display their talents. Magically, the frog princess always excelled the others; she seemed to have powers that only witches and fairies had. The king announced a grand ball, at which all of his daughters-in-law were commanded to dance. The third son wept again in frustration, wondering how he could dance with a frog. But she consoled him and said she would meet him at the ball. Meanwhile she cast off her frogskin and stepped forth as a radiant, royal beauty. When she appeared at the ball with her consort, she enchanted everyone. She seemed to have magic powers to create worlds beyond the ordinary.

When the ball was over, her husband arrived home first. The young prince went in search of her frogskin, and when he found it, he burned it. When the princess lay down with him that night, she warned him that at daybreak she would vanish because he had destroyed her frogskin. The next day she was gone.

A year and many months went by, and the young prince longed so much for his wife that he embarked on a long journey to find her. After many adventures, he found her and loved her with his whole being, and the princess was released from the spell that had been cast over her.[2]

A friend of mine – a man blissfully happy with his wife of a few months, then suddenly widowed by an appalling accident – once told me his definition of love. I think it is one of the most profound and insightful I have ever heard: "Love is the absolute affirmation of another's meaning."

In the fairy tales frogs are always associated with sexuality and eroticism, but in this tale the frogskin is much more: it is a symbol of the meaning, the reality of the princess herself – the part that the prince cannot take into himself, because he has not affirmed a part of himself. In a contemporary idiom, the frogskin might be symbolic of the prince's failure to connect with the real person beneath the facade of appearance. Indeed, the "ugliness" of his beloved deters him from maturity in love. What does a man want from a woman? Too often it is only skin deep.

The fairy tale works on the level of personal consciousness and also on the level of collective meaning – the frogskin is an apt metaphor for the disturbing impact that the energy and spirituality of women are having on contemporary male-centered culture. The frogskin symbolizes the magical, mystical, creative powers of the princess, a Dionysian energy that leaps beyond the boundaries of the rational order. It is skin, a point of intimacy and connection, but also a public expression of her subjectivity. The prince is unnerved, uncomfortable with this aspect of his beloved. He tries to burn it – control it – by destroying it. And so they are both cast under a spell: he, alienated from himself by a spirituality of mask and appearance; she, excluded from his society by her reality. Indeed "The Frog Princess" is a parable of the estrangement from men that many women experience today.

3.

THE MYTH OF MAN-KIND

My fondness for the story of *The Wizard of Oz* has generated many delightful and insightful conversations during the course of my myth workshops. One woman who also loved the story told me of her refusal to permit the story to end. Her imaginative child's mind continued to invent adventures for Dorothy long after she had finished the book. She literally created her own mythic saga in which Dorothy starred as hero in her fantasies night after night.

Evidently there were many who responded to *The Wizard of Oz* with a similar desire and urgency for more about Dorothy and the Land of Oz. Four years after the first publication of *The Wizard of Oz*, L. Frank Baum published a sequel, *The Land of Oz*, the first of thirteen subsequent books that continue the adventures of Dorothy and a variety of other characters. Baum notes in his preface to the second book that he has received "a thousand little letters from a thousand little girls" asking for more stories about Oz.

The Land of Oz[1] chronicles the adventures of Tip, a boy brought up by the Sorceress Mombi who, with the aid of her magic Power of Life, becomes the creator of such memorable characters as Jack Pumpkinhead, the Saw-Horse, the Gump, and the Woggle-Bug. A series of entrapments, flights, and escapes complements the dominant motif of the attempt to restore right order in Oz. The Scarecrow, who had taken the vanished Wizard's place as ruler of Oz, has been displaced by a revolutionary army of girls under their leader, General Jinjur, who makes herself Queen of Oz. After a series of adventures, including the reconstruction of the Scarecrow by stuffing him with money bills (after his straw had been scattered by the Jackdaws), Glinda the Good Sorceress appears and reveals that neither Jinjur nor Scarecrow is the legitimate ruler of Oz but that the throne belongs to the heir of Pastoria, from whom the Wizard usurped it in the first place. Pastoria's heir was a daughter, Princess Ozma, who as a child was changed by the Sorceress Mombi into the boy Tip in order to disguise her and protect her from harm.

Glinda marches on the Emerald City with her own army of girls and restores Oz to its rightful heir. When the truth is revealed, Tip is unhinged: "Why I'm not a girl!" He excuses himself, "Let Jinjur be the Queen! I want to stay a boy, and travel with Scarecrow and the Tin Woodman, and the Woggle-Bug and Jack—and my friend the Saw-Horse—and Gump! I don't want to be a girl!" Finally he succumbs to his fate and, after his transformation into Princess Ozma, she says: "I hope none of you will care less for me than you did before. I'm just the same Tip, you know; only—only—." In the final sentence of the book, Jack Pumpkinhead responds, "Only you're different!" and, as Baum notes, "everyone thought it was the wisest speech he had ever made."[2]

Perhaps the early readers saw Baum's Tip as an author's effort to please both his devoted girl and boy readers. Some undoubtedly saw the satire on the suffragettes which provided the backdrop for the action. A few might have detected a slight tongue-in-cheek social commentary:

As they passed the rows of houses they saw through the open doors that men were sweeping and dusting and washing dishes, while the women sat around in groups, gossiping and laughing. "What has happened?" the Scarecrow asked a sad-looking man with a bushy-beard, who wore an apron and was wheeling a baby-carriage along the sidewalk. "Why, we've had a revolution, your Majesty—as you ought to know very well," replied the man; "and since you went away the women have been running things to suit themselves. I'm glad you have decided to come back and restore order, for doing housework and minding the children is wearing out the strength of every man in the Emerald City."[3]

After the adaptation of the book for television in 1960, there was an outcry from parents' groups concerning the subversive nature of the content of *The Land of Oz*. It is doubtful if Baum intended to initiate a revolution in sex roles or a discourse on the merits of androgyny. Once again his imaginative inspiration struck a hidden and persistent nerve in the culture. His imaginary voyages consistently loosed female power and autonomy. The real meaning of the sequel to *The Wizard of Oz* may lie at the unconscious level. The theme of decapitation recycles throughout the stories. The Tin Woodman, who once chopped off his own head, cuts off the head of a Wildcat. The Lion kills the Spider-monster by striking off its head. The Scarecrow twists the necks of the Crows. The Scarecrow's head is removable. Oz first appears as an enormous head, hairless, armless, and legless. The Gump is all head. Jack Pumpkinhead is preoccupied with fears that his head will rot and fall off.

The decapitation theme is suggestive of a rejection of or a threat to the rational mode of experience, certainly the preferred and dominant masculine mode in the culture. The castration associations that the decapitation theme also suggests reveal an archetypal content that may explain the persistent appeal of the stories for men as well as women. One reviewer notes, "In psychoanalytic language, the boy-girls of Oz are phallic, and thus deeply reassuring to boys (or men) with castration anxieties. The reassurance is against their unconscious fear that girlish girls are what they seem to be, castrated boys."[4]

If the Freudian explanation seems too subtle, there is a more obvious interpretation that may shed light on the contemporary male predicament. Real power and identity in men is connected with the release of the authentic feminine in the self and in the body politic. Everything else – all the typical male masks – are defense mechanisms at best and pathology at worst.

The "tough warrior" is one of the masks that contemporary men can choose to wear. However, rather than bear the weight of its pressure, many men will opt for the mask of the "eternal boy." The hallmark of this mask is avoidance of responsibility. Everything becomes a game – even politics – and the crucial strategy is the escape. Peter Pan, the epitome of the eternal boy, has had many incarnations from Rip Van Winkle and Huck Finn to Ernest Hemingway and Teddy Roosevelt. Whether it's lived out by going down the river or off to war, embracing the drug culture, the Playboy philosophy, sports, the gay subculture or the Cosmos Club (men only), or through the constant abdication of responsibility for domestic order in his world to a "Wendy," the eternal boy role is a tempting option in a culture that places heavy demands on the male gender.

The burden of being somebody is so heavy in our society, and the imperative of dominance so strong, that masks are required as props for these difficult scripts. Primarily it is the male who must carry the weight of these myth-scripts in our culture. Women enjoy a qualified exemption from the dominant myth, making these masks unnecessary to their self-definition – except in certain instances; but women have scripts of their own, as we shall see in the next chapter. The tough warrior and the eternal boy are both aspects of a masculine myth that has left men orphaned from their own selves and from the "other" in the social context.

Beneath the masks, who is the New World male? Current research on the male role suggests that, with some ethnic and class variations, the following characteristics are part of a typology of the American male:

- low self-disclosure
- repression of feelings
- excessive task and instrumental orientation, i.e., an emphasis on performance
- detached autonomy and narcissism (with consequent inability to connect, empathize, collaborate)
- abstract projection that often overrides reality
- obsessive need to win, to be on top
- fear of vulnerability (or any threat to self-reliance)
- dependency[5]

Not all males exhibit these characteristics but, by and large, these are the qualities that are typical of men who enjoy a degree of privilege and real or nominal power in society. The ability to analyze; to keep feelings under control; to maintain emotional distance with subordinates; to have a capacity for concentration, ambition, decisiveness, and determination – all of these qualities are necessary for achievement and enterprise. The typology is a prescription for efficient task-completion, indeed for building the kind of civilization we are accustomed to. The qualities in some respects are indispensable, at least in the short run. We are only beginning to understand the long-run cost of such qualities to the personality as well as to the culture, unless balanced by complementary capacities.

The inclusion of dependency in the typology may come as a surprise to some – especially since the male myth feeds on the notion of self-reliance. But it should not be surprising that persons who repress the part of themselves that is vulnerable, compassionate, emotional, and relational should come to depend on someone else to provide or take responsibility for that dimension of personal reality. The myth of male dominance – the imperative of power – will inevitably produce a society of dependent males. Let us examine this paradox.

First, we must understand the birthright that connects every baby boy to the culture in which he is born. This birthright was portrayed very graphically for me in a photo I discovered while assembling materials for a congressional hearing. At first glance the photo appeared to be a typical family portrait: an attractive, sari-clad Indian woman, sitting in a modernized urban setting, with her three children. Her ten-year-old son was sitting next to her, holding one infant. She was holding another infant in her lap. The baby on his lap seemed robust, squirmy, and alert. The baby the mother was holding, by contrast, resembled some of the hollow-eyed children of Ethiopia we have seen on the evening news. The caption on the photograph read:

The emaciated baby girl on the left and the sturdier baby boy on the right are twins. The difference in their condition is entirely due to the boy being nursed first, and his sister getting what was left over. The healthier boy cries for attention and gets it; the glazed little girl no longer even tries.

Few portraits could illustrate so graphically the birthright of the male and female child in our civilization. It is a snapshot of a myth, a false consciousness that has crippled both men and women. This myth has three clearly defined elements: first, son preference; second, male entitlement to dominance and power; and third, the worship of what is male-identified—what I like to call "androlatry."

Son preference is a universal phenomenon. Some research holds that, globally, 90 percent of parents would prefer a son as the first child. Son preference extends from sex-selection to inheritance rights and privileges of education, from access to basic nurturance to resources of empowerment. Moreover, there is implicit acceptance in the culture at large, that males are entitled to preference, privilege, and power. They are born to dominance—or at least the surrounding culture makes them assume so. One way culture does this is by promoting the worship of what is male-identified. What is valued is associated with male experience and social functions and is, therefore, superior. What is not valued is associated with female experience and functions and is, therefore, inferior. These values are transmitted and imprinted in our consciousness by the family, religion, the law, schools, medicine, commerce, and the political structure. Masculinity and femininity are constellations of value that have constructed our world, have taught us who and what shall be respected, valued, rewarded, and empowered.

Since that which is valued is the birthright of the male, the cultural messages of entitlement to dominance are inevitably accompanied by messages of defensiveness, especially in an open, democratic society. The characteristic low self-disclosure of the American male has been shown by researchers to be related to the maintenance of dominance: males generally avoid self-disclosure in order to maintain control over people and situations. The characteristic has undoubtedly been reinforced by the perception that highly disclosing males are deviant. High self-disclosure is a quality that is associated with the constellation of female-identified traits. In general, masculinity requires a certain armor. Sidney Jourard, distinguished for his research on male psychology, says, "The male role requires man to appear tough, objective, striving, achieving, unsentimental, and emotionally unexpressive. . . . If a man is tender, if he weeps, if he shows weakness, he will probably regard himself as inferior to other men."[6]

Thus men typically reveal less personal information about themselves to others than women and cap more of their inner experience. Jourard and other researchers connect this symptom with the greater neuromuscular tension (stress) in men and with their lower life expectancy. The strong, silent Western hero and the cool corporate manager have much in common. Even research studies of leadership have been biased by the stereotype; they show that "effective" leaders often maintain an optimum distance from their followers, avoiding the intrusion of personal knowledge of feelings and needs that might compromise their performance.

Moreover the imperative of performance requires that men develop the external mask. Experience in processing the inner life will atrophy by default as well as by repression. In the last few years men's consciousness writers have made us more aware of this affective deficit and the long-term costs it exacts. Herb Goldberg was among the first to describe the successful "male zombie" and the social autism that leaves him terrified of feelings, except in very controlled, limited settings. Because parts of his own being are numb or atrophied, he is not sensitive to the emotional signals of others. Characteristically, he exhibits a low capacity for empathy. His insight into people is often minimal because he cannot, in Martin Buber's terms, "imagine the real." His socialization as male, in addition to his class and cultural conditioning, removes him even further from being able to receive "the actual other." He will often guess wrong, or be mystified and surprised when others reveal their inner dispositions. He will experience difficulty in maintaining intimacy. Because he does not know what he feels, he does not know what he wants and, more importantly, needs. He cannot love, in the total sense of the word.

(Parenthetically we might speculate on what will happen to those women who in growing numbers are exposed to the socialization patterns of men and male-dominated groups. We will return to this in the next chapter.)

Ironically, the socialization patterns of our culture seem to provide more experience of "others" in group settings for the young man than for the young woman. Sports, scouting, clubs, schools and colleges, military or professional or religious training, the themes and sociology of rock music, and a host of other group rituals enhance the phenomenon we have come to describe as male bonding. Although these experiences cultivate relational skills of a sort, they do not tap the deeper affective levels. Lillian Rubin, in her book *Intimate Strangers*, has made a helpful distinction between bonding and intimacy:

It's when we separate bonding from intimacy that we can explain the relationships we sometimes see among American working-class men—relationships which seem at once so intensely connected yet so lacking in verbal expression. In my research, I came across a few such friendships, where all kinds of activities from work to play were shared, where the depth of the bonding was undeniable, but where feelings—whether about one another or about self—were talked about only when tongues were loosened by too much drink. . . . Intimacy, as we think of it, is possible only between equals—between two people who have both the emotional development and the verbal skills to share their inner life with each other.[7]

It is precisely what Rubin identifies as the "sharing of inner life" that is the key to the affective disability that so many men experience. As one man confided to me, "Talking about it makes me uncomfortable—I'm used to operating at another level." The deficit goes deeper than the repression of feelings or the lack of socialized practice in the expression of feelings. It involves deep fear, hatred, and denial of what is most fundamentally female.

There is speculation that the origin of this denial may lie in the asymmetry of the mother-son relationship—in contrast to the mother-daughter relationship. The mother-child bond establishes the core of the inner life of the child while at the same time it provides a gender specific object of attachment and separation. As Rubin explains, it is the mother's imagery of the self that is internalized by the child and provides the representation that the nascent self is measured against. For the young female child, attachment to the mother and the development of a feminine identity are experienced as a continuity. Even in the separation process—when the child develops her own independent identity—there is no need to repress the early primary identification with the mother as an ego archetype. For the young male child this attachment-separation process is much more problematic (although certainly no more complicated than it is for the female child). The mother cannot be a model for his emerging masculine identity. Therefore separation from what is mother-identified and female-identified becomes functional in his development.[8]

This asymmetry is reinforced by the familial child-rearing patterns in our society. The female monopoly of child care and the relative absence of the father that characterizes many American families probably intensifies the experience of difference and discontinuity in the young male and can impoverish his inner relational life (his ability to project objects of intimate attachment) by the need to repress the early primary identification with the mother. L. J. Kaplan observes that "many men who have been well-nurtured in early childhood cannot revive the memories and emotions associated with good mothering, because in our culture the values associated with masculinity require that male children renounce their ties to the mother and reject dependency and neediness."[9]

The fundamental core of identity for both sexes is what Robert Stoller calls "protofemininity," and the transition from it to masculinity is hazardous for young males. When the developing boy begins to construct his masculinity beyond the core identity of impulses toward femininity he must create a protective shield inside himself, in the form of fantasies that, if successful, endure and become a character structure. According to Stoller,

the behavior that societies define as appropriately masculine is filled with the forms of this defensive maneuver: fear of female anatomy; envy and resulting derision of women; fear of entering their bodies; fear of intimacy (of entering even more than their bodies—into women's inner selves); fear of manifesting and thereby revealing that one possesses "feminine" attributes, in many cultures categorized in such qualities as tenderness, affection, uninhibited expression of feelings, generosity, caretaking, or the desire to envelop others; fear of female attributes such as roundness, hairlessness, high voice; and fear of being desired by a man. Therefore, be tough, loud, belligerent; abuse and fetishize women; find friendship only with men, but also hate homosexuals; talk dirty; disparage women's occupations. The first order of being a man is: don't be a woman.[10]

Stoller notes a higher incidence of sexual aberrations in men and suggests that buried beneath many perversions is fear of women and unsureness of one's own gender identity. Another study concludes that the impetus of this ambivalence propels men into task orientation. Male entitlement to dominance and power is, in this view, a fundamental revolt against the boy-infant's initial experience of absolute power in the mother, the female. The male escape into world-making is an expression of both fear and envy of female power. Dorothy Dinnerstein observes:

As we leave infancy the possibility of transferring dependent, submissive feeling to the second parent—whose different gender carries the promise of a new deal, a clean sweep – entices us into the trap of male dominion. . . . [A]s we rush into the trap of male tyranny the big, immediate thing we are feeling the need to escape is not freedom. It is an earlier, more total tyranny: female tyranny. . . . [T]he male-governed world-making enterprise has had at its heart, then, our ongoing struggle to carve out, and fence around, a realm for the exercise of sober self-reliance.[11]

The flight from female power is also a flight from the sensual, the natural, the emotional, the concrete, and the real. As a result the world-making enterprise is polluted with bluff, fantasy, abstraction and objectivity, with violence and "death-ridden, pseudoactivity." Dinnerstein concludes that the culture as a whole, and men in particular, "go on paying heavy, hostile, costly magic homage to the original magic protector: not to woman herself, but to an abstraction of woman as captive goddess of a more archaic realm."[12] The exile of this real, primordial female power to the realm of fantasy and abstraction has left the masculine consciousness vulnerable to the seduction of the Snow Queen. Is it any wonder that the Nazi fascists who invented the V-2 bomb in World War II could so easily be converted into scientists for the U.S. space program? The allegiance is to an abstraction that transcends the vicissitudes of culture and value.

Abstraction allows the mind – and fantasy – to play freely with nature and events, to exert a kind of absolute control over creation that is impossible when all of the exigencies of the real are taken into consideration. The culture of male dominance cannot survive without abstraction. It permits the invention of esoteric languages and the hoarding of information coded in that language by the empowered caste. The notion of male dominance is in itself a fiction, an abstraction. Robert Martin, a senior research fellow of the London Zoological Society, in noting the sudden resurgence of popular books defending male dominance and aggressiveness as natural traits, has observed that such notions develop because of man's inability to be objective about himself.

The engagement with world-making enterprise and abstraction finds its apotheosis in the absorption with and manipulation of technology, another means of mimicking or displacing female power. A machine is a multiplied male, a promethean abstraction of power. According to Charles Ferguson, "The machine offered man the prospect that he might become as important as woman in the life process. . . . [T]hrough the nexus of the machine he could exercise the function of both the male and the female. . . . [I]t would enable him to feel what he had not been able to feel before."[13] Ferguson goes on to demonstrate that the American culture – that is, the dominant white male culture – has largely been shaped by mechanisms: the sailing ship, the gun, the bottle (a coping mechanism), slavery (a labor-saving device), the pen, the machine, and money (a mechanism for controlling all mechanisms).

Despite the efforts of the male culture to control and displace female power, and the apparent success of such ventures, males continue to strive internally for separation from the female. Further confirmation of the male development conflict surrounding separation is provided by research in men's fantasies and dreams. Studies in the difference between male and female projective fantasies and dreams confirms a higher content of catastrophe, destruction, and loss experiences in men's fantasies by comparison with women's. Dream content also reveals greater frequency of violence in male dreams. Story completions invented by men consistently reflect a movement from enhancement (happiness) to deprivation (loss); whereas the stories made up by women reveal a movement from deprivation to enhancement.[14] The male fantasy and dream contexts show a greater tendency to end in catastrophe, disruption, and destruction. The female contexts tend more toward resolution, reconciliation, and reconnection. Furthermore, the studies show a higher scale of paranoia and a more unrealistic evaluation of capacities (hubris) in the men.

Neither socialization nor sociobiology can fully explain these differences or their roots in the evolution of the species. Indeed, the phenomenon of male consciousness and behavior must be dealt with or it may undermine the survival of the species. It has its roots partially in culture and partially in a developmental pattern. Modern civilization is fundamentally grounded in the separating, ego-consolidating behavior of the male culture. The very notion of "ego" is a concept that is viable only when maintaining distance between the self and the other. Social historians have pointed out how the demise of feudalism and kingship coincides with the emergence of a new "self-distancing" perception of the human person. When Descartes declared "I think, therefore I am," the observation of the self and the distinctions between self and other in the body politic – as well as in the human person – became paramount considerations. "Ego" became a psychological reality because it was a social and political necessity.

Klaus Theweleit, in his provocative study of *Male Fantasies*,[15] would prefer to call this development a split in consciousness that emerged in the sixteenth and seventeenth centuries, decisively altering the way human beings relate to themselves and to reality. Theweleit points out the extent to which this capacity for spiritual "splitting"– a capacity for dividing one's inner reality from the outer reality—is dependent on the cementing of divisions in society, particularly sexual ones which, as we have seen, determine the two primary constellations of symbols, myths, and values in the culture. Out of these divisions emerges the conception of an unconscious life separate from the conscious awareness of the person.

Freud and Jung were among the most articulate interpreters of this new perception of the person. Both transformed the sociology of their times into a psychology of human nature. Freud saw the unconscious as the reservoir of primary instincts and drives; Jung saw the unconscious as a kind of repertoire of collective scenarios and vectors that he called archetypes. Freud recorded the real experiences of many of his patients and later seems to have reinterpreted them as fantasies (psychoanalytic theory). Jung recorded the dreams of his patients and sifted them for significant, mythic patterns (depth psychology). Unfortunately Jung's archetypes, like Freud's Oedipus complex and penis envy, were contaminated with culture-bound stereotypes. Nevertheless, as Demaris Wehr notes, "Jung offers a more imaginal description than Freud does of the inner world of women and men bound by a patriarchal culture."[16]

Jung's concepts of anima and animus, in hindsight, offer us a lopsided view of the inner reality of men and women. The anima is represented as the tender core and idealized soul of every man; the animus as the internal, critical voice of every woman. Wehr suggests that such gender-linked archetypes can be seen as "inner representatives of socially sanctioned, seductive but oppressive roles and behavior patterns."[17] Nevertheless, Jung's concept of the anima offers us a unique view of the inner world of the male who struggles to accept a side of himself which is devalued by society, that constellation of female-identified experiences and feelings that he inevitably suppresses—an alienation that arises out of fear of women.

So sweeping, so comprehensive and all-powerful is this psychic phenomenon that the renowned French philosopher-psychoanalyst Luce Irigaray ventures to say that "to an extent, the unconscious is historically censored femaleness."[18] The male psyche is thus divided into inner life (female) and exterior armor (male). Fear and alienation from woman are so deeply rooted in the male that he is orphaned from himself. The final words spoken by the survivor in the movie *Platoon* express the truth about men at war and the deeper alienation of men from their very selves: "Is the enemy we're fighting in ourselves?"

Whence comes this awesome and awful fear of femaleness? Many psychologists posit a developmental flaw, a deficit in the symbiosis-separation process between mother and son which we have described previously. Some theories suggest that the attachment to mother persists in its threatening aspect because the dissolution of the earlier symbiosis was too abrupt or independent behavior prematurely forced. Some believe it may be the magnification of female power that is the result of nuclear families, female monopoly of child care, and the demise of the extended family and multiple surrogate parents. Others believe it is primarily the effect of the transference of the young male's identification from the mother (valued in the personal sphere) to the public sphere (the dominant culture) where mothering and femaleness are devalued.

To what extent is the self-esteem of the mothering parent, or the degree to which she may trade vicarious experience through her own child for owning her own experience a crucial factor? Clearly, there are many possible interacting factors that may contribute or accelerate the male's critical developmental passage to an identity and individuation that is premised on not being like mother.

Moreover, it appears that there are many factors in our culture that coerce men to despise and suppress in themselves the natural primary object of their need for attachment—woman and mother. Barbara Ehrenreich draws a compelling social thesis from this phenomenon:

Under these conditions, men will continue to see the world divided into "them" and "us," male and female, hard and soft, solid and liquid—and they will in every way possible, fight and flee the threat of submersion. They will build "dykes" against the streaming of their own desire. They will level the forests and pave the earth. They will turn viciously against every revolution from below—and every revolution starts with a disorderly bubbling over of passion and need. They will make their bodies into hard instruments. They will confuse, in some mad revery, love and death, sex and murder. They may finally produce the perfect uniformity, the smooth, hard certainty that transcends anything that fascism aspired to: a dead planet.[19]

Whatever the causes, femaleness has gone into exile, has gone underground in our culture. The most visible evidence of the repression can be observed in the psyches of men. There are three primary expressions of this ethos. First, of course, is the overwhelming sense of fear and dread—fear of submersion, of losing control, ultimately of dissolution, of being swallowed up, engulfed, drowned. Thus, in men's dreads as well as their fantasies we encounter the association of women and women's bodies with floods, abysses, pits, swamps. Even since ancient times, natural wells, springs, and seas have been closely identified with mother goddesses. In the semantic and mythic universe, as in the psyche, "woman" becomes a code word for a whole constellation associated with natural phenomena, bodily processes, feelings, vulnerability, and the unconscious. To be engulfed by the "flood" is to be vulnerable and out of control.

The second expression of this ethos is more pathological. It is in fact a "refusal of the real." In his investigation of the German Freikorps (volunteer soldiers), Theweleit describes the fascist impulse as a terror of the real, the concrete: "it is above all the aliveness of the real that threatens these men. . . . Their mode of (re)production is the transformation of life into death, and dismantling of life." The threat of the "flood" and being engulfed by the real is combated with monuments, towering cities, weapons and missiles, and standing tall. Theweleit notes that in the fantasies and dreams of the volunteer soldiers the political enemies and the hostile principle of femaleness are identified with floods in much the same way. He sees these images as embodiments of the eruption of the soldier male's unconscious.[20]

The response of these Freikorps volunteer soldiers to the *real* and its association with female-identified functions, while extreme, is in many ways a microcosm of the contemporary malaise: the flight from suffering, the denial of death, the fear of aging and vulnerability, the abuse and neglect of children and the environment, the paranoia about illegal aliens and about national security. The exploitation of money, sex, power, drugs, and a variety of other escapisms have become the dominant culture's way of avoiding intimate contact with the *real*, with what the culture has repressed, with problems to be solved.

A third expression of this ethos is the projection of the ideal. Jung, for one, has ventured an explanation of the exaltation of woman, a phenomenon that has occurred repeatedly in cultures as well as in the psychology of men. He suggests that the more remote and unreal the personal feminine is, the more intense is the male's yearning for a projection of the eternal feminine onto social institutions that can signify a maternal character in embracing, protecting, nourishing, always welcoming, approving the individual. Examples of this projection range from the Virgin Mary and the university as alma mater to the feminine personification of ships and machines, cities and countries, sciences and revolutions, and perhaps most of all, the Church.[21]

Thus the oppression, adulation, exploitation, and exaltation of woman is all of a piece. It is the displacement of the repressed femaleness, the eruption of the unconscious of a culture.

The universal male birthright of entitlement to dominance is amplified in our culture by the American myth of empowerment through violence – production and control achieved by force – and through the exclusion or exploitation of "the other." Likewise, the male developmental dilemma of separation is intensified by the New World myth of self-creation. The negation that both of these cultural imperatives implies – the rejection of otherness in the environment (the enemy, the alien) and in the self (femaleness) leaves the American male dependent and impotent. He must hide behind the masks of the tough warrior and the eternal boy, or risk being an outcast or deviant.

The first time that I understood this clearly was a painful and terrifying experience in my own life. As a congressional aide I had been assigned to the investigation of the murders of four American women missionaries in El Salvador. After several years of immersion in and relentless excavation of the horrors that surrounded that case, I found myself sitting in a ramshackle courtroom in a remote Salvadoran town, sitting just a few inches behind the accused murderers. As an official congressional observer I was there for the duration of the marathon trial which lasted twenty-five consecutive hours. I had plenty of time to study the five guardsmen who were on trial. With the exception of one, who was sick and wept continuously throughout the long, humid day and night, they all sat passively through the detailed recitation of their atrocities as if they were accused of merely stepping on a few troublesome insects.

I was troubled by the emerging pattern of mindlessness and numbness to violence, cruelty, and mutilation that seemed characteristic of these young men and of the entire military subculture. Four of the five were short even by Salvadoran standards; they came from desperate poverty and had few skills or opportunities. Most of them were not good enough to make the army, so they had to settle for the national guard. In a world that promised them nothing and had deprived them of so much, being a national guardsman was a ticket to power. In return for absolute loyalty, the *caudillo*, (the chief) offered these social castoffs perhaps their first pair of shoes, regular meals, a uniform, and weapons. Thus socialized into a ritual of militaristic seduction, they acquired a sense of power and status that was denied them in the ordinary social structure. They followed their sergeant's orders and whims like abused dogs. The sergeant, who had ordered the rape and murder of the women, was much bigger, bullish, sullen and surly in his self-importance. Classic macho, he was the perfect enforcer for the *tanda* system of feudal militarism that infects so much of

Central America with corruption and violence. (The Contras in Nicaragua are among their alumni.) It is a network, a web of terror, that makes the Mafia look like a Boy Scout troop.

Why were these four women missionaries such a threat to this pathetic man and these sad creatures who followed him so blindly? The women were a threat because they were perceived as having power, the greatest power of all – the power to win the hearts and minds of the people and to empower them with hope for change. Nothing could be more threatening to an established, entrenched military elite that has nothing to gain and everything to lose by social change. That in itself was enough to make them a threat. But the fact that they were *women* – this unleashed the unconscious in many men just like the sergeant whom I confronted during my work in Central America. Women, the despised part of the self and the denigrated half of the culture, should not have that kind of power. They had to be crushed, eliminated – and above all, they had to be humiliated in order for these men not to feel impotent.

I have never forgotten the faces of those guardsmen or the sad, pitiful details of their histories – so filled with deprivation, rage, and impotence, so bound by dependency and self-defeating bursts of violence. When I read M. Scott Peck's chapter on "Mylai: An Examination of Group Evil" in his book, *People of the Lie*, I sensed something was missing in his analysis.[22] It was more than "regression under stress" and the "fragmentation of conscience," more than psychic numbing and group narcissism that caused at least fifty ordinary American soldiers to slaughter 350 unarmed women, children, and old men in several Mylai hamlets in South Vietnam in 1968. In addition to these factors and symptoms, it was an eruption of the unconscious and all its associations with femaleness, vulnerability, and "otherness." The men of Charlie Company projected their fear, rage, and impotence on the most convenient symbolic target: unarmed, feminized "gooks."

In his study of the German Freikorps volunteer soldiers, Theweleit notes that in their fantasies, Reds, communists, and women are associated with the same negative images (floods, red tides, pits, swamps, bloody flows, etc.). In this twisted pathology, femaleness and all its associations with feeling and sensitivity are repressed, but the real woman becomes the necessary object of the male's confirmation of dominance, bravado, and conquest. Another interesting study of two hundred Green Berets who admitted participating in terrorist campaigns in Vietnam found that they were frequent, compulsive womanizers. The study showed "there was significantly high agreement among them, however, on being 'left cold' by their first sexual contacts with women. They had been disappointed by their lack of feeling, which then became habitual, though it never stopped them from chasing women."[23]

Domestic violence provides another evidence of impotence and dependency in men. Leaving aside the effects of the longitudinal history of violence in families, rage against women is implicated as the immediate cause of domestic violence – rage in response to woman's failure to conform to the expectations of a particular male. Battering is an attempt to put women down and keep them in their place – it is no different than the child's tantrum when it cannot command the attention of the mother, from whom it fears to be separated. It is the primary way that many societies have given men permission to vent their feelings of lowered self-esteem and powerlessness. The rage masks the fear, the impotence, and the dependency. One clergyman who has worked extensively with batterers observes, "Virtually all men are angry at women and a man who batters is acting out in extreme form what most men feel, at least part of the time."[24]

The same tendencies that often characterize the behavior of male soldiers and many domestic relationships are magnified in the phenomenon of pornography, where women are consistently the primary objects of violence: rape, battering, mutilation, humiliation, sadism, annihilation, and bondage. These same slick and glossy images of oppression and atrocity are used as sales gimmicks by the advertising and record industries. No one seems to notice, so numb have we become to the victimization and dehumanization of women. No one seems overly concerned that these images become the stored repertoire of appropriate objects for violence, for acting out our most irrational impulses.

Nature and nurture issues will never be completely resolved, and perhaps we will never know for sure just how much maternal omnipotence-impotence and father absence (which can be affective and expressive as well as physical) have contributed to the repression of femaleness in our culture. Ultimately, the evidence from experience suggests that it is a heavy dose of *myth* rather than *mother* that is responsible for the male predicament in the current era. The problems hinge on *expectations*: the culture's expectations of men, and the male's expectations of what the culture and women, in particular, owe him. And so we come full circle, back to the universal environment of son preference and male entitlement to power.

The fear of women and the threat of their power, is real and is connected with these expectations. What men really fear is the loss of their entitlement to power. Joseph Pleck, in his study of male power, describes two forms of power that men perceive women as holding over them. The first is *expressive power*, the power to express emotions (an interesting corollary to the documented low self-disclosure in American males). As Pleck notes, in the traditional male-female dyad, men have learned to depend on women to help them express their emotions, indeed, to express their emotions for them. (This vicarious expression is analogous to women's presumed dependency on men for vicarious expression of their needs for achievement.) A second form of power that men attribute to women is what Pleck calls *masculinity-validating power*, a myth that requires women to perform in certain ways in order for men to feel their masculinity validated, confirmed. Thus men, having abdicated from exercising these dimensions of power themselves, are dependent on women for fulfilling these expectations. When, for whatever reason, women refuse to behave according to the script, men feel lost and bereft, impotent, and usually attempt to force or bribe women back into the expected roles.[25]

Men's need for power over women derives from their own self-interest as well as their psychological needs. At a very early age, small children perceive who is empowered in the social context. Many little girls often wish they were boys; almost no little boys are on record as wanting to be girls. Even preschool males perceive that masculine identity and power is achieved by at least partial isolation from female things and by disproportionate aggressive behavior. One of the most interesting correlations in behavioral studies on men is the fact that males who rank high on masculinity scales as youths often display considerable maladjustment and sociopathic tendencies in adulthood.[26]

Recently I discovered another interesting corollary to these developmental issues in men as a result of some research I was doing on pedophilia (the pursuit of sexual activity with children or young persons). After reviewing the research literature on approximately 150 cases of pedophilia, I was struck by the fact that pedophiles as a group are capable of acting out with either sex: the choice is that of an immature person rather than a particular homosexual or heterosexual object. The psychological assessments of these individuals showed that almost all of them had conflicts and anxiety about "dominance" and, characteristically, fear of adult females. It is well known that much of the traditional therapy for these individuals – aversion therapy, behavior modification, even chemical treatment with anti-androgens – is relatively ineffective in really curing the disposition. More recent experiments with social skills and assertiveness training have been a little more successful. Needless to say, the phenomenon of pedophilia provides a pertinent gloss on the analysis of male psychology presented in this chapter.

There is reason to anticipate more stresses and developmental tensions among males in the light of recent sociology of adolescents. The time during which young people exist in a nonsexually charged social environment has been considerably shortened. Dating and pairing are occurring more universally and at younger ages, and the demands on young men to be emotionally and empathically "controlled" and to prove masculinity through relating to women have become much stronger. Pleck and others conclude that "exaggerated masculinity, rather than being a reaction to inner insecurities, may reflect an overlearning of the externally prescribed role or an overconformity to it. This alternative interpretation, part of the emerging new theory of sex-role strain, puts the burden of responsibility for destructive, extreme male behavior on society's unrealistic male-role expectations . . . and not on the failings of individual men and their mothers."[27]

Many new stresses have been introduced into the social environment by the women's movement, the rush of women into the job market, the rising number of two-earner families, women's entry into male preserves, and the new sexual assertiveness and experience of women. William Goode believes that the most important change that men experience is "a loss of centrality, a decline in the extent to which they are the center of attention."[28] Expectations!

These stresses have generated a rising tide of male rage, Neo-Right ideologies that celebrate male headship and entitlement, competitiveness with women, and in general a smorgasbord of backlash symptoms. As in the nineteenth century, the increased visibility of women's militant demands has drawn forth cries of "sexual suicide" and neo-determinism in sophisticated circles. In some circles it has generated wimp hysteria and, in society, increased assaults on women both physically and psychologically.

The workplace has become the most visible arena of these emotions. Anthony Astrachan has identified some of these fears in his book, *How Men Feel.* One response to change has been fear of female talent and energy. Astrachan maintains, however, that "on a deeper level it is fear of the combination of competence and sexuality; many men (and women too) see a real and painful conflict between them. At its most basic, it is fear of female rage and of the threat of emasculation that men sense in that rage."[29] Another response is related to men's refusal to share power or relinquish it in appropriate circumstances. Most men are socialized to feel superior to women and require someone to look down on to prove that they have that power. Astrachan says, "In business that translates into the belief that we belong above women at any level of any hierarchy. That makes it very difficult for some men to accept women as peers, and even harder to accept women as bosses."[30] The annals of sexual harassment cases and sex discrimination lawsuits provide evidence of the lengths to which men will go to prevent women from having power.

The impotence and dependency of men is a condition of their membership in the dominant culture. The pyramid structure of power in society demands that men, too, play subservient roles in return for some of their privileges. Viewed from this perspective of the political economy, sexism is a narcotic that keeps men from rebelling against their own exploitation. To illustrate this symbiosis many examples might be cited, but one scene in the film *Men's Lives* is particularly graphic. In the scene a worker from a rubber plant describes how his bosses pacify him to get maximum output from him, but seem very little concerned with his fundamental human needs. He then throws water on his little show of feistiness and succumbs to resignation, remarking that he is only a worker and can't really understand what is going on. Then he is asked whether he would want his wife to take a job in order to reduce the pressures he feels to help support his family. In contrast to his earlier passivity, he aggressively asserts that he will never allow her to work, and furthermore he would never help with the housework after he comes home from work if she did take a job outside the home. Pleck illuminates the significance of this vignette:

The man expresses and then denies an awareness of his exploitation as a worker. Central to his coping with and repressing his incipient awareness of his exploitation is his false consciousness of his superiority and privilege over women. Not scrubbing floors is a real privilege, and deciding whether or not his wife will have paid work is a real power, but the consciousness of power over his own life that such privilege and power gives this man is false. The relative privilege that men get from sexism, and more importantly the false consciousness of privilege men get from sexism, play a critical role in reconciling men to their subordination in the larger political economy. . . . [W]e cannot fully understand men's sexism or men's subordination in the larger society unless we understand how deeply they are related.[31]

Thus many men will continue to wear the mask of the tough warrior–leader of the family wagon train–to compensate for the social disempowerment that they experience but deny. Other men will opt for the escape mode and don the eternal boy mask. In recent years the manifestation of the eternal boy has undergone an interesting transformation in the American culture. As a species, the single yuppie male emerged as a prolific mutation in the 1970s and 1980s. The number of men living alone rose from 3.5 million at the beginning of the 1970s to 6.8 million at the end. Although there are more women living alone too, their number has increased only half as fast as men's. Almost two-thirds of the men living alone are in the never-married category and view marriage as restrictive of their autonomy.[32] Advertising and marketing have nourished the emergence of the species with strategies that exploit the consumer orientation of these individuals. The profile is by now well developed: single or divorced professional males, earning substantial or more than adequate salaries, spending it on themselves. As one marketing manager told an interviewer: "Divorce helps everybody [except women]: the men get a bigger share of the good life, and we double our orders for stereos, refrigerators, washers, microwaves."

Ehrenreich and others have identified this "commitment phobia" as evidence that the male revolt against the breadwinner role has been much more successful than women's revolt against the feminine mystique. As women were struggling for a very basic kind of moral and psychological autonomy, men were carving out a kind of autonomy in the social space, one that endorsed self-indulgence and detachment from the claims of others. Many women also mistook this form of autonomy for the real one.

We see this kind of autonomy in the myth of the loner, the orphan hero, which is very much alive in the popular media. Prime-time TV heroes–among the chief conservators of our national mythology–have added a layer of sensitivity to their personalities, but almost all of the serious prime-time fantasy heroes are singles. (Hunter, Spencer, Magnum, Sonny Crockett of "Miami Vice" being a temporary exception). The ones who are married are rich, patriarchal robber barons ("Dynasty" and "Dallas"). In contrast, more of the nonserious (comic) heroes are portrayed as *connected*, embedded in the context of family systems ("Bill Cosby," "The Jeffersons," "Family Ties"). This absence of connectedness–taken seriously–in the sociological reality of increasing numbers of men and in the cultural projection of fantasy life suggests that somewhere between

Leatherstocking and the Equalizer the myth of self-creation has been transformed into living by and with, if not for, oneself.

The gay subculture is in many ways a microcosm of the crisis in masculinity that pervades our relationships and our times. Within the gay community (our consideration is limited to men for the moment) we find a bipolar psychology and sociology. We find one group of men migrating toward the pole of authentic autonomy that would release them from the culturally determined and stereotyped male role and the myths that underlie the role. Whether it is men struggling to express repressed femaleness (caring, homemaking, noncompetitive, aesthetic instincts) or to liberate their maleness from conformity to others' expectations, these men in recent years have often found their inspiration in the women's movement and personal support from close women friends. They do not hate women; they simply prefer to express their sexuality with men; they fantasize men as sexual partners. In discovering women as role models and friends, they have discovered the lost sister in themselves.

This contingent of the gay world is often more successful at negotiating friendship and nonsexual relationships with women. As Astrachan notes, most gay men seldom have deep friendships with straight men because of the tensions that may arise out of homophobia. Their relationships with other gay men are also affected by tensions similar to those of nonsexual relationships between heterosexual men and women: "they might become sexual, which changes the nature of love and trust."[33] Seymour Kleinberg believes that the richest and most moral relationships gay men form are with women. Neither partner in this kind of relationship is pressured by the demands of conventional sex-role playing. Women also have testified to a certain kind of freedom in these friendships, since the gay men neither patronize them or treat them as objects as most straight men do.[34]

There is another segment of the gay subculture, however, that is motivated by misogynism and narcissism rather than by an authentic autonomy. In fact, these gay men often mimic the worst features of the dominant culture: exaggerated physical strength, promiscuity and sexual violence, dominance. Kleinberg suggests that they are in fact "eroticizing the very values of straight society that have tyrannized their own lives. . . . The perversity of imitating their oppressors guarantees that such blindness will work itself out as self-contempt."[35] These men, perhaps more than all others, have repressed the femaleness in themselves.

No amount of movement rhetoric or gloss can hide these two tendencies in the gay culture, or disguise the implications for women and for the culture at large. The world of gay men, incorporating as it does both of these attitudes toward women and female-identified experience, is a microcosm of the larger male culture. Moreover, it is symbolic of the struggle of a disempowered masculinity to achieve its authenticity and maturity in the social context.

The study of another microcosm underscores these implications. The Church has been one of the primary conservators of misogynist myths about women. Fear of the power of women and the need to control it has generated all kinds of teachings, attitudes, and practices concerning women from contraceptive prohibitions to the *Malleus Maleficarum* on witches. But there is evidence that the tradition of clerical celibacy grew out of more than the effort to control the power of women (sexuality); it seems to have been directly related to a contempt of women (therefore a desire to simply eliminate them). This misogyny is characteristic of the second strain in male homosexuality described above. Bishop John Shelby Spong argues, "The church filtered misogyny through a Manichean dualism and then overlaid that negative attitude with a male priesthood that was in significant numbers homosexual."[36] Like some historians, Shelby Spong suggests that the dominance of a large number of misogynist gay men in the clergy was a critical factor in the Church's mandatory requirement of celibacy and of its continuing antiwoman bias.

As the dynamics of power in male-female relationships undergo adjustment and change, there will undoubtedly be much pain. Many men are experiencing symptoms of abandonment in response to changes in women's roles and behavior. Women are often blamed for the failure of male expectations. A *New York Times* survey in 1983 found that 28 percent of American men felt that the women's movement had improved their lives; 63 percent said it had not. Astrachan estimates only 5 to 10 percent of men really support the changes precipitated by the women's agenda. Men will continue to experience the symptoms of abandonment until they "cut the cord"–not the ambiguous attachment to mother, but the chains of privilege and myth that bind them to a patriarchal system that in fact keeps them impotent and dependent.

Today many of the men we know and love are like Peter Pan's "lost boys," dependent on Wendy, searching for a father-connection. In J. M. Barrie's play, the boy John says knowingly, "Peter is not really our father. He did not even know how to be a father until I showed him." These are boys who, unconsciously for the most part, long for fathers who embrace them, who touch them, who express their emotions, who know how to take care of themselves. They long for fathers who mother, who are not afraid to share power as well as their own vulnerability; fathers for whom the care of children and of a home are valued activities. They are looking for fathers who are present, who know how to play as well as work. They need fathers who are free to be all these things.

Sam Osherson, in his book *Finding Our Fathers*, identifies men's journey of liberation as a process of "healing the wounded father." He says,

Ultimately it is the internal image of our fathers that all men must heal. All sons need to heal the wounded fathers within their own heart, on their own. The process involves exploring not just the past but also the present and future – ways of being male that reflect a richer, fuller sense of self than the narrow images that dominated the past. In truth that is the task of all men today: to explore the masculine nurturer and caretaker within.[37]

Speaking for many women, Phyllis Chesler echoes his insights:

I began to understand that father-wounded sons never recover, never confess, never remember; slowly I began to understand why women can never satisfy the longing of boys who are love-starved for their fathers; why women can never exorcise the grief of men, lured by their fathers into wanting the impossible . . . God Almighty's benevolent protection: against other men, against the original female parent, a magic male amulet, a son's shield against the rising hot shame of childhood vulnerability.[38]

Men are doubly orphaned – once by the culture which has idolized "fatherlessness," and twice by the genderizing process which estranges men from themselves and from women, and hypnotizes all of us with an abstract myth of manhood.

The ancient world debated the question, "Can women be saved?" Today many women are asking the question, "Can men be saved?" They ask this in a much more fundamental way: can men develop the behaviors that the future of the family, society, and the world seem to require?

The answer to that question fortunately does not depend on the bad news presented in this chapter. Men are experiencing their orphaned state in unprecedented ways in our time. Many are being left by the women they love; a significant number are being forced to learn skills they always assumed to be women's work. Many more are now primary caregivers for children; they are partnered with women who are their equals as spouses, parents, professionals in collaborative enterprises and in public life. Some men are learning to value and participate in the world of experience that is female-identified and thus are liberating the repressed feminine – the caretaker, the nurturer, the protector of Gaia – in themselves.

Perhaps the churchmen who once told us that "women will be saved in childbearing" (1 Tim. 2:15) will have to revise their instruction. Perhaps men will now be saved by child-caring—that is to say, not only in the literal sense taking up responsibility for children and their development, but entering more fully into the existential world of female-identified, basic human functions. In a symbolic sense it will mean caring about all forms of life in the Gaia and relinquishing political and personal priorities that displace or threaten those values. It will mean caring for the child in the man, surfacing and honoring the vulnerabilities, the feelings, the powerlessness that have been repressed and latent, even in the most powerful. Men have a story to tell and a journey to make, and when they find the words and the way, the myth of man-kind will no longer have power over us.

The Hunter Maiden

ong ago, among the Zuñi people of the Southwest, there lived a young maiden. She lived alone with her aged parents in their pueblo. Her two brothers had been killed in warfare, and it was her responsibility to supply the family with food and firewood.

The little family lived very simply. During the summer, when the girl grew beans, pumpkins, squash, melon, and corn in their garden, they had enough to eat. But when cold weather came, there were only dried beans and corn to feed the family.

To keep hunger at bay through the winter, the Zuñi people had to hunt game. The stone axes and rabbit sticks of the young maiden's brothers hung on the walls unused–for it was the custom that only men could hunt, and her father had grown too old and feeble for hunting.

One year the cold weather set in early and the first snow had fallen. Now was the time the girl must gather brush and firewood. "We have little to eat," she said to herself, "but at least we will be warm."

As she worked she watched the young men of the tribe go forth with their rabbit sticks and stone axes. Later in the day they returned to the village with strings of rabbits.

"If I were a boy," she thought, "I could hunt rabbits, and my parents would have meat to nourish them." She pondered this, saying to herself, "There's no reason why I can't hunt rabbits." Indeed, when she was a child she had often accompanied her brothers on the hunt.

So that evening, as the girl sat by the fire with her parents, she told them she intended to hunt rabbits the next day. Her father said, "No it is better to live with hunger. Hunting is not women's work." Her mother said, "No, no, it is too dangerous. You might lose your way in the mountains. It will be very cold."

In the end her parents reluctantly agreed to let her go. Her father prepared a stone axe for her. Her mother prepared a small lunch and a warm wrap. The girl rose very early in the morning before the young men set out to hunt. Carrying the stone axe, she set out for the river valley beyond their pueblo. She soon found many rabbit tracks and improved her snaring skills as she went along. By the end of the day she had added many rabbits to her string.

Soon it was growing dark and snow had begun to fall. The string of rabbits grew heavy on her back and she began to feel tired. She looked behind her to retrace her steps. The snow had wiped out her trail. She had lost her way. She realized it was foolish to go on in the blizzard and the darkness and began to look for shelter for the night. As she moved along the rocky cliffside, she discovered a small opening that led into a cave. She gathered twigs and piñon, bringing in several armloads to keep the fire going throughout the night. She cleaned one of her rabbits and roasted it over the crackling fire. Soon she was ready for sleep.

Suddenly from the dark stillness outside the cave came a long, mournful wail. Fearing some other hunter might be lost in the darkness she went to the mouth of the cave to investigate. A huge figure loomed out of the darkness. She stood frozen in terror and fear. Huge red eyes glared at her and she realized it was one of the Cannibal Demons that haunted the world from ancient times. She ran to the back of the cave and hid. The Demon roared at the mouth of the cave, trying to get in, but the opening was too small for his huge body.

"Let me in!" he roared. "I'm hungry and cold."

The girl did not answer.

Then the Demon called out slyly, "Come out here and bring me something to eat."

"I have nothing for you. I've eaten all my food," the girl answered.

"Bring out the rabbits you caught," he demanded. "I can smell them. I know you have rabbits."

The girl threw out a rabbit. The monster seized it in his long, clawlike hand and swallowed the rabbit in one gulp.

"More!" he demanded. "Give me all your rabbits!"

Now the girl was angry. "I have no more. Go away!"

The monster threatened her, "I'm coming in there to eat you and your rabbits!" Lifting up his great flint axe he began to chop away at the stones near the entrance, gradually making the opening a little larger.

The sound of the flint axe on rock traveled through the night air. Far away on Thunder Mountain, two Warrior Gods heard it. They knew at once that it must be the Cannibal Demon's axe and that he must be causing trouble.

Picking up their weapons they flew through the darkness to the cliffside where the Demon hammered away at the entrance to the cave. They saw the predicament of the hunter maiden and quickly dispatched the Demon. He fell at their feet, dead.

"You are safe now, maiden," they called to her. "We will sleep out here at the entrance to your cave and protect you until morning."

The next day as the sun rose and the white snow glistened, the girl came out of the cave with her string of rabbits. The Warrior Gods praised her strength and courage. Then they walked with her down to the snow-covered valley to the outskirts of her village. While they were walking the two Gods taught the maiden much hunting wisdom.

When they could see the pueblo in the distance, the girl turned to her two companions, bowing low and breathing on their hands to thank them. When she straightened up, they had disappeared.

The girl walked into the village, proudly carrying her string of rabbits. All the people stared in wonder. Never had they seen a maiden hunter, and the number of rabbits she had caught astonished everyone.

She did not stop but hurried on to her home. When she entered, her parents cried out with joy that she had returned safely. "Now we have food to eat," she cried. "I'll cook a fine rabbit stew to make you strong. And there will be furs for the bitter cold winter."

"You have done well, daughter . . . and hunter maiden," her father added, smiling. "From now on you will hunt for our family, and your brothers' axes will be yours."[1]

4.

WOMEN – OUT OF THE CAVE, INTO THE DESERT

In the early 1970s I thought I had found the yellow brick road – I had discovered the women's movement. I knew instinctively that something was going to happen in women everywhere that would profoundly alter the evolution of humankind and of our planet. The transformation had begun in my own consciousness – it was exhilarating to be part of something that daily offered new revelations psychologically, intellectually, and socially. So much personal and political dis-ease suddenly had an explanation. The exorcism had begun. Women, and some of their male companions, were awakening from sleep. "Somewhere over the rainbow" a new country existed that would enable us all to be whole. It was wonderful to be one of the early explorers, pioneers in the quest for that country.

The awakening gave me new eyes to experience my own reality; Kansas would never be the same. Everything ahead was in technicolor; everything behind was grey, sterile, and passionless. I couldn't imagine anyone ever wanting to go back there. In 1978 I wrote a book about the awakening of women: *Kiss Sleeping Beauty Good-Bye*. The basic premise of the book was women who do not have the power to make choices, to act, and to take responsibility for their own lives cannot be whole. They are ethically and spiritually dwarfed, perfect in their own way, perhaps, but artificially stunted.

It seemed to me then that there were only two basic spaces that women could occupy: they were either "formula females" who were still asleep, or they were lucky enough to be waking up. You could find your way along the yellow brick road with the help of a Good Witch or two, and you had to be careful to avoid the Wicked Witches who could keep you in bondage or destroy you. Men, like Dorothy's companions, were not the chief protagonists of the story after all; it was the female figures that embodied real power in the Land of Oz. It seemed so simple.

Today the situation and the story seem so much more complicated and overwhelming – more inexorable and cosmic, and at the same time more fraught with regression and tribalism; more exhilarating, and at the same time more frightening. It reminds me of Dorothy's adventures in *Ozma of Oz*, the third in Baum's series of Oz sequels.[1]

Dorothy has been washed ashore after a shipwreck. She finds herself, accompanied by her pet hen Billina, on the beach of the Land of Ev (Eve?). Ev is a magic country on the other side of the Deadly Desert that separates Oz from the real world. Ev is a matriarchal fairyland, currently ruled by Princess Langwidere, who is said to have thirty different heads, one for each day of the month. (The princess prefers changing heads to changes of clothing, coiffure, or makeup, and demands that Dorothy exchange heads with her – Langwidere, it seems, is a "fad" feminist!)

The former king of Ev had sold his wife and children into slavery to the Nome King before committing suicide. Langwidere is ineffectual against the Nome King who has turned the inhabitants of Ev into bric-a-brac. Queen Ozma of Oz comes to the rescue of the Evs and Dorothy. Dorothy and Ozma experience immediate solidarity: "as soon as she heard the sweet voice of the girlish ruler of Oz, she knew she would learn to love her dearly." Roquat of the Rock, the Nome King, lives deep beneath the earth, the emperor of legions of hardworking nomes. He succeeds in transforming Ozma and her company into bric-a-brac. But Dorothy and her pet hen outwit Roquat, discover his secret code as well as his Achilles heel (hen's eggs), and disenchant Ozma and all the other victims of the Nome King. Roquat desperately summons his army, but, blinded and poisoned by two of Billina's eggs (uniquely feminine missiles!), he is unable to prevent the theft of his magic belt and the loss of all his prisoners.

The Land of Ev(e) looks and feels familiar. For many of us the yellow brick road of awakening has not led through the magical country of Oz to the transformation of Kansas. We're still on the road and the way is fraught with detours and death valleys. Since the early 1970s I have had the privilege of accompanying hundreds of women on the journey. Whatever the time we had together – brief, as it is in many workshops; or enduring, as it is in community or with friends – it has been a time of shared stories, solidarity, struggle, and the discovery of wisdom. But we are still in a place that is unfriendly to women – and there are many pockets of self-hatred and mistrust in our own hearts. We are more diverse than I first surmised; the differences between those who are awake and those who are asleep are not so simple.

To make sense of this Land of Ev where so many of us find ourselves now I have developed my own "liberation index," a sort of guide to the diversity of levels of feminine consciousness in the present era.

The first level, of course, would be the state of *innocence.*. I see many young women in this category. They come out of families where they had strong, nurturing parents who were to some degree role models of an egalitarian marriage. They may have attended private schools where girls were affirmed and encouraged. They pursue (often in Dad's footsteps) law degrees, or medicine, or MBAs. When they graduate professional doors open wide to receive them. Many of these women could only be described as innocent. But when you hear them say, I don't consider myself a feminist because it might "affect my professional relationships," or because it might "scare off available men," then you know that the innocent has begun the retreat into denial.

There are many poor women in the world who are also innocent. Their situation is so desperate, so degraded and subservient, so closed off from the extended social reality that they are unaware they could exist in any other way. I am reminded of an incident told by a black woman who was teaching a literacy course in one of our inner city ghettos. She had just learned that she was pregnant and wanted to share the good news with her students. One woman in the class grew very disturbed, even angry with her, as if the teacher had violated a taboo. Her response to the teacher's good news was, "And how come your husband didn't beat the hell out of you for that?" Violence in relationship is the norm for many women – they cannot conceive of alternatives.

Millions of women exist in the state of *denial*, a second level of consciousness. They are vaguely aware that there are alternatives to their situation, but prefer the security and rewards of the expected role. Their need to be approved or their need to be needed is so ingrained that they cannot conceive of disturbing their small universe. Their own self-denigration often conforms to the social projections of women. They have been described as codependents in a system that is, at best, unfriendly to women. No cyclone has as yet blown them out of their garden of dependency.

There are some women for whom the consciousness of their situation becomes so painful and unbearable that neither rebellion nor conformity is possible. *Escape* is their coping response; these are the women who go mad, commit suicide, or numb themselves through addiction. I believe one of the reasons for the popularity of talk shows like Oprah Winfrey's is that it allows women – primarily – to reveal and process this constellation of denials and escapes.

Then there are the *defectors*, converts to co-optation. Today there are a significant number of women who have experienced, at least initially, the consciousness and conscience of feminism. Sometimes they burn out; sometimes professionalization or upward mobility seduces them into investing in "the white, male system." And there are far too many, perhaps, who make incredible compromises with themselves because of their need for a particular relationship. Books about women who love too much have become a cottage industry.

No doubt there are thousands of women who start out as "missionaries" to an oppressive system. For awhile they have one foot in, one foot out. They are extremely conscious of what the corporation – or a particular kind of relationship – does with and to women. All too often they drift into defection, perhaps because they have no peers who are also awake or because the trade-offs are too great. There are a few who survive with their vigilance and integrity intact. If a woman "dressed for success" in the beginning, sometimes she reaches a level of power where she can be herself. But what does it mean to be a powerful woman in a system that is fraught with oppression? Is it possible to be a change agent while still being an insider?

Innocence, denial, escape and defection – these are among many varieties of "bric-a-brac" that keep women under a spell and that threaten women's wholeness and happiness today. What is left? At some point every woman must come to terms with the final option: *deviance*. It becomes a matter of degree, rather than a total identification or engagement – although it may lead a woman to exit every space of acceptability. Sooner or later it seems, the social systems – marriage, family, professions, institutions, politics, corporations, churches, peer pressure, class expectations – push us to the boundary of deviance. We reach a certain point where it becomes clear that the primary motive of a system is to perpetuate unequal distributions of power and resources, to exploit and/or abuse us. Or we gradually come to realize that an intimate partner is incapable of relating to us except from a position of dominance or manipulation. Resistance, deviance, or departure becomes a necessity. Women undergoing these redefinitions and transitions experience an overwhelming sense of not belonging, of being alienated from the social norm – of being orphaned.

More than anything else, women fear the loss of connection; yet it is often those very connections that keep women prisoners, their psyches conditioned to a kind of house arrest. The roles assigned to women by the culture are primarily those of relationship, of caregiving. Seen in the broader social context, the roles assigned to women are a kind of compendium of the culture's unsolved problems. For centuries women not only have attended to the "fallout" from the violence and inadequacy of our social and political systems, but their own bodies and psyches have born the brunt of its failed experiments. Nevertheless, when a woman steps out of any of these assigned roles, she risks being thrown into the terror of abandonment.

But the casual observer will object, why should women feel more orphaned now? So much has changed in the last thirty years—women are so much better off. Yes, there are many ways in which some women's lives have improved, certainly for women in the dominant sector of the culture. Women have more entry into education, into many new professions and jobs. They play new privileged roles in corporations, in the Church, and in other institutions. They are making many more distinctly personal choices about lots of things: what to wear, who to love, whether to have children. They take more interest in and participate more in public life. They seem to be more comfortable with their sexuality. Why then these pronounced symptoms of loneliness, guilt, and powerlessness?

The fear of being alone is the worst of all female terrors. Like most human capacities, the need for relationship, a nurturing presence, and a holding environment has both positive and negative aspects. In recent years, thanks to the work of women researchers like Jean Baker Miller and Carol Gilligan, we have gained a new understanding and respect for the positive bias that women have toward connection and relationship.[2] One study cites the responses of several adolescents to the question, "What is the opposite of 'dependency'?" The answers of the boys and girls were characteristic. They boys' typical response was independence; the girls were more likely to suggest that loneliness or isolation was the opposite of dependency.

In a culture that fosters individualism and detached autonomy, where the conditions of advancement and improved status often require separation—the new location, the new job, the new spouse, the new self— the maintenance of connection and continuity in relationships is extremely difficult. Thus the fact that women have a lower threshold for loneliness and feelings of disconnection seems to be a healthy adaptation in a social milieu that is ridden with isolating forces. The loneliness that many women experience is fundamentally authentic; it is anxiety doing its job—warning us about something in our social fabric that is not hold-ing together.

And there is a particular loneliness that has to do with men. The popu-lar articles about the dearth of available men are really a camouflage for a more crucial problem. Recently a woman who came to me for counsel exploded in my office. She raged against fate, against the world's leaders, the world's mothers, against God, against everything that selected her to be born in this era. She grieved over the fact that so many women, like her-self, were caught in a "myth-warp," doomed never to find a life companion because this generation is incapable of producing the evolutionary male that a woman's changed consciousness needs and expects. If the feminiza-tion of poverty is a reality of our times, so is the feminization of loneliness. In her book *Alone in America*, Louise Bernikow notes, "In all of the surveys of how lonely we are, women said they were lonely far more often than men did. . . . The quality of relationship that satisfied most of the men I talked with left women hungry."[3] Although the Hite Report's methodol-ogy has been held in question, the most recent edition, *Women and Love*, is an extraordinary revelation of the pain and truth of women's relation-ships and the particular kind of loneliness that they endure.[4]

There is the loneliness of the mother at home with small children, the loneliness of the woman whose spouse doesn't communicate his feelings, the loneliness of the single woman looking for a significant other, the loneliness of the woman in the corporate law firm where, "The people who are rewarded are the sickest ones, the distorted personalities, men unwilling to feel anything. Work provides them with an excuse not to feel anything . . . . It's amazing that people could survive on so little, without emotional sustenance."[5] There is the loneliness of single mothers and children without roots and extended family; there is the loneliness of elderly women, whose numbers are growing astronomically; and there is the loneliness of being single—which is now the condition of a third of the adult population of the U.S.—in a transient, mobile society.

If women suffer acute attacks of loneliness today, there are reasons enough in the surrounding social milieu. But there are also reasons of the heart, within woman herself, that are likely to provide seasons of extended loneliness. Bernikow suggests that loneliness is really unab-sorbed change. But the process of adjusting to changes in the way we live, in the conditions of modern life, is only one aspect of "unabsorbed change." Women, more so than men, are trying out a new myth. They have no role models or generational anchors to lean on in trying out a new story, and so it is scary and lonely. We forget that Freud summed up the accepted view when he defined female dependence as an essential attribute of femininity. For centuries we were convinced of it ourselves. What happens when a new consciousness breaks through and we begin to see new possibilities for ourselves? When we begin to see the possibility of personal autonomy? Could loneliness be, Nelle Morton asks, "the awful abyss that occurs after the shattering and before the new reality appears?"[6] The orphaned woman has broken with many of the old codes of normality, but has not yet found what will take its place.

And if we go even deeper, into the mother lode of our emotional life, we might discover another reason for our loneliness—most of us are undermothered. Two experienced therapists sum up the problem: "All the women we have seen in therapy have come with problems and confusions about their sense of self because they did not embody enough of mother to allow them to separate."[7] Women who have absorbed the traditional myths about femininity can smother, but not mother very well. The sense of self they transmit to daughters is not anchored in a solid, self-centered identity; and so the daughter develops a self-anxiety rather than a healthy sense of self-worth. She is uncertain of her boundaries because of the "push-pull" dynamics in her emotional dependency on her mother. She often carries a lifelong, but unacknowledged, neediness because of this ambivalence. Her developmental pattern often has not prepared her to receive caring from another woman on a psychologically consistent basis, and this will complicate her relationships with men and women.

Undermothered women, women starved for "matrimony," often grow up as successful "daughters of the father," women well-adapted to coping in a patriarchal culture. But this is often at the cost of a deep alienation from their own feminine ground and from a personal mother. With Adrienne Rich, they can say, "The woman I needed to call my mother was silenced before I was born."[8] So, like men, women also carry a separation anxiety that is different but no less intense; it is one that sets the thermostat of a woman's need for and expectations of relationships very high. Moreover, her socialization as a female does not actively support and reward her for being separate, nor does it give her the necessary inner resources to cope with it.

Loneliness, finally, is not about women who love too much, or men who can't love, or about smart women who make foolish choices, or about men who hate women. It is about recovering those resources, that inner content with our own presence and a caring social environment that mediates our existential aloneness. Dependence and independence are not, in themselves, inherently healthy or unhealthy. Cultural influences have distorted and crippled dependence as a means of domination; likewise cultural influences have overvalued male-style independence. Thus feelings of dependency can be extremely painful in our social milieu. When these needs are met by someone, we fear the loss of our own identity and power; and when they are not met, they reinforce our feelings of unworthiness and emptiness.

Women often feel guilty for having these needs – needs for closeness, intimacy, dependency, sharing, nurturance – and they fear the loss of relationships because they are afraid their need will drive others away, especially men. On the other hand, men have traditionally denied or disguised their need for emotional dependency while getting it met. Women's role has been precisely to take care of men's need for nurturance. Women have felt more needy, more orphaned than men because, by and large, they have not gotten their needs met by men. Nurturance is something most men have gotten (and still get) from women, but they have not known how to give it (for all the reasons we have suggested in the last chapter). No wonder women in our culture seem needy – they have not had "wives"! This is what therapist Miriam Greenspan calls "patriarchal doublethink."[9]

Women experience in a most profound way the orphan's feelings of worthlessness. When they express their genuine need for nurturance and affiliation, they are made to feel guilty for a kind of excess. When women do attend to their own needs for a change, they are made to feel guilty for shirking their caregiving responsibility. When they express their sexuality without pretense, they are treated like temptresses or deviates. When women say "no" they often feel they are pushing another person away and feel guilt for that rejection. And when they surface anger for all these double binds, they are made to feel guilty again.

A lifetime of these received messages – from within as well as without – adds to the erosion of self-worth that is often flawed from infancy. By the time she reaches school age, a woman's habit of inner self-criticism is well developed. (As every teacher knows, most young boys tend to overrate their prospects and capacities; young girls tend to underrate theirs.) Carrying this dynamic into her relational life, a woman will often convert her needs for getting closeness and nurturance from men into self-criticism. Greenspan calls this tactic "a doomed effort to control reality," based on the false assumption that a woman's problems in relationships will be solved if she can just "get her head together."[10] This assumption may be a more comforting way of thinking than facing the fact that there may be precious few men available for the woman whose myth of herself does not match the traditional one. Thus women, whom mythology has burdened with a primordial guilt for everything, continue to prime the pump in their own psyche.

Women's socialization to femininity as a caregiver (responsible for others' emotional sustenance) and to finding her identity and fulfillment in living for another has been the reservoir of a great deal of self-hatred and guilt. What happens when she adopts the culturally approved autonomy and independence that has been the prerogative of males? She risks falling victim to another double bind: implicit understanding that in order to be an exceptional, accomplished woman, "You have to think like a man." But beneath that stereotyped compliment lies another implicit corollary: "You're not a real woman" (because women are complementary to, i.e., inferior to, not competitive with, men). Today, many women newly arrived in male-dominated professions are suffering the fallout from this new form of feminine self-hatred. One wonders if it explains some of the backsliding into comfortable traditionally feminine roles.

There are few women who do not experience at some time in their lives the orphan's feeling of being a hostage to fate, of having no power over what happens to them. Pregnancy and the vulnerability to it brings a woman much closer to this experience of powerlessness than most men. The economic jeopardy and exclusion that most women experience in terms of salaries, opportunities, benefits, and advancement is intensified by the fact that most of them have children who depend on them for support. Moreover, our entire political economy is geared to the survival of the fittest, who are assumed to be men who are providers. (In fact it most benefits single men who are providing for themselves.) Women who want to work, women who must work also feel powerless in trying to provide for their children. There has not merely been apathy, but aggressive opposition to surrogate care for children in our society. Children unfortunately are often a "noncompute" in considerations of providing equal opportunities for women. Moreover, women have little or no voice in the formulation of public policies that directly impact their own quality of life and the lives of their children—whether that is comparable pay, health care, or defense policies.

It is in the area of domestic relations that the powerlessness of women is so dramatically evident. Domestic violence is experienced by one in every three women in our culture. It is one of the most compulsive and continuous forms of victimization. Women are imprisoned in its tortured cycle by their fear for themselves and their children, by their own naive expectations, their lack of resources, by their desire not to hurt even when they are being hurt, and certainly by the lack of social understanding and support in their predicament. Women who stay with batterers feel trapped and helpless. And nowhere is the connection between guilt and low self-worth more insidious than in the battered woman who blames herself for her spouse's explosive behavior.

The powerlessness of women begins with the little girl's perception of who it is that is empowered in her world—males, for the most part. She masters the language of the disempowered, full of qualifiers and deferential syntax; she masters the restricted gestures that sexual politics will require of her. She may also adopt the dialect and swagger of her male peers, but circumstances will require more practice with the female script. She will probably come to believe that it is an authentic expression of herself. Peer pressure and the surrounding culture will complete the task of shaping the self she presents to the world. It should not be surprising then that women can be disconcerted by events or questions that cause them to consciously evaluate their lives. In my work with women in workshops and counseling I have confirmed the observations of Judith Bardwick, that "a larger number of women compared to men will evade an evaluation of their lives, because any assessment heightens their perception that they do not determine their life style but, relatively powerless, are limited to responding to the directives and initiatives of others. For a certain kind of woman, even asking the questions, 'Who am I?' 'What do I want to do?' is decimating."[11]

But the questions must be asked. We must face and name our radical orphanhood. Empowerment can only come if we confront our powerlessness together.

There is a wonderful print over my desk, a painting of a woman astride a magnificent, galloping spirit-horse. It is full of flowing, powerful energies, and the artist has inscribed this caption under it: "It is woman who will unleash the feminine energies which will heal and unify our planet. First she must make her own journey." This journey is the key to our own wholeness and liberation, and ultimately that of the world. Our experience will be, already is, a paradigm for the evolution of humanity itself.

The journey begins with a recognition of our orphaned condition and a coming to terms with our orphan self. If men must struggle to reclaim and value parts of their experience that they have delegated to women,

women must struggle to name and value their own experience – the experience of the *real* rather than the pseudofeminine.

The recovery of the authentic feminine begins with the experience of *emptiness*, or *nothingness*. History and culture have orphaned women from their own experience; they have internalized this, it is part of their pseudo-self. I have described the process elsewhere as a kind of "heteronomy" in which the myths and expectations of the dominant culture are impressed on the consciousness by internalization and self-repression. It is destructive of the moral personality, and in its most extreme form leads to the "despair of not being willing to be oneself."[12]

To exorcise this pseudo-self – along with the self-negation, self-hatred, and alien values it signifies – one must pass through a profound experience of emptiness, nothingness. This is the return to the cave, so symbolic of the journey of women. We must enter it, be in darkness, fear, and self-doubt for awhile, and emerge after our confrontation with our own demons, especially the demons of needing and being needed. The cave is that inner space where the authentic self is created from the broken pieces of our lives, where we become empowered and content with ourselves, and unafraid.

In my own experience this return to the cave came after my awakening or consciousness change. Exposure to women's lives and their stories was an important catalyst in that awakening, as was a more catastrophic awareness of my own oppression. As one of the first women on the faculty at the University of Notre Dame in the early 1970s, I was plunged into and surrounded by a male culture layered over with a clerical culture. The Christian veneer could not disguise the blatant gynophobic atmosphere, and in due time most of us went out the proverbial revolving door for women. From that time on, I knew in my bones what it was to be oppressed – the scales had fallen from my eyes and revealed my own history from childhood of being disvalued, envied, and displaced by males as well as male-identified women. My anger became a positive source of energy to work for social change.

Still, like many other women who were "awake," I had not yet experienced the cave – the emptiness and the emptying. This second, more profound liberation of the authentic feminine in myself came in the wake of failed relationships (two in particular) and of other significant losses (the sudden deaths of three close friends and of my father, and a catastrophic fire). These losses sent me down to the roots of my being, searching for an understanding of my own behavior and the discovery of what I had substituted for my own reality.

The cave experience begins with an encounter with the life experience in reverse. Early in life is the need for love, then the hurt over not getting what we needed, and finally, the desperation and anger to ease the hurt. The cave experience reverses this process: moving from anger and desperation, through hurt, to deal with the neediness for love. The confrontation with parental ghosts is crucial to this process. For some, the deficient parenting is obvious. For others, it is more subtle. One post-cavewoman says it for all of us: "I was an orphan with parents. They were parents to the invented, phony me, while no one took care of the real me."[13] And another: "I gave myself up to get love from my mother; when that didn't work, I tried my father; and when that failed, I tried God."[13]

In some fundamental way, we have all been deprived of love, of mothering—if not of love, then of the feeling that we have been loved. Knowing we were loved is not enough; we have to *feel* it. If the early deprivation is not acknowledged and owned, life can become a series of failed or unsatisfying relationships in which we unconsciously reconstruct the original holding environment and attempt to resolve it. We attach ourselves to lovers and spouses who are like the parental ghosts: critical people, so we can overcome our judgmental parents; or cold, aloof persons, so that we can make our parents warm and expressive. We set up a vast array of defenses to defeat and repress our awareness of our neediness. In the cave experience the superstructure of defenses comes tumbling down; we feel naked and exposed, our handicaps revealed, our pseudo-self shattered in the terror of realizing that our unconscious needs have been totally out of control or invested in controlling.

Relationship losses are critical for women. Separation—a condition of masculine selfhood conveyed by the culture—has never been an imperative for feminine selfhood. Our sense of self is organized around being able to make and maintain relationships, rather than based on self-enhancement through projects, careers, or achievements. Thus for many women the disruption of an affiliation is perceived not just as a loss of relationship but as something closer to a total loss of self. Jean Baker Miller and other feminist psychologists have proposed that this psychic starting point represents an alternative starting point for a more evolutionary approach to living and functioning, decidedly different from the approach fostered by the dominant culture.

The self-in-relation model of selfhood is based on the premise that for everyone—men as well as women—individual development proceeds only by means of affiliation. Indeed, this premise would lead us to challenge as archaic the modern theory of healthy male development which posits disconnection from the mother and the separation from the world of female-identified experiences symbolized by the oedipal situation. The new model would allow for the evolution of relationships, for a rhythm of closeness and distancing in every relationship, for expanding networks rather than painful amputations. Unquestionably it would be a difficult model to achieve in the present configuration of our social and political economy, which so often rewards separation and causes disruption of bonds.[14]

Nevertheless the recovery of the authentic feminine requires that we see our identity as a "self-in-relation" rather than as one who "lives for another," or one who enjoys a kind of absolute autonomy. Unfortunately, defining ourselves through relationship is fraught with problems because so many of our affiliations grow out of a distorted power model, "one up, one down." Women have been seeking the kind of relationships that are almost impossible under the present arrangements, and they have been willing to sacrifice parts of themselves – the true self – for scraps of attachment. In this sense women have been truly orphaned by the culture, by history, and made desperate for safety and satisfaction in their relationships. Women's needs as well as their expectations can set in motion a debacle of manipulation.

Thus part of the cave experience is getting in touch with our own familial, social and historical deprivation. The fault lies not so much in ourselves as in the constellation, the context in which we find ourselves. In the self-in-relation model, it is the girl's mothering relationship with her mother that forms her most fundamental self-definition. As we have noted before, the qualities which the mother values and devalues in herself as "mother"– as caring person – are transmitted in a powerful but subtle manner. This mutual caretaking and identification – often remaining unconscious – becomes the core structure of feeling for the daughter, making it very difficult for her to act in ways that violate this intense interpersonal connectedness. Janet Surrey notes, "Whatever the expense to herself, it becomes intensely difficult for the woman to act in a way that might hurt another person. This often explains the difficulty some women have in separating from self-destructive or ungratifying relationships with men or women – they cannot tolerate being an 'agent of abandonment' and continue to feel totally responsible for the other person's feelings."[15]

For many women in our culture the confrontation with parental ghosts means recognizing how the dynamics of the family system make us vulnerable to neediness and needing to be needed. A father often presents to us a more socially empowered personality than our mother. If he is not punitive or abusive, our feelings reach out toward him when we begin to try on selves that would distinguish us from mother. Moreover, a father is often not there enough or not mothering enough. This leads us to identify with and idealize male approval, and leaves us with a feeling deficit in respect to male closeness. (It could be just the reverse, but the situation as I've presented it is more typical in our culture.)

Because of the uniqueness of the mother-daughter relationship, this feeling deficit will often manifest itself as a dis-identification with mother, which is really a cover for a very profound unconscious identification with her. In the exorcism of the father's ghost may come the discovery of who the woman's mother really is, who she has been struggling to be underneath all the deficits, the props, and the poultices.

Since the early 1970s I have been working with women through workshops, retreats, and counseling. Much of what women bring to these settings is the task of recovery from internalized patriarchy. Sara Maitland has described this internalized pater-ego in her essay on her "two fathers," her real father and the Father inside: "The Father in my head holds me in a double blackmail: if you are good I will cherish you and if you are bad I will punish you. But I will never ignore you or leave you alone or let you go your way."[16] She describes the way that this internal Father monitors her relationships with others, even with herself; monitors her professional life, even her mothering of her own children. "Women's approval, companionship, makes me feel happy, but it does not ever make me feel virtuous, safe or good. Men's approval, which does make me feel virtuous, does not make me feel happy, safe or good."[17]

This internalization burdens us with normative expectations and rules. It is the core of women's depression, self-doubt, and self-hate. The internal monitor intimidates us, keeps us from admitting to ourselves the truth of our inner reality: that our terror of man hating is a defense mechanism to ward off the realization that, in a patriarchal society, most women unconsciously hate men.[18] Anger becomes a very important midwife in helping women to purge the unconscious, hidden forms of this man hating, to bring it to the surface, and finally to pass through it to liberating ways of relating to men and other women.

The internal Father intimidates women into guilt and self-hate in four areas in particular: first, the body and sexuality; second, the need to love and to be loved; third, competition with men for power; and fourth, pride in one's giftedness. Over and over again women's inner conflicts focus on these four areas, precisely the areas of personal energies that women need to befriend and cultivate in order to be wholly, authentically woman.

Like many other women I had once imagined these conflicts as a struggle between the "masculine" and "feminine" energies in myself. I sometimes avoided dealing with the conflict because I assumed that one would have to triumph, the other be defeated in myself. Then I discovered the wonderful model of wholeness that was first developed by Toni Wolff, a disciple of Jung who was dissatisfied with the oedipal model as a paradigm for female development. Her model described four dominant female energies under the aegis of four goddesses, ancient symbols of female power, archetypes of feminine experience: the Magna Mater, the life-giving power of the mother, of nurturing and mentoring; the Hetaira (or Aphrodite), the goddess of love, the lover and companion; Artemis, the virgin-amazon, earth-protectress and rival to man; and the Sybil (or crone), the seer, the wise woman.[19]

As I worked with these archetypes in the company of other women, they became an important aspect of the cave experience—images and presences that assisted women in reclaiming parts of themselves that they had denied or repressed, even mutilated in their efforts to heed the internal monitor. We discovered that most of us were more comfortable on the Mother-Aphrodite axis because it liberated our relational energies and mimicked the approved roles for women in society. We were less comfortable on the Artemis-Sybil axis, because that was the axis of power in the culture, the power to name, shape, build the major sectors of the social order: politics, science, the arts, religion, medicine, and law. We were less comfortable there not because these were masculine capacities or pursuits, but because feminine energies and values had been largely excluded from these sectors.

Moreover, role models in these sectors are not abundant; therefore each of us has to make contact with the archetype deep within ourselves, bring it to the surface, affirm it, and be affirmed for releasing those energies. This process would be incomplete and impossible for a woman alone; and so the mediation of other women—the midwifery of the spirit—is an essential part of this journey. Support groups and networks, "kin-spirits," are indispensable in a woman's passage to a fuller life.

The Mother-Aphrodite axis—although more consciously expressed by women—is also in need of healing. These affiliative energies have largely been distorted, exploited, and even perverted by a patriarchal society. The primary event in the patriarchal consciousness is the split between the spirit and the body. It has spawned any number of aberrations from pornography to state-sponsored torture to anorexia. Women's association with the body, with nature and natural functions, and with sexuality, estranges her from the concerns of the spirit and the life of the mind – or so our cultural apparatus implies. This despisal of embodiment is branded, as it were, in women's flesh – it should come as no surprise that women's self-hatred and feelings of inadequacy are often symbolized in their feelings about their bodies.

One of my favorite exercises in the women's workshops I have conducted is asking the participants to decide which part of their body they dislike the most. This simple exercise becomes a springboard to discussion of the self-loathing and self-laceration that women absorb from the social environment as well as, sadly, from significant others in their lives. Women's poetry is filled with these images and with testimonials to their exorcism in the recovery from possession by the pater-ego. I think especially of poems like Robin Morgan's "Network of the Imaginary Mother" which describes her conversion from flesh-loathing to flesh-affirmation while nursing her dying mother. She describes aspects of embodiment in terms of goddess figures: Kali, Demeter, Isis, African and pre-Colombian goddesses. So many of the physical features that modern women dislike in their femaleness are the very aspects that were most admired in the ancient goddesses.

Women fear rejection because of their bodies. Woman's body is her "frogskin"– a profound symbol of the unity and connectedness of her sexual, erotic, magical, mystical, and creative powers. To separate these from her embodiment is an incredible, intolerable mutilation of her spirit. Embodied spirit is the very means and condition of authentic relationship – the medium of love, joy, and communion. Reduced to nothing but her body, woman is totally "other," alienated from herself. Reduced to nothing but spirit, she is alienated from all that is real. The stereotypes of the whore and the virgin are forever at war inside a woman's pseudo-self and in the consciousness of the culture. (We see this acted out in teenage runaways from strict, pious families who end up as prostitutes; we see it acted out in the woman who is an "ideal wife and mother," who begins to exhibit "nympho" tendencies at cocktail parties.)

The authentic feminine, the true self is a self that is connected with everything, and in whom the experiences of sexual love, religious experience, and the creative impulse are not separate. Novelists, poets, and biographers have sometimes captured woman's sense of this connectedness, portraying women who believe that sexual love, the creative urge, and religious zeal are aspects of one and the same life force. Recent interpretations of the lives and works of many of the women mystics reveal this same fusion of powerful female energies.

If the normative ego structure of our society has been defined by separation from something or someone, then perhaps women are indeed the harbingers of the future. Once liberated from relational power distortions, we are able to connect–in an embodied way–to everything: not just to persons, but to ideas and feelings, to creatures and the earth itself, to the cosmos–and to God, the ultimate Being-in-Relation.

Modern culture has been the history of the masculine objectification of reality, even to the point of the reification of the tenderest of relations. The pornographic objectification of the body of woman has been symbolic of this violence. We can hope that the next era will be the era of feminine subjectification, the transformation of objectified reality into body (that which I can see, feel, and touch; that which I care for), matter and mind embodied in an ecology of interdependence and mutuality. We can hope that the body of woman will emerge from being an object or instrument of exploitation into that of a paradigmatic, metaphoric force. As philosopher Charlene Spretnak observes, "The experiences inherent in women's sexuality are expressions of the essential holistic nature of life on Earth; they are 'body parables' of the profound oneness and interconnectedness of all matter/energy."[20]

But if women assumed that sexual freedom would fulfill the paradisal promise of this symbolism, they were sadly mistaken. There is a blight on the rose of sexuality. Because the erotic has been both idolized and mistrusted, it has been narrowed, specialized, genitalized. Because it has been the prerogative of males to awaken or inspire (even in the religious dimension!) the erotic in women, its power has been mechanized, diminished in us. Moreover, the dominant male culture is unnerved and perplexed by the fact that women in solidarity seem to be able to liberate the erotic in all of its spiritual and sensual power–between and among themselves through the sharing of experience and personal stories, creative expression, ritual and social struggle–in ways that transcend what sexual experience ordinarily connotes. This is because in the normative cultural paradigm it is not sex but *dominance* that has been eroticized in the sexual encounter. In fantasy, men eroticize possessing and conquering; women eroticize being possessed, being transported. Male and female, we have all learned that resistance often heightens eroticism. An honest examination of the dynamics of power in actual sexual relationships suggests that the prevailing paradigm of sexuality in our culture is one of pursuit and capture, of dominance and submission, and that—contrary to the popular myths—this is neither fulfilling nor natural. And although the dominance/dependence is usually stereotypically assigned according to gender, it is neither an exclusively heterosexual problem nor a consistently male-in-pursuit-of-female dyad. Whatever the configuration, the sexual encounter can easily fall into these dynamics if the same myths are being projected by the partners.

The implications are obvious: sexuality must be freed from these dynamics if the erotic—with its spiritual as well as sensual elements—is to be liberated and creatively expressed. In this context, celibacy becomes a liberating option to pseudoeroticism. On the other hand, when the celibacy option is acted out within the context of the same power dynamics, it can become a seductive, repressive mode of manipulation and control. As in the case of sadomasochism, it can reinforce dominance and dependency as a condition of relationship and debase the authentic feminine.

The wholeness women are seeking is compromised in another way. When the Artemis-Sybil energies of the feminine are repressed and violated by the surrounding culture, they are split off from consciousness and submerged in the psyche. When touched, contacted, and released in a woman, these powerful feminine energies may surface, accompanied by destructive forces of rage and aggression, of negation and depression. Women have not been allowed to struggle visibly and openly with their own demons—these too have been suppressed by the culture. As the earth-community moves into a phase that marks the "return of the goddess," a return of the authentically feminine, we can expect to experience signs and symptoms of what has been described as animus.

Some years ago, during a very troubled time in a relationship with a male friend I awoke one morning from an intense dream. In the dream I saw a very still, almost stagnant sea. There were several fish lying on their sides on top of the still waters, flat, with staring empty eyes as if they were dead. Suddenly the sea began to churn and roll, and a huge sea serpent, eyes flashing, breathing fire, burst through the surface from the depths. As the serpent writhed and coiled, the waves pitched, the sky darkened with clouds, and a roaring tempest broke the placid stillness. The fish that had been lying on the surface suddenly came to life and many disappeared into the depths beneath the stormy sea. Time passed; the serpent and the storm disappeared. Then, when the waters grew calm with gentle rolling waves, I saw pairs of dolphins playing in the sunlit sea.

I have pondered this dream many times since, and marveled at how it seems to capture so much of the agony of woman-man relationships in our times: the selfishness and ruthlessness, the explosiveness of repressed feminine energies; the emptiness and shallowness of the approved masculine roles. In hindsight, the archetypal significance of my dream has gradually emerged. A stunning parallel is found in the Sumerian myth of Inanna, who descends to the underworld in a confrontation with her destructive sister Erishkigal, then demands her male consort as scapegoat and sacrifice; he is dispatched to the underworld as the price of transformation and redemption from her own demons.[21] Thus, our dolphin selves, and gentle mutuality, will come – but only after much struggle and pain.

There is no turning back from the cave, the desert, or the depths on the other side. We can't stop the tide of women's consciousness and get off. Something happened in the late 1960s that changed everything forever. Some women's lives were turned upside down. Some women's lives didn't change very much, but they were conscious that something was changing around them. Nothing has really been the same since.

Today we sense it is happening on a global scale. Saudi women, Iranian women, Kenya women, Argentinian women, Native American women are discovering their collective power. In our culture, as we might expect, it began with an emphasis on consciousness change and personal autonomy – our national myth of self-creation and individualism influenced the style and structure of the women's movement in the United States. In other cultures, the starting point will be different, perhaps with more emphasis on the collective – precisely because the national myths differ. The agendas will differ in terms of priorities, but the goals are inevitably the same: the restructuring of the power dyad between men and women, between the valued and the less valued, the privileged and the powerless.

No, what we're on is not the yellow brick road – it's more like a people mover. Some women are walking, running faster than the moving tide. Some are simply standing still, but moving willy-nilly. Some are walking more slowly alongside the people mover, following their own rhythm. A few, perhaps, have leaped onto the mover going in the opposite direction. Some women change directions more than once. We are all on board, one way or another, participants in the most universal social change since the dawn of the idea of democracy, and perhaps since the invention of tools and fire.

Women are all at different places on the people mover. What do we have in common? Something Sylvia Marcos of Mexico calls "permanent rebellion." She distinguishes "primary rebellion" from "permanent rebellion." Primary rebellion erupts from the first horrifying realization of oppression. It is usually marked by aggression against the enemy; censorship of those who are not committed or ideologically pure; little capacity for compromise and long-range strategy. Permanent rebellion, a later stage, is a capacity for sustained commitment, rain or shine; a quality of will – a willingness to work, knowing that we will never completely attain the goal that we seek; a willingness to sacrifice perfect attainment in order to work toward it as a value that orients our life; a willingness to struggle to transcend barriers of class and culture that keep us from communal action for the future.

Marcos concludes that there are three essential elements of this permanent rebellion: first, the value of the body and the affirmation of the body; second, the value of action and the necessity of being an activist; third, the value of spirituality and the sustaining energy of the spirit. Women can survive on such things – perhaps the world will, too.[22]

There was a time, perhaps, when male dominance, son preference, and androlatry promoted some limited evolutionary end. Or possibly it was, from the beginning, a historical aberration. We may never know. But the contemporary social reality clearly demonstrates that it has become a primitive holdover that is now dysfunctional and disruptive to the further evolution of the species. Not only our own personal wholeness, but the survival of world order and ecology is at stake.

For now, the men are simply "not there" in so many ways. Like Dorothy's male companions they lack the feeling heart, the experiential insight, the courage to let go of their scraps of power and their pseudo-selves. For now, we wander just the other side of the Deadly Desert in the Land of Ev, struggling to rescue ourselves and our lost sisters from the Nome King, struggling with our own demons in the cave, discovering new strengths that will astonish and nourish the world.

A Dream in the Desert

live Schreiner (1855–1920) was a remarkable and gifted woman who knew better than most what it was like to live between the "no longer" and the "not yet." Her writing was to distinguish her as the first major South African writer in English to gain international esteem. Her inner journey—out of a racist Boer background and missionary upbringing—gave her insights into the struggle for female identity and integrity, and into the black African's situation, that were prophetic and that preceded by decades other more easily remembered voices. Self-educated, she forged her own self-determination in the crucible of work, ill-health, friendships, loss of faith, and a long search for a life partner who shared her convictions about egalitarian marriage. Her book, *Women and Labour,* became the "bible" of early twentieth century feminism; her novels and stories made the plight of women and the South African working classes brilliantly transparent.

Schreiner was by temperament a philosopher and writer, not a revolutionary. But her influence was international and iconoclastic. She was one of the first to link the causes of women's liberation, black freedom, and world peace. Her tales of Africa gave strength to the British suffragettes who were imprisoned and force-fed for acts of resistance. She knew instinctively that women would have to write their own myths, tell the story of their own experience, speak in their own voice. Her myth seems now like a prophecy of our own times:

I saw a desert and I saw a woman coming out of it. And she came to the bank of a dark river; and the bank was steep and high. And on it an old man met her, who had a long white beard; and a stick that curled was in his hand, and on it was written Reason. And he asked her what she wanted; and she said, "I am Woman and I am seeking for the Land of Freedom."

And he said, "It is before you."

And she said, "I see nothing before me but a dark flowing river and a bank steep and high, and cuttings here and there with heavy sand in them."

And he said, "And beyond that?"

She said, "I see nothing, but sometimes, when I shade my eyes with my hand, I think I see on the further bank trees and hills, and the sun shining on them!"

He said, "That is the Land of Freedom."

She said, "How am I to get there?"

He said, "There is one way, and one only. Down the banks of Labour, and through the water of Suffering. There is no other."

She said, "Is there no bridge?"

He answered, "None."

She said, "Is the water deep?"

He said, "Deep."

She said, "Is the floor worn?"

He said, "It is. Your foot may slip at any time, and you may be lost."

She said, "Have any crossed already?"

He said, "Some have tried!"

She said, "Is there a track to show where the best fording is?"

He said, "It has to be made."

She shaded her eyes with her hand; and she said, "I will go."

And he said, "You must take off the clothes you wore in the desert: they are dragged down by them who go into the water so clothed."

And she threw from her gladly the mantle of Ancient-received-opinions she wore, for it was worn full of holes. And she took the girdle from her waist that she had treasured so long, and the moths flew out of it in a cloud. And he said, "Take the shoes of dependence off your feet."

And she stood there naked, but for one white garment that clung close to her.

And he said, "That you may keep. They wear clothes in the Land of Freedom. In the water it buoys; it always swims."

And I saw on its breast was written Truth; and it was white; the sun had not often shone on it; the other clothes had covered it up. And he said, "Take this stick; hold it fast. In that day when it slips from your hand you are lost. Put it down before you; feel your way: where it cannot find a bottom do not set your foot."

And she said, "I am ready; let me go."

And he said, "No—but stay; what is that at your breast?"

She was silent.

He said, "Open it, and let me see."

And she opened her garment. And against her breast was a tiny thing, who drank from it, and the yellow curls above his forehead pressed against it; and his knees were drawn up to her, and he held her breast fast with his hands.

And Reason said, "Who is he and what is he doing here?"

And she said, "See his little wings . . ."

And Reason said, "Put him down."

And she said, "He is asleep, and he is drinking! I will carry him to the Land of Freedom. He has been a child so long, so long, I have carried him. In the Land of Freedom he will be a man. We will walk together there, and his great white wings will overshadow me. He has lisped one word only to me in the desert—"Passion!" I have dreamed he might learn to say 'Friendship' in that land."

And Reason said, "Put him down!"

And she said, "I will carry him so—with one arm, and with the other I will fight the water."

He said, "Lay him down on the ground. When you are in the water you will forget to fight, you will think only of him. Lay him down." He said, "He will not die. When he finds you have left him alone he will open his wings and fly. He will be in the Land of Freedom before you. Those who reach the Land of Freedom, the first hand they see stretching down the bank to help them shall be Love's. He will be a man then, not a child. At your breast he cannot thrive; put him down that he may grow."

And she took her bosom from his mouth, and he bit her, so that the blood ran down onto the ground. And she laid him down on the earth; and she covered her wound. And she bent and stroked his wings. And I saw the hair on her forehead turned white as snow, and she had changed from youth to age.

And she stood far off on the bank of the river. And she said, "For what do I go to this far land which no one has ever reached? Oh, I am alone! I am utterly alone!"

And Reason, that old man, said to her, "Silence! What do you hear?"

And she listened intently, and she said, "I hear a sound of feet, a thousand times ten thousand and thousands of thousands, and they beat this way!"

He said, "They are the feet of those that shall follow you. Lead on! Make a track to the water's edge! Where you stand now, the ground shall be beaten flat by ten thousand times ten thousand feet." And he said, "Have you seen the locusts how they cross a stream? First one comes down to the water-edge, and it is swept away, and then another comes and then another, and then another, and at last with their bodies piled up a bridge is built and the rest pass over."

She said, "And of those that come first, some are swept away, and are heard of no more; their bodies do not even build the bridge?"

"And are swept away, and are heard of no more–and what of that?" he said.

"And what of that . . ." she said.

"They make a track to the water's edge."

"They make a track to the water's edge . . ." And she said, "Over that bridge which shall be built with our bodies, who will pass?"

He said, *The entire human race.*"

And the woman grasped her staff.

And I saw her turn down that dark path to the river. . . .

And I dreamed a dream.

I dreamed I saw a land. And on the hills walked brave women and brave men, hand in hand. And they looked into each other's eyes, and they were not afraid.

And I saw the women also hold each other's hands.

And I said to him beside me, "What place is this?"

And he said, "This is heaven."

And I said, "Where is it?"

And he answered, "On earth."

And I said, "When shall these things be?"

And he answered, "In the Future."[1]

SYSTEMS AS FAILED PARENTS

The Wizard of Oz was a fantasy created for children, but reality bursts through that fantasy with unexpected force. L. Frank Baum's idyllic daydream contains bits and pieces of the nightmare of history, echoing in the consciousness of an author who was deeply affected by the events and trends of his own times.

The symbolic allegory lies just beneath the surface of the story; the characters and the episodes resonate with the anxieties and conditions of the 1890s. *The Wizard of Oz* is a modern *Pilgrim's Progress,* a book of disillusionment and of spiritual restoration. In contrast to the earlier classic with its Calvinist, introspective tenor, Dorothy's journey is a social parable, a New World democratic allegory.

The bright, technicolor optimism of the characters creates an entertaining and delightful mirage on one level, while on another the story is permeated with social despair. As we have noted in chapter two, the book was incubated in the American milieu of the 1880s and 1890s, times not unlike our own.

The moral idealism of the Reconstruction had given way to the new oppression of segregation. Increasingly conservative Supreme Court justices began reversing the progressive trend in civil rights. By the 1890s lynchings of blacks by white mobs occurred on the average of one every 2½ days; state legislatures passed laws that made it illegal for blacks to vote, hold office, to hold property, find jobs, and seek education equitably. Grant left the presidency under a cloud of scandal and reformers accused politicians of being in bed with big business. The rise of the trusts and the robber barons spawned an unprecedented level of corruption in public offices and in the financial community. The unregulated stock market, runaway borrowing, and lust for profit precipitated the Wall Street Panic of 1893. A depression ensued, swelling the tidal wave of unemployment and farm bankruptcies.

By the time he turned to writing Baum had suffered several business failures himself and bankruptcy more than once. On the verge of his Oz opus he was a curious amalgam of populist sympathies, cynical conservatism, and detached journalism. Dorothy's companions are emblems of his mixed feelings: a Scarecrow who, like the American farmer, has been victimized but shows little capacity for converting to new ways; a Tin Man, a worker who is rusting away because industrialization is replacing the independent craftsman, but who seems to have little heart for organizing to improve his status; a Lion who can master a politician's rhetoric and a good cause, but whose claws are powerless against monied interests and exploited workers; a Wizard who represents the debasement of the electoral process, a president who governs by popular choice and by smoke and mirrors. Baum often spoke out against American policies toward Cuba, Latin America, and the Philippines. William Jennings Bryan, a pacifist and anti-imperialist whom Baum supported in the election of 1896, didn't have a chance. As we have noted, Baum enshrined Bryan's "silver crusade" forever in Dorothy's magic silver shoes – fated to be lost forever in the desert. In the end, Dorothy has to get herself back to Kansas. Baum's final wisdom seems to say, "We are in a social and political mess, but only realism – not quixotic schemes – will get us through to a better future."

The Emerald City of Oz is perhaps Baum's most satirical metaphor, mocking the populist and greenback democrat as well as the greedy capitalist and plutocrat. Everyone in the magical city wears special spectacles to protect their eyes from the brilliance and dazzle of their surroundings. Everything is green: rays of the sun, skin pigment, clothes, buildings, food, pavement, furnishings, and of course, the local currency. Baum may have been suggesting that everyone – rich and poor alike – shares a belief in the system, everyone believes in the same illusion, and so it works. When that collective trust begins to erode, the system teeters precariously.

Today we are experiencing what happens when segments of a culture begin to take off the green glasses. Suddenly the myths that have driven our institutions are exposed. We look at each other and ourselves through eyes squinting in the unaccustomed glare, bereft of our green glow. Who are we? Who have we become? How much of ourselves have we given away?

- A forty-three-year-old woman in Washington, D.C., wife of a government executive, wakes up after twenty years of an abusive marriage.

- A middle-aged businessman in Omaha struggles with the onset of depression in the midst of his most successful year.
- An elderly woman, receiving her first Social Security check after the death of her husband, realizes she will be poor for the rest of her life.
- A young serviceman stationed in Subic Bay, Philippines, over-whelmed with fear and guilt, requests a medical discharge.
- A thirty-six-year-old priest, disenchanted with his lifestyle, seeks counseling for alcoholism.

For all of these individuals, the Emerald City of their hopes, expecta-tions, and self-image has dissolved. Each may feel victimized, overcome with vague anxiety, or simply numb. A few, perhaps, will struggle to some light at the end of their tunnel of darkness. They will discover and realize that their unhappiness is connected with the loss of an authentic self and its replacement by an artificial substitute. They have been colonized by a myth. The project of the true self has been abandoned.

Colonization is subtle. It is partly the fault of our own passivity and lack of vigilance, but it is also an inexorable effect of the systems that absorb us: family, workplace, class, gang or peer group, education, profes-sion, and media. Each of these systems imprints its own myth on our con-sciousness; it becomes a ritual text that can estrange us from our real, true self. Instead we are left with a kind of laminated persona, each layer easily exploited by a culture in which many systems are in a runaway state. Awareness can be dangerous: we can panic or break down. But the alterna-tive is worse: we can be hypnotized into compliance, robotized, and never know who we really are.

Reclaiming our personal power, our sense of belonging to ourselves and to others as fellow human beings, requires that we challenge the myths of power that have shaped us. There are two primary myths. The first is our *faith in dominance and, consequently, hierarchy*. There are many subcorollaries attached to this myth such as "men take charge," "father knows best," "heroes are loners." We will see how some of these expres-sions of the myth have colonized our consciousness and distorted our world. The second is our *denial of our mortality and fallibility, of our finite capacity*. There are many subcorollaries to this myth also: the idolization of technology, denial of death in life, perfectionism, compulsive celebrity, "more is better," organization over organism.

We have acted in complicity with these myths by treating systems and institutions as if they were parents. When they fail, we suddenly awake to our own dependency, to our own failure to mature into an authentic self-responsibility.

There are two primary systems in which we spend most of our lifetime. One is *the family,* and the other is *the workplace* with its consumer adjunct, *the marketplace.*

Gone are the days when we could romanticize the family as a haven and enclave set apart from the world, a sanctuary where moral nurturance and emotional sustenance were assumed benefits. Even the Norman Rockwell magazine covers of the 1940s and 1950s celebrated a mythic family that had long since disappeared. Today we are mostly satisfied with what we have, recognizing that every family has its problems. Yet our own history reveals how much of our family of origin we try to paint over in our own relationships. It is never perfect, it is never finished.

It is popular these days to bewail the disintegration of the family. Blame is cast upon working mothers, absent fathers, single parents, inadequate caretakers and latch-key children, lesbian mothers, gay couple parents, the falling birthrate, and the dissolution of the extended family. Much of the blame falls on the changing constellations of family. But the constellation of the family is not the problem. The problem is how we participate in family, and how we care for each other.

The veil of secrecy and privacy that has cloaked the nuclear family for so long has been shredded. More and more we can see what a fragile and flawed, yet flexible and sustaining environment it is. Night after night our television screens document family tragedies like incest, and family triumphs like the welcoming of an abandoned child or a Down's syndrome baby. In families miracles are wrought by love, and wounds are inflicted by violence.

The revelations about the extent of violence in families should make us question not the structure of families today, but the myths that persist in the interpersonal dynamics of the family. To great extent, the nuclear family has become a victim of its own isolation. It is cut off from many of the familial and communal connections that would support its functions and moderate its pathologies. From time to time the theater recalls for us the painful loneliness and isolation that pervades the self-destructive family, as in Eugene O'Neill's *Long Day's Journey Into Night* or in Arthur Miller's *Death of a Salesman.* The same burden of self-creation and self-reliant individualism that taxes the American's personal myth also deeply affects the family.

When we learn that interpersonal violence probably occurs in one out of three American families, we need to ask why. What ritual text is operating? (Violence in American families – perhaps in all families – is not an aberration. It is too frequently the norm.) I would suggest that the ritual text is the myth of *dominance* – a myth that divides valued and privileged persons from the not-valued within the family circle. Indeed, in most instances it is not a circle, but a hierarchy. The myth of dominance and control, of valued and not-valued has persisted for aeons and has been sustained for centuries by religious and social traditions, from which we ordinarily expect more humanitarian insight.

Wife beating is a case in point. I remember as a child being vaguely aware of the black and blue marks on a girlfriend's mother's arms and face, believing what I was always told: "She bruises easily – and she's always running into something." Years later I discovered the truth.

I remember, too, in the years when I was researching the legal basis for women's status, the despair I experienced when I realized that English Common Law, which contained so much of the basis of a humane and democratic society, the basis of our own Constitution, also gave permission to husbands to beat their wives. And I recall the rage I experienced when I first read Genesis 19 where Lot offers his virginal daughters for gang rape in order to protect his male guests. Or when I read of the Levite in Judges 19 who turns his concubine over to the rapists in order to protect his guest and safeguard the ethic of hospitality. Over and over again the tradition, in the process of exalting a principle or appeasing evil, sacrifices women.

Perhaps the saddest commentary on human fallibility is the way in which the human sciences, from which enlightenment might have come, reinforced the same myths and ritual texts, with a perverse intensity. Witness the history of the development of gynecology in the U.S. Countless women – mostly black women and immigrant women – endured years of almost unimaginable agonies after early surgical experimentation. Much of the surgery was an attempt to cure women's excess capacity for sexual pleasure. Even respected psychologists like Freud and Helen Deutsch popularized the notion that women's masochistic disposition required some emotional coercion and/or threat of violence to heighten erotic pleasure.

The preponderance of women as patients for psychosurgery provided one more opportunity for the expression of male dominance and control over women's bodies and psyches as well as a justification for battering. As late as 1972 an introductory text on psychiatry suggested that:

A depressed woman, for instance, may owe her illness to a psychopathic husband who cannot change and who will not accept treatment. . . . [W]omen patients of this type are often helped by anti-depressant drugs. But in the occasional case where they do not work, we have seen patients enabled by a leucotomy [lobotomy] to return to the difficult environment and cope with it.[1]

We can perhaps take some small satisfaction in the fact that since 1970 battered women's shelters have begun to replace drugs and lobotomies as one interim solution to abusive husbands. Unfortunately since divorce is a frequent outcome of domestic violence, women and children often endure economic and social punishment for their escape.

The terrifying profile of a battered spouse or child in one out of every three or four American homes illustrates our negative potential as a species. The ritual text of permission to abuse is an implicit assumption in many of our institutions and social arrangements. The battered woman syndrome is so familiar that we do not recognize its viciousness or its many manifestations. It is a cumulative cycle of tension, belittlement, violence, remorse, and reconciliation that can lead to paralysis of will and extinction of a person's sense of self-worth. The memory of the violence and the threat of its recurrence becomes the batterer's means of absolute control. The terror and trauma alter one's thinking in ways that are not unlike what American prisoners of war suffered in Vietnam. There are many persons in our society who are hostages to what has been called "conjugal terrorism."

The victim's consciousness is so traumatized that with the loss of self-worth and any sense of control often comes a distorted sense of blame and responsibility. How does one assimilate psychologically the fact that the person who loves you is beating you? Most men who batter don't just hit their wives and children, they isolate and intimidate their victims, destroying their self-confidence; they imprison them in a sense of inadequacy as well as fear, a conditioned helplessness. Paralysis is the result. For some, the trauma ends in suicide or homicide. And as the evening news attests, children get caught in the cross fire.

It would be no exaggeration to suggest that men's violence against women is the most common form of violence experienced by most adults. This violence encompasses a range of coercive behaviors that are certainly aberrant, but most of which overlap with "typical" male behavior –

hence the difficulty for women and children in separating what is appropriate from what is destructive. For example, although rape is a gross abuse of power, it incorporates some of the implicit rules and myths about heterosexual encounter, male aggression and conquest. Likewise, incest represents an exaggeration of patriarchal dominant norms, not a departure from them.[2]

The myth of dominance and the "right" to batter goes beyond sexual politics. Women, too, are capable of abusive behavior—as many male victims and battered children evidence. Elder abuse, physical and psychological abuse of the elderly by adult children or caretakers, is a growing problem.

Even if the level of violence never reaches a physical level in families, many of us are scarred by other more subtle forms of violence—verbal battering, intimidation, devaluation, humiliation. Perhaps the most subtle and destructive of all is what has been called the SAD theory. Simply put, this theory suggests that if human beings do not receive enough touching and physical care-gestures at crucial times in their development as infants and children, their brains are neurologically deprived—the appropriate synapses and receptor sites simply do not develop.[3] This condition leaves the organism starving for inappropriate forms of stimulation; these individuals are often susceptible to chemical substance abuse in later life. Deprivation is a form of violence.

We have come a long way from the Freudian view which assumes the innocence, or at least neutrality, of the parents and the guilty, instinct-driven urges of the child. The pathology of the child is more often rooted in child abuse than in an Oedipus complex. Alice Miller has done much to dissolve the narrowness of psychoanalysis and the myopic attitudes of society in her works on early childhood. She maintains that:

Behind every act of violence there is a history. A history of being molested, a history of denying. The denial is a law governing us, but it is ignored by society and still not investigated by the professionals. . . . Our culture is so violent because as children we learned not to feel. . . . As a child, Hitler had no witness. His father destroyed everything his son did. He could never tell anyone the pains he was suffering. . . . [T]hat child looked for a glance, but was constantly treated like a dog. One of the Ten Commandments says, "Honor your father and your mother, that it may go well with you." Nowhere does it say, "Honor your children so that they will be able to honor others as well as themselves. . . . The repression of early childhood trauma required in our society by the Fourth Commandment leads to a state of collective repression.[4]

If so many families fall short of our expectations and batter women and children, especially, through physical or psychological abuse, or passively, through deprivation and devaluation, we might well ask, Are there any families that are OK? To the extent that all families are infected, to greater or lesser degree, with the myth of dominance modeled in the dynamic of gender roles and social class, the answer would have to be no. To the extent that families are struggling to evolve new dynamics of interaction, the answer would be a qualified yes. In other words, the only OK families are probably recovering families who are processing their pain and their pathology.

So much of this happens to us, of course, before we can even begin to think about it or process it. How do we survive the violence of our origins? It is not the pain of recognized truth that is so devastating, but denial of the fact that in some way we were unloved as a child. If we cannot face the pain and the truth, we may go through life trying to earn love, or manipulate it, or "fix" it in substitute experiences.

As Alice Miller so wisely observes, spiritual survival depends on mourning the lost child, the child in each of us that was partly maimed, killed, or abandoned, the part of us that is an orphan:

Avoiding this mourning means that one remains at bottom the one who is despised. For I have to despise everything in myself that is not wonderful, good, and clever. Thus I perpetuate intrapsychically the loneliness of childhood: I despise weakness, impotence, uncertainty—in short, the child in myself and others.[5]

If the family is the source of the learned repertoires of abuse and violence that pervade all of our institutions, then obviously it must be a focus for intervention. We might take heart from the fact that the horizontal quality and fluidity of the American family seem to offer a potential for self-healing as well as self-destruction. In contrast to the earlier, more rigidly organized patriarchal family, the contemporary American family, like so much of the economy in which it is embedded, is a deregulated family structure. In the New World democratic milieu the family has evolved into a voluntary association—in principle all adults are equal and children also have a voice and rights. No one can be incarcerated or totally disenfranchised in the family, at least in principle.

Thus the family constellation can change rapidly, reassess, consolidate resources, and seek outside help. The emergence in our era of family systems therapies (even multiple group family therapy) and of a variety of support groups for recovery from dysfunctional families is a harbinger of a self-correction process that can flourish in a voluntary society. As the negative feedback reaches a critical mass, individuals break loose from the hypnotic sedation of deprived families and then push and pull other family members into a recovery process. I see this happening in families across our nation, which suggests that our culture has a unique capacity to nurture these self-correcting, self-healing voluntary processes. Recovery groups are epidemic. There is a pragmatism in our national character that says, "If it's broken, we can fix it."

Unfortunately, to rescue one's real, true self from the facades, flaws and failures of the family is not to guarantee survival. To parody Grimm, we may be out of the oven, but we're not out of the woods yet. Practically all of the institutions that are the pillars of civilization – and in which we will spend as much or more time than in the family – are founded on the myth of dominance. Church, school, university, courts, hospitals, corporations, governments, professions – all of these are elaborate structures and rituals for acting out the myth of dominance and, presumably, for perpetrating violence on the constituents to whom they are accountable.

It is particularly the workplace and its adjunct, the consumer marketplace, which embody the myth in a most uncompromising way. The family version of the myth of dominance – patriarchy – was the structure that Aristotle saw as the most felicitous design for government and social institutions. What is patriarchy but a fundamental model of power? To be more precise, it is a model based on the *hoarding of power*. In institutional terms patriarchy requires that resources of power be consolidated in the hands of a few. Patriarchy and the structures of domination and control that model it are, ironically, expressions of impotence, of the compulsion to transcend natural realities with man-made mechanisms of control – thus begetting a second myth, the denial of vulnerability and fallibility.

Understanding how societies and institutions of domination function is the first step toward identifying the violence and pain of our own experience in the social milieu, then mourning and exorcising it. For the myth that is most alive and insidious is not perceived as a myth until it is seen through. To see through the myth of dominance is to see the way in which patriarchy was perpetuated by the control male elites exerted over the symbol systems of our civilization, and the intentional denigration of female (or alternative) competence, authority, and experience that this depended on.

Closer examination of these power elites reveals some common characteristics: for example, the clerical caste, the warrior caste, and the medical caste. Each of these exhibits a specific group bias highly invested in perpetuating its own power-hoarding ethos. All are based on a mutually assumed, self-granted superiority as the basis of their entitlement to power and expectation of preference. The myth of superiority is often sustained by pseudocompetence. (The Vatican believes it has "infallible" notions of what is best for women; the military brass believe that they know what is best for national security.) Each caste acquires a monopoly of information or esoteric knowledge that enables control. Doctors and defenders of the faith have much in common. Each exerts almost exclusive control over resources and operations. Knowledge or experience that does not emanate from the caste is trivialized.

The myth of superiority is often maintained by the notions of divine right, natural law, or some other variation of "royal" consciousness. Thus priests are "ontologically different" from ordinary mortals; colonels pursue their higher calling ("above the law") to the cause of national security; Federal Reserve bankers see themselves as the guardians, gatekeepers of the monetary system. These royal attitudes assume that all decision making in these categories should be relegated to them and not to laypersons.

This caste mentality is maintained by the same principles of internal socialization that have allowed the Ku Klux Klan to survive for so long: conformity (compulsory membership and code); cronyism (you do things together you wouldn't have the nerve to do alone); cloning (don't exhibit too much originality); exclusivity (let's keep this just between us). Members of the elite caste share vicariously in the inflated status of the group and develop a peculiar psychology.

Perhaps the most outstanding quality of the caste psychology is the need for control. Power elites fear the unpredictable, the playful. Any form of disorder presents the threat of chaos. Messy, protracted operations are to be avoided. Thus power elites exhibit low tolerance for ambiguity, dialectic, and dialogue. Another quality is the competitive complex: the need to win, to be on top. Hence a great deal of reality is seen in terms of "one up, one down." Caste psychology is schizoid in its value judgments. There is a tendency to have one set of values for private life, another for one's public functions. The personal and the political are separate. (It is said that Patrick Henry, a classic instance of patriarchal consciousness, could plead eloquently for liberty and human freedom before the Virginia House of Burgesses while he kept his abused wife locked in the cellar of his home.)

Characteristically, power elites objectify the "other." Women become sex objects or caregivers, sin objects or sacred objects. Men become status objects, success objects, defense objects. Persons become objects of conversion, or profit, or treatment, or therapy; they become "things," "commodities," "statistics," means to an end. The style of power elites is secretive and distanced from the consequences of policy. (Directives and memos are favored over face-to-face encounters.) Paternalistic gestures are another means of control (favors, mentoring, touching). Overt emotion is usually excluded, and information and experience are reduced to quantitative data, abstract theory, or dogma. Control over the agenda is imperative. Information is passed up; decisions are passed from the top down. There is often an assumed immunity from sanctions within the caste.

Studies of many institutions and corporations dominated by male power elites have also revealed how "kin categories" tend to evolve in these settings.[6] This phenomenon provides additional evidence that the imprinting of the basic power model – man-over-woman – and the family structures it generates are replicated in our larger social institutions. Sociologists point out how often in the corporate setting allocation of resources, privileges, and rewards are distributed unequally, not according to contribution or production, but according to role. The roles or kin categories tend to follow gender lines. The Boss/Father is usually an experienced male who absorbs the most office/work space, holds tenure, has the freedom of flextime, receives substantial wages and benefits, enjoys immunity from sanction, the luxury of specialization, etc. He basically makes the decisions and the rules, and he exerts absolute control over his own tasks and time. The Wife/Secretary or Executive Assistant comes next in the hierarchy, but with a considerable reduction in all of the above benefits, if she is a female. She is totally dependent on the Boss/Father but is really in charge of the other employees, for setting the framework for their tasks, for discipline, and for transmitting communications. The Brothers are the young men on the rise. Their upward mobility is high, their wages good, and they have access to mentoring and skill training. They are looked upon as insiders and the Wife is expected to give them preference. In many law offices today, young women are beginning to push their way into Brother slots, and they are easily seduced by the socialization that goes with those roles.

It is the fourth kin category that is the most disempowered and certainly the most numerous in typical organizations. The Daughter's role demands generalized rote skills (rather than the specialization that goes with higher status). It carries no personal work space or tenure; wages and benefits are minimal. The tasks are transitory and the expenditure of energy sustained, intense, and rigidly controlled. The Daughter has no control over her own tasks and time. The Daughter role in the company resembles the job description of a waitress. Needless to say, there are many unskilled males holding Daughter jobs, and more and more women are swelling this lower tier of employment ranks.

But there are highly trained professionals in institutional settings that suffer as much from disempowerment as unskilled workers do. Ultimately, patriarchy is not a respecter of sexes. When it comes to caste preservation, women too can internalize the hoarding of power, the patriarchal consciousness. (The pre–Vatican II model of female religious orders is a classic instance.) The disparity of power between doctors and nurses is a classic case of the disempowered professional. Their grievances have become so hurtful that the best nurses are removing themselves from the control of doctors, whether male or female; their replacements are often less experienced and more compatible with the Daughter role. The subordinate role, when it is subjected to flagrant patriarchal behavior and disempowerment, has a severe, negative impact on mental and physical health and on the sense of social connection. Oppressed groups everywhere share some of the same characteristics, whether they are nurses, women actuaries, clerks, or seasonal agricultural workers. Research has identified a set of behavioral syndromes that are consistently identified with the experience of being a member of a disempowered, devalued, subordinate group:

- high stress levels
- low self-worth, self-hatred
- passive aggression, covert manipulation
- envy and envy-avoidance (no one should stand out, no one should move up or out)
- intolerance and exclusivity (the oppressed often internalize the mind of the oppressor)
- horizontal violence (the oppressed redirect their rage and rebellion against Boss/Father toward each other, because they cannot risk Boss/Father's disapproval)
- colonized consciousness (change, which the oppressed most need, is what they most fear, "backlash")
- addictive behavior (dependency becomes an addictive adaptation, marked by denial, drivenness, compulsive symptoms, and often by secondary addictions such as chemical substance abuse and eating disorders)

As many social analysts have observed, people who exhibit these characteristic behaviors are cut off from any kind of communal action directed toward the future. Deprived of power, orphaned from participation, they are orphaned from each other and from future possibilities.

Whenever I fly on a jet airliner I am reminded of what a striking metaphor it is for the impact of many modern systems – the law, health care systems, education, government, finance, or corporations – on our lives. On a jet airliner passengers are completely at the mercy of the pilot, crew, and the technology itself. The pilot and crew are a highly trained elite caste given the power to monitor feedback from the technology, and to make all crucial decisions necessary for a safe flight. In contrast to older forms of travel such as horse, stagecoach, or even boat, if some catastrophe occurs, no one escapes – at least rarely. Whatever happens affects everyone totally. We are connected in a shared capsule and a shared fate for a space of time. Buckminster Fuller once compared our new awareness of our common planetary fate to a shared spaceship in which Euro-Americans, Africans, Asians, and others are hurtling through space toward a common future. The world has grown so complex, interlocked, and interdependent that we can never again imagine ourselves as lone travelers – we are now passengers, sharing a common space and fate.

In so many ways, the experience of flying by commercial airliner today, including the experience of being processed through a typical airport, is an experience of being totally powerless, of having absolutely no control over your fate. It is a metaphor for the myth of dominance and power hoarding which is the blueprint for so many of our social structures. Reflecting on some of the air disasters in recent years reveals an interesting pattern.

I missed the Air Florida disaster in Washington, D.C. in 1982 by twenty minutes. If my own plane had not been late in arriving I would very likely have been driving across the fated bridge at the moment the crash occurred – it was a night I will never forget. Recently I was told by a government researcher that a careful analysis of the tapes and other evidence from the crash indicated a strong possibility that the copilot had been too intimidated by the pilot to insist that the acceleration was not providing enough lift before it was too late to abort the flight. Moreover, research on pilot cockpit-styles in several accidents over the last few years show that air disasters are more related to human failures than to mechanical problems. The loner/hero, the macho individualist – the myth that is so embedded in our culture – is the unfortunate institutional model of the

Boss/Father, and the role model for many pilots. This type of individual has many personal resources but often discourages feedback. This quality might be insignificant if you are riding a horse or pulling a wagon, but it could be lethal if you are a pilot, a doctor, a psychiatrist or any other boss dealing with a very complex process.

The space shuttle Challenger disaster and the ensuing investigation revealed the same problem on a corporate scale: management so determined to get a vehicle into space that they ignored the expert feedback of engineers. Even the engineers were so naive about their own technology that they did not expect O-rings to wear out or be affected by colder temperatures. The myth of the machine that never fails thrives on our fantasies of omnipotence. And when there are no checks on the decision-making power that is hoarded at the top, the scene is set for catastrophe.

And what did the investigation of the crash of Northwest Flight #255 in Detroit reveal? Another dominant captain who was so sure of himself that he or his copilot turned off the feedback, the checklist warning system? A pilot who was too eager to take off? Was this a case where the very expertise of the pilot made him trust too much in himself, or too much in the machine? If nothing else, the persistence of the myth of dominance today increases the risk in highly complex processes. Deviations and "slips" have far greater consequences. In hindsight many financial experts agree that "Black Monday" of 1987 happened because so many people in the system ignored so much feedback.

Systems fail us when there is no accountability. The completion of the feedback loop demands accountability as well as vigilance. A mechanism or intervention may produce a different result from the one intended. We see this all the time in systems designed to promote health and healing. A patient can enter the system with a minor dysfunction and end up more ill than before. Wherever people relinquish some or all of their power to someone or to a system that hoards expertise, the necessity of having accountability and feedback monitors is even greater.

The national debacle of Contragate is a classic instance of a system out of control because of the absence of accountability and feedback monitors. The McFarlane/Poindexter/North/Casey fantasies of foreign policy coups and extragovernmental operations demonstrate how a power elite infected with individualism and omnipotence can put an entire system into a runaway mode. The Contragate cabal, like Greedgate (the Wall Street scandals) and Godgate (the PTL scandal), had all the marks of runaway, destructive systems that we have described: the hoarding of power (decision making) and information, secrecy, monopoly over resources and access, cronyism, disregard for those who might have to bear the consequences of decisions and transactions, the need to win, and schizoid value judgments.

Modern bureaucratic systems, large and small, are essentially capitalistic, that is, of their very nature they hoard power, profits, resources, and constituencies. Even in a controlled state such as the U.S.S.R., power is capitalistic, a translation of the myth of dominance into the managed social economy. Modernity has set in motion a kind of inevitability of bureaucracy which seems to operate by default in our civilization. Foucault, Ferguson, and others have illustrated the double bind in which these systems confine us. The first effect is obviously the totalization of power, and the second is the individualization and isolation of the participants. Bureaucratic structures separate us from others without freeing us, resulting in the loss of autonomy as well as connection. (The only connection that ultimately matters is the one with your manager, a relationship of control.) Bureaucracy ties us to roles and rules rather than to each other, weighting us with connections that deny community. Participation is entirely framed as control, leaving little room for creative unfolding of potential or the capacity to shift priorities and resources to emerging realities. Feedback itself is controlled and human flourishing within these systems is minimal.[7]

The same self-correcting process that is crucially needed in families is obviously needed in our larger systems. The introduction of participatory structures into the workplace has proved to be one place to begin. Research on cooperative and participatory work experiments has revealed some helpful modifications of our default bureaucratic model, but, surprisingly, even more significant changes in human behavior outside the workplace. For example, two studies showed that the participation of male workers in quality circles and group feedback sessions significantly modified their own behavior toward their spouses (more egalitarian, more expression of feelings) and children (more democratic). Some of the workers also showed greater participation in the civic community as a result of these influences.[8] Evidently the workplace is one of the most neglected sources of socialization in our society. The introduction of participatory and family-related structures into the workplace is a hopeful catalyst for change. These trends suggest that the workplace may accomplish more behavior modification than the family, church, and school.

Power hoarding, power elites, and bureaucratic structures have left us orphaned in so many ways. Here again the proliferating self-help recovery groups may represent the leading edge of the future. Most of these groups are small, operate on a shoe-string budget, have no formal "top-down" structure, are egalitarian and personal. They share leadership and information, emphasize individual participation and responsibility, mutual support, group self-examination, and incremental change. Well over 500,000 such groups meet regularly throughout the U.S., involving an estimated 15 million Americans. Likewise, family support centers have been appearing and multiplying across the country in recent years. Grassroots mediating modules such as these may be the seeds of a new consciousness that will nurture institutional and structural reform in our culture.

The foundation of the new consciousness must be an evolutionary attitude: the recognition of life systems and of human beings as error-making, error-correcting processors; and the realization that we cannot act or grow in isolation. If systems fail us and diminish us, we have to change ourselves if the systems are to change. The first priority must be the completion of the feedback loop in our social arrangements and institutions. We are a culture that has maximized "feedforward," but we have not given equal priority—as nature does—to the self-correcting mechanisms of feedback. This demands, in social organisms, equal valuation and full participation of every cell, every individual. It demands that we place a priority on cooperation and caring. Above all it demands the discipline of *forgiveness* of ourselves, of others, of history. It demands a readiness to "turn around." There is no place for perfectionism, dogmatism, and the denial of our fallibility in an evolutionary universe.

The dominance model (bureaucratic, capitalistic) is probably the most significant factor in the production of violence that victimizes and estranges us from each other. Historically Western civilization has also produced a consciousness that places great faith in technology, which can be seen as an attempt to achieve maximum consolidation and acceleration of power. Some would suggest that this is simply another description of patriarchy: the hoarding of power in order to transcend natural realities with man-made instruments. Thus, our culture tends to convert all problems into technical problems, and to believe that machinelike organizations can solve everything. There is much that technology can solve, but when it comes at the expense of a massive denial of the organic and systemic nature of human life and social polity it plants dragon's teeth that one day will sprout in destruction.

Life perseveres and flourishes in a delicate balance—what scientists like to call "homeostasis" and philosophers, "holonomy." Part of that delicate equilibrium is the acceptance of the reality of *mortality, vulnerability, falli-bility,* and *limits.* Technology and unchecked, machinelike growth–"if it can be done, it should be done," and "more is better"–can distance us from a reverence for the proportion, rhythm, and mutual interaction that holonomy demands.

The model for life is embedded in our body and in the planet earth. A few months ago while researching the nature of the synaptic transmission, I was awestruck when I learned that there are probably over ten trillion synapses in the brain alone, each one representing a highly complex interfacing of neurons, substances, vesicles, ions, receptors, electrical charges, channels opening and closing, some in 1/10,000 of a second, the process reversing at just the right millisecond–an incredible, vastly intri-cate system of feedforward and feedback, outlay and uptake, of chemical production and conversion, of supreme cooperation. I suddenly realized that I was looking at the blueprint for the universe from the inside, as it were. Could anyone imagine that preserving life on earth could be mod-eled on anything so crude and primitive as patriarchy or technology? Could anyone doubt that we would somehow have to honor and imitate Mother Earth herself–the embodiment of the divine purpose of creation? Are we so compulsively a male culture that even in our social, political, and economic arrangements, we are still struggling to separate from our Earth-Mother? Are we still pasting scraps of omnipotence and dominance on ourselves to reinforce our separated egos?

And what of consciousness? In an organic, living system conscious-ness resides not only in the head but in the entire system. Gregory Bate-son, in describing the holistic system says, "No part of such an internally interactive system can have unilateral control over the remainder or over any other part. The mental characteristics are inherent or immanent in the ensemble as a whole."[9] Participation is the key to the preservation of consciousness in the organism. A living structure is one in which the parts communicate and cooperate. A dead structure is one in which the parts have ceased to communicate and cooperate. This pervasive quality of consciousness in an organic system is a stark contrast to the purely technological or machinelike system.

The treatment of the elderly, the handicapped, and the homeless in a culture might be a case in point. In societies that are not organic, there is a tendency to put away the diseased, the misfit, the aging, or the handi-capped–to hide them from view, perhaps to eliminate them (as in Nazi Germany). In much the same way early medical treatments sloughed off a sick or deteriorating limb whereas today there are increasing and improving efforts at rescuing and rehabilitating the sick or diseased body part. Today we struggle to develop ways of integrating mentally deficient persons with the normal environment; we provide care that improves the quality of life for the weak or impaired. These subtle changes in social policy and community attitudes – at least in awareness, if not in practice – are harbingers of a growing awareness of lost connections and the essential oneness of all living creatures in an ecosystem.

Systems are ultimately the layers of skin that the human social organism develops to protect its vital functions, to secure the food and stimuli it needs to survive and flourish. Systems are at the same time extensions of ourselves and molds that shape and imprint our consciousness and social behavior. Systems are the chief sources of socialization. Today many of the traditional systems or "skins" are being displaced by more powerful influences. We underestimate, for example, the extent to which the economy and the marketplace – the skin of a consumer society – shapes and molds us. Sociologist Harry Braverman says:

The industrialization of food and other elementary home provisions is only the first step in a process which eventually leads to the dependence of all social life, and indeed of all the interrelatedness of human kind upon the marketplace. . . . The population no longer relies upon social organization in the form of family, friends, neighbors, community elders, children, but with few exceptions must go to market and only to market, not only for food, clothing and shelter, but also for recreation, amusement, security, for the care of the young, the old, the sick, the handicapped. In time not only the material and service needs, but even emotional patterns of life are channelled through the market.[10]

The fact that I have received at least a dozen direct mail ads for computer matchmaking services in the past year graphically illustrates Braverman's thesis. The phenomenon of the marketizing of social relations and the displacement of more personalized individual and community connections and transactions has an increasingly atomizing and objectifying effect. It results in the overwhelming paradox of our contemporary society: increasing fragmentation and emotional distance in the very midst of increasing interdependence. Even as our social life on the planet becomes a dense network of interlocked activities in which people are more interlinked and interdependent, we are becoming more separate. There is more risk that our contacts with one another, which are accelerating, will divide us instead of bringing us closer together. The system will teach us to behave like commodities rather than like persons.

Television is another example of a skin that molds us even as it stimulates and feeds us. Like most of the systems that have an impact on us, it is dominated by a power elite of about one hundred people in Hollywood and New York who determine about 95 percent of what we will see on the tube. Television is not just one influence operating in the socialization process; it is the overall socializing process superimposed on all the other processes. George Gerbner's research has revealed that children absorb thousands of hours of living in a highly compelling world of images. They see everything represented: all the social types, situations, art, politics, and science. From television very young children learn certain assumptions—myths—about life that bear the imprint of this early and continued daily ritual. Television keeps us imbedded in the marketizing matrix of our culture. "Turning the set off is not liberation, but an illusion. You can turn the set off, but you still live in a world in which vast numbers of people don't turn it off. If you don't get it through the 'box,' you get it through them."[11]

The marketizing matrix propagates the myth that consumption will allow us to override, or at least numb our awareness of, our own mortality and vulnerability, the fragility and insecurity of our existence. It is designed to deny suffering—not necessarily to cure it. It is designed to privatize our experience rather than to strengthen the bonds of connection and belonging—those authentic bonds which belong to the realm of "gift" and cannot be marketized or organized. It is precisely this displacement that to great extent explains the fact that two major forms of dis-ease affecting our culture today are greed and addiction.

Philosophers have described at least three possible behaviors that a system can exhibit: self-correction (steady state), oscillation, or runaway. Morris Berman notes: "In a self-corrective system the results of past actions are fed back into the system, and this new bit of information then travels around the circuit, enabling the system to maintain something near to its ideal or optimal state. A runaway system, on the other hand, becomes increasingly distorted over time, because the feedback is positive, rather than negative or self-corrective."[12] Moreover, a healthy system mimics the pattern in the neuronal synapse where the electrical charge reverses the process in an infinitesimal instant. Greed, very simply, is a structure of accumulation in a runaway mode. Addiction is a system of consumption in a runaway mode. Both estrange us, orphan us from the organic pattern of life imbedded not only in our own neurons but in the universe itself.

The denial of death and mortal limits, the denial of our fundamental unity as one finite biosocial organism, is often expressed in a heightened pursuit of symbolic immortality. This pursuit, and the myths that feed it, can be as compelling and universal as the drive for dominance and power. It is expressed in the overwhelming need to maintain an inner sense of continuity and self-perpetuation over time and space. It can be a way of experiencing our connection with all of human history and with the ultimate purpose of the universe, or it can be a disease of the mind and body.

Robert Jay Lifton has observed the diminishment in our times of the sense of biological immortality (the sense of surviving in one's own family, tribe, nation, organization, and species) and likewise the sense of theological immortality. (This has been blunted by the spirit of secular materialism and ethical nihilism.) Moreover, a third and fourth mode of immortality, the immortality of works and of nature itself, are particularly threatened by the prospect of nuclear or environmental apocalypse. Lifton suggests that the postindustrial culture is severing us from virtually all of our symbolic modes of immortality, and we are abandoning ourselves to the fifth mode, that of experiential transcendence.[13] The drug and sex revolutions, the New Age phenomena, the proliferation of experiential radicalism in politics, art, or lifestyle can be seen as expressions of this narrowing of our symbolic range. This compulsion for experiential transcendence is ambiguous. It can trap us in the net of greed or addiction—or it can launch us into the pursuit of fundamental spiritual change.

A memorable expression of our vulnerability to indulgence came recently from the lips of a young stock trader on Wall Street: "Yes, I love my job—it's like having an unlimited license to gamble. High stakes, high risks—lots of 'high's'!" No wonder we have a market that shudders now and then, with so many and so much in the runaway mode.

Perhaps it is this infantile sense of infinite potential and omnipotence that orphans us most from ourselves and from each other, from peace (*shalom*) on earth and in our hearts.

Perhaps it is our adolescent dependence and carelessness that blames the system for everything and indulges in the rhetoric of rebellion—but fails to take responsibility for the power we have given away.

The Legend of Hiawatha

art of my heritage as a child growing up in the Great Lakes region was the good fortune to have a father who could evoke my imagination and enchant me with stories of the Indians—Iroquois, Huron, and Mohawk—who used to live in the territory we called home. I would not have been surprised if a departed Indian spirit had appeared one day over the railroad tracks or from behind a garage.

When I was a bit older my pursuit of arrowheads and Indian lore turned to a more conventional, but less imaginative interest in such subjects. One of my first educational experiences was the inevitable exposure to Longfellow's poem "Hiawatha." Longfellow's version of the legend, I was to discover many years later, was really a clever interweaving of several folktales, not all of which concerned the legendary Hiawatha. But Longfellow's images remain: the story of how the woodpecker got his red stripe, the origin of the peace pipe, how the Indians discovered corn, the origin of picture writing. Most of all, Longfellow's poem was a love story, a story of treachery and retribution; the characters of Hiawatha, Nakomis, and Minnehaha still loom in our school memories.

Some years later when I discovered that someone like Hiawatha had actually existed and learned more of the bits and pieces of history that were the source of the legend, I again mythologized this figure, who was so often referred to by the Indian tribes as "the promised prophet." Haion-Hwa-Tha was reputed to be an Iroquois statesman, lawgiver, and shaman who lived around 1570. According to some sources he was born a Mohawk but sought refuge among the Onondaga when his own tribe rejected his teachings. His efforts to unite the five Great Lakes tribes were opposed by a powerful chief, Wathatotarho, whom he eventually defeated, but who killed Hiawatha's daughter in revenge. The alliance he inspired, the unification of the Onondaga, Oneida, Seneca, Cayuga, and Mohawk tribes in the Iroquois League of Five Nations, eventually produced a compact which became one of the models for the U.S. Constitution. Excerpts from the legend go something like this:

The slumber of the great Sky God was disturbed by the sounds of anguish coming from earth, where human beings were enduring great suffering and violence from cruel giants. The Sky God, determined to change himself into a mortal, swiftly descended to earth and told the frightened humans to follow him. By trails known only to him, he led the group of shivering, fearful refugees to a cave at the mouth of a great river where he fed them and told them to sleep undisturbed. After many years of living content-edly near the cave, growing strong and numerous, and learning hunting and growing skills from their guide, the Sky God told them to disperse along the great river into five separate tribes. To each nation the Sky God gave a special gift. The Sky God looked upon the peaceful, productive tribes and was very pleased. He decided to take a human shape and live among the Onondagas, taking the name of Hiawatha. He chose a wife from that tribe and from their union came a daughter Mni-haha. Hiawatha was a great teacher and adviser, and above all he preached peace and harmony.

There came a day, however, when the peace and safety of the tribe was threatened by a fierce, wicked people from the north beyond the Great Lakes, "untutored nations who knew nothing of the eternal law." They devastated Hiawatha's people. He called the five nations to a council and told them to await his coming. While he was on the journey to the great council in his canoe, his small daughter was snatched from him by a great eagle. Hiawatha, stunned with grief, mourned his daughter for three days. The people wondered if the gods had demanded Hiawatha's daughter as a sacrifice for the deliverance of his people. Finally, Hiawatha purified himself in the waters of the Great Lake and assembled the council. Part of what he said is recorded:

"What is past is past; it is the present and the future which concern us. My children, listen well, for these are my last words to you. My time among you is drawing to a close. War, fear, and disunity have brought you from your villages to this sacred council fire. You have drifted apart, each tribe thinking and acting only for itself. Remember how I took you from one small band and nursed you into many nations. No tribe alone can withstand those who care nothing about the eternal law, who sweep upon us like the storms of winter, spreading death and destruction everywhere. My children listen well. Remember that you are brothers, that the down-fall of one means the downfall of all. You must have one fire, one pipe, one war club."

Hiawatha then asked the five tribal firekeepers to unite their fires to the big sacred council fire, and chiefs and wise men withdrew to seek their own counsel. The next day they pledged their compact and Hiawatha rejoiced. He gathered up the dazzling white feathers which the great eagle had dropped and gave the plumes to the assembled leaders of the tribes. "By these feathers," he said, "you shall be known as the Ako-no-shu-ne, the Iroquois." Thus with the help of Hiawatha, the mighty League of Five Nations was born.

The elders begged Hiawatha to become the chief of the united tribes, but he told them:

"This can never be, because I must leave you. Choose the wisest *women* in your tribes to be the future clan mothers and peacemakers, let them turn any strife arising among you into friendship. Let your leaders be wise enough to go to such women for advice when there are disputes. Farewell."

With that, Hiawatha stepped into his white mystery canoe, and instead of gliding away on the waters of the lake, it rose slowly into the sky and disappeared into the clouds.[1]

When I first heard the original legend I was fascinated with Hiawatha's pacifism and his relinquishment of power – both evidence of an ethos that contradicted the invading white European notions of power. Later anthropology and ethnography confirmed the significance of the legend. The testimonies of missionaries and explorers reveal that among the Iroquois all real authority was vested in the matrons of the tribe. The lands, the fields, the organization of the planting, and fruits of the harvest all belonged to them. They were the "souls" of the Councils, the arbiters of peace and war (men fought the wars, but only the women could declare wars and ratify treaties), and the managers of the public treasury. Although women could not serve on the Council of Elders, the hereditary eligibility for office passed through them, and elective eligibility was largely controlled by them. They spoke on the Great Councils through their male spokesmen. The position of matron was open to any woman who qualified as a head of household.

In addition to these powerful matrons, some women were designated "keepers of the faith" who had an equal voice, along with the male shamans, in all ritual and religious matters. Marriages and divorces were arranged by mothers as well as the spacing of births. In contrast to almost universal practice there was usually greater delight at the birth of a daughter than a son. The mother conferred the name on the child. A crucial element in consolidating the power of the women was the tradition of the family longhouse, a large multifamily dwelling in which communal sharing was the way of life. (The longhouse was the metaphor which inspired the League, and the Iroquois often referred to themselves as "the people of the longhouse.") The female ownership of the land was nominal because, in the view of the Iroquois, the land belonged to future generations as well as to the present generation. In general, however, much of the power that women exerted among the Iroquois was the result of their control of the economic organization of the tribe.[2]

Historical evidence suggests, however, that the distribution of power did not insure the triumph of Hiawatha's pacifism. The warrior consciousness persisted in the Iroquois, no doubt encouraged by the presence of European interlopers. But the myth also persists. It is a way, as it was for some colonists, of imagining political reconstruction.

When I was working in the U.S. House of Representatives several years ago, there were many occasions when I fantasized what it might be like if the wisest matrons in the land had the power of veto over military interventions, defense budgets, and the power to organize the public economy and priorities. What an interesting prospect! In any case the legend of Hiawatha is another of those unique tales in which a charismatic orphan figure recognizes, models, and—in this particular case—institutionalizes the values of the return to the feminine, the preservation of the Gaia, the earth community. Women become the carriers of the values of nonviolence and sharing, even the sharing of power.

6.

SPIRITUAL ORPHANS
IN SEARCH OF A GOD

When I was young the character of Dorothy in *The Wizard of Oz* inspired many of us who were on the threshold of adolescent rebellion, but were not likely to act it out in socially unacceptable ways. Dorothy was curious, imaginative, longing for adventure, and bored with routine family life in Kansas. Her sudden translocation to Oz is one of the most wonderful wish fulfillments in all of literature.

As an adult woman I found in Dorothy a mythic symbol that resonated with many of the major turning points in my own growth to moral maturity – most of which would be described as acts of rebellion. No longer was she a childhood fantasy figure, but suddenly she took on a more heroic aspect. Especially in her encounters with the Wizard Dorothy seemed to portray so much of the reality of our experience of awakening and of seizing our own inner authority and autonomy as women.

In her first encounter with the Wizard, Dorothy is the innocent who unquestioningly accepts the Wizard's command that she first destroy the Wicked Witch of the West (her shadow?) before he will help her find her way back to Kansas. Her worthiness, her goodness is dependent on the difficult task and the approval of the mysterious Wizard.

After Dorothy and her companions have successfully (even if unwittingly) dispatched the Witch, they return to the Great Oz to claim their promised rewards. This time she and her companions are more assertive with the Wizard. Dorothy, with the help of her dog Toto, rips away the screen that keeps the Wizard hidden from their eyes. Suddenly he is revealed as a charlatan – not Oz, the Great and Terrible, but a little bald-headed retired circus balloonist, who fooled everyone with his smoke and mirrors. Why, she says, "you're a humbug!" And as her rage peaks, she calls him "a very bad man." His reply has always represented for me the other half of the experience of disillusionment and the disintegration of an idol: "No, my dear, I'm really a very good man; but I'm a very bad Wizard."

When the Wizard finally speaks the whole truth to Dorothy and her companions, they discover their own personal resources. Discovering that the emperor has no clothes has always been the passage to self-empowerment. Whatever or whoever the idols are that we depend on to prop up our sense of identity and security, these must be shattered if the real person is to emerge in her or his own strength and self-knowledge. We discover that this is the pattern of growth, and one by one the idols fall: parents, teachers, peers, authorities, philosophies and institutions, creeds, codes and cults, friends and lovers, self-image, and – the greatest idol of all – religion. Even our notion of God must be shattered over and over again if we are to stand in truth with ourselves and with all that is.

Some cling desperately to the God image of their youth or of their first conversion because it represents unchanging values and the reassurance of a world and spiritual economy that makes sense. Its static aspect reinforces a sense of security and wards off the threat or necessity of change. Others, perhaps, manage without a notion of God because it was simply absent or denied in their original holding environment; but these persons usually find something else in life that becomes a God-substitute and can have the power of an idol.

There are many, no doubt, who through negligence or deliberate repression lose their early notions of God. Finding those early notions irrelevant to their experience, they simply abdicate from any necessity for spiritual search. Then there are others of us who over the period of a lifetime shed our notions of God like so many worn-out husks or snakeskins. Our disillusionment with God keeps pace with the demystification of human behavior and world reality. So many of the forms that unconsciously gave shape to our lives and our self-image turn out to be "humbug." And so we cast them off. We are left, like the legendary emperor, with only a sensitive, raw, totally vulnerable, and exposed skin. Who am I? Does life have any meaning? What is appearance, what is reality? Why is there suffering and evil in this world? God's face and intent are elusive.

In the past the solidity and continuity of creed, code, cult, and caste was assured by the proximity and rhythm of life and community cycles. Today all of these scaffolds are teetering, if not already collapsed. The forms that shaped our lives and our self-image vanish like mirages. The myths, like the gods of old, have faded into a twilight. Our vision grows dim, our pathway in the dark uncertain. There is no longer a Supreme Director or Ultimate Good Provider in the universe, no Judge or Arbiter of right and wrong, no unconditional Amnesty or Providence. Recently, a man told me that he felt as if he were a passenger in a driverless vehicle, careening on into the future toward inevitable destruction. "The only reality," he said, whether cosmic, physical, or ethical, "is entropy." A rather grim prospect. Is this where the process of "dehumbugging" reality and belief structures inevitably leads?

This man's bleak perception is counteracted by many others for whom the confrontation with this stark possibility is unthinkable. They have pasted the shreds of the old notions of God on themselves and constructed what Freud called a "prosthetic God." In his *Civilization and its Discontents,* he observed that man, once a vulnerable and feeble organism, has through science and technology fulfilled his longings for omnipotence and omniscience—desires which he once embodied in his gods. Freud wrote:

> To these gods he attributed everything that seemed unattainable to his wishes, or that was forbidden to him. . . . Today he has come very close to the attainment of his ideal, he has almost become a god himself. . . . Man has, as it were, become a kind of prosthetic God. When he puts on all his auxiliary organs he is truly magnificent; but those organs have not grown on to him and they still give him much trouble at times. . . . Future ages will bring with them new and probably unimaginably great advances in this field of civilization and will increase man's likeness to God still more. But . . . we will not forget that present-day man does not feel happy in his Godlike character."[1]

Freud was the first contemporary philosopher-psychologist to claim that God was a "humbug" and be respected and listened to. In *The Future of an Illusion* he asserts that religion is a "childhood neurosis." Ironically Freud was not free of the idol-making tendency himself, since he succumbed to the illusion that science was illusionless. Moreover in his theories of libido and the Oedipus complex, his own projections are evident, and subsequent historical probing has placed these theories in context. Nevertheless his view that humankind had simply switched clothes from the omnipotent, transcendental, judgmental God of the Middle Ages to the "prosthetic God" of self-creation and technological hubris is still very relevant.

In one sense Freud ushered in an age of repression. Religious experience was pushed back into the subconscious, submerged in a kind of cultural amnesia, no longer regarded as a powerful social engine in an explicit public consciousness. Repressed, it became for the cultural elite what Hans Küng has called "the last taboo."[2] Privatized, it became for thousands of mainline churchgoers a social ritual and mere adjunct to the real business of living. It is precisely in this climate of secularization, of the repression of religious experience (and of the creeds, codes, rituals, and symbols that give it expression) that an archetypal vacuum develops. Into that vacuum flow the most powerful unconscious myths that drive the culture. These tacit myths are a ritual text that shapes social attitudes and institutions and spawns a political logic. Authentic religious experience is often a corrective to these tacit myths.

The most powerful, comprehensive, and energizing tacit myth and engine of legitimation in most cultures is, ironically, its myth of God. The God myth is the ultimate legitimating metaphor and model for social and political structures, for language and for the dynamics of interpersonal relations. The values, power structure, and social arrangements of a culture make the God myth necessary. The God myth is an anthropological reality, not a religious reality. In an existential sense it is almost always a caricature of the Holy One who is Truth beyond all images. Too often it bears the residues of the primitive totemism that preceded its development. The Aztec Jaguar god, with its gaping receptacles for human hearts ripped out of living human sacrifices, is an example that carries the residue of a more ancient past as well as the imprint of the social structures that required it for legitimation in the Aztec world.

The paradigmatic God myth of Western civilization is most clearly represented in the creation story of Genesis. What is depicted there is a world of matter and energy created in one momentary flash of divine power as a finished product. Monotheism and divine autonomy are very emphatic. The creator is depicted as an anthropomorphic Father God, a patriarch. The patriarch sets up a hierarchy of life systems, one that carries the implication that each one will rule over the next one down on the ladder of life. God is at the top, man is next, then woman and child, then animals, earth. God's hegemony is absolutized in terms of dominance and dependence. Autonomy in one who should be dependent at any point on the ladder is regarded as a negation of God, as sin. Thus the notion of God's omnipotence, in cultural terms at least, negates our participation in Being. (The enculturated God myth is largely the product of later application and interpretation, not necessarily of the intent of the original biblical narrative.)

Thus we have inherited a God who is transcendent, remote, judgmental, omnipotent, omniscient, and, by historical implications, white, male, and celibate – a God who has been busy replicating himself in patriarchal structures of dominance everywhere. It is a myth that implies "one up, one down," and has been used to legitimate racism, religious bigotry, classism, imperialism, and sexism. It has reinforced a world of dominance and dependency in the private and public domain, divided us between control and the fear of chaos, between a world of "haves" and "have-nots," a world of the valued and the not-valued, the disposable. Above all, this God seems to have little to do with authentic religious experience, with the numinous and the holy.

The Genesis creation story also presents us with a myth in which humanity is disobedient–in which humanity attempts to participate in God's power. The myth that has become most influential in our culture is not the generalized, benevolent view of the first chapter of Genesis ("And God saw that it was good"), but the view that is presented in the third chapter, which was written by a different author of another time. This is the chapter that recounts the fall. Eve is portrayed as the occasion of the human fall from grace – a curse becomes the foundation of society and the source of death and pain. Authority is vested in the male. Man is required to rule over woman and to subdue the earth.

It is important to understand the priority that this myth had in its own time in order to understand its persistence. There were other myths available at the time – for example, the Sumerian myth in which a male was the source of the fall and the curse upon humanity. In fact there were many myths in which men ("heroes") who aspired to divine knowledge or power were blamed for bringing evil into the world. In these myths the means by which humans acquired divine knowledge or power was always through eating and drinking certain substances or through sexual experience. Typically, we find all of these elements in the early parallel myths: the tree of knowledge, the forbidden fruit, the snake. But the Genesis myth so obviously inverts many of the tropes of existing myths. It canonized an emerging social reality of patriarchy.

There are two things happening to this God myth today. Both are destined to have far-reaching effects on human events and global politics.

The first is a phenomenon that we are all too aware of: the hardening of the myth into a rigid, fascistic, narrow-minded, militant fundamentalism–whether that is expressed in the Islamic extremism of the Iranian mullahs or in the creationism and moral puritanism of the Neo-Right in the United States.

The second thing that is happening is the dissolving of the myth. There are two primary expressions of this evident in our culture today. One is the New Age phenomenon. If fundamentalism projects the illusion of God in control of everything, then the New Age devotee projects the illusion that the individual is in charge. The fundamentalist must conform the self completely to the heteronomy of God's absolutism. The New-Ager must conform the self to one's own aspiration, and inevitably to one's own needs, gratifications, and illusions. The New Age believer runs the risk of displacing the traditional God myth with the absolute autonomy of the self: "You are God; you can create your own reality." Nevertheless, the New Age phenomenon in many instances represents the growing edge of the human quest for a new God myth. The latter is clearly a modern variation on the traditional American myth of self-creation. In the extreme reincarnation and channeling might be seen as another prosthetic solution to the problem of self-creation.

There is another expression of the dissolving God myth that seems to offer even more possibilities for personal and social transformation; this is the experience of women, so many of whom are today forging their own authentic spirituality across generations, across cultures and class. In the passage through alienation from the old patriarchal myth to the reconstruction of a God myth through the lens of their own experience, women point the way to the future beyond illusion. The primary vehicle of this transformation is the process by which women, so long alienated from their own disvalued experience, are learning to give voice and passion to their own story and myth. Women are at once orphic tellers and affirming listeners who mediate and validate each other's reality through sharing, solidarity, and community. Out of these come new images and wonderful experiences of the divine, the holy.

No one has captured this more vividly than Alice Walker in her novel *The Color Purple*. In her stunning conversation with Shug, Celie realizes that the reason she feels estranged from God is that she has been imaging him as white, male, aged, uncaring, and distant. Shug, a woman who has helped her to know real love, assures her, "you can't see anything at all, until you get man off your eyeball."[3]

Patriarchy, embedded so graphically in the creation myth of Genesis, is the universal religion, and the spiritual exodus of women today from that caricature of the divine is the most profound sign of our times, of a transformation that is coming. Why is it so threatening? What explains the vehemence, the viciousness, and the relentlessness of the backlash? To answer that question it is necessary to look at another aspect of the creation and God myths.

The creation myth of Genesis marked the establishment of monotheism and the legitimation of patriarchy as a way of nature, as God's will, and the natural law. Social historians and anthropologists, building on the work of biblical scholars, have offered new insights on the myth in recent years. Gerda Lerner in her study *The Creation of Patriarchy* points out the significance of the prohibition not to eat of the tree of knowledge of good and evil, and the consequence of a double transgression.[4] First there is sexual transgression: "They knew they were naked." In the ancient world, images of the snake were always associated with the goddess of fertility, the goddess of life. Thus, the snake is the symbol of preeminent female power and also of the threat of chaos – female energies out of control. The banishing of the snake is the banishing of the goddess and, symbolically, Eve's free and autonomous expression of her sexuality. Henceforth its only expression would be through motherhood, pain, and sorrow.

The second transgression is one of power: "You shall be as gods." Because of her autonomous act, her curiosity, and her aggressive desire to know, Eve is to be punished by being excluded from knowledge and experience that is power. Eve is cursed, punished by being subordinated to her husband – "he shall rule over thee." Eve will have the power to reproduce in the physical sense, but no creative power in the social sense.

And so the curse of Genesis – visited most visibly and one-sidedly on woman – is the split in civilization between reproduction and the creation of culture, between procreation and power. We are the inheritors of the world that Genesis legitimated. When we ask, who creates life? Who speaks to God? Who rules over and names creation? Who creates culture? The answer is man. And when we ask, who bears children? Who gives her body and labor to care for them? Who brought sin and death into the world? For centuries, the answer has been woman.

The development of monotheism was an evolutionary leap that advanced human beings toward abstract thought and the definition of universally valid symbols. No one would deny this, and thus in its time it could be considered providential. Nevertheless, the birth of the process of symbol making – the fundamental process that shaped our society – occurred under circumstances that marginalized women. Monotheistic patriarchy advanced human capacity but institutionalized the exclusion of women from the creation of symbol systems, from the castes that name, validate, define, and judge. From this came a philosophy of history – the split between the mind and body, and between spirituality and sensuality. There is considerable evidence that social class divisions began with the dominance of men over women in the creation of culture, and developed into the dominance of some men over other men and all women. Gender dominance and preference–legitimated by the dominant myth of our culture–underlies all forms of invalidation and exploitation–class, race, caste–that today threaten to rend the fabric of the planet.

If today women are slowly and painfully being admitted to the symbol-making systems of politics, religion, the arts, and sciences, it is often on terms dictated by the ruling caste: "Behave like a man, and we'll let you into the club." If the Father God is alive and well, so is the Eve myth. As long as the myth persists women will be associated with sin and the seductive, perverse aspects of nature. They will be burdened with responsibility for the moral and domestic economy. (Women are convenient guilt-catchers and rescue squads when people or things go wrong.) And women will be feared for their power; femaleness is an energy, a force that must be controlled (otherwise, chaos, or men overwhelmed by eros, may result).

What, then, is the meaning of the existence and persistence of this God myth and creation model? In short, it means the aggrandizement of masculine self-sufficiency and the denial of the feminine. Catherine Keller in her brilliant book *From a Broken Web* spins out more of these implications. If God is traditionally seen as omnipotent, all-powerful, all-controlling, and ultimately responsible for all evil and unjust suffering, then divine self-sufficiency must imply divine impassivity. Indeed, God's inability to *feel* seems to have been acknowledged by Aquinas, tutored by Aristotle. God the Father images a "reflexive selfhood: self-knowing rendered infinite and exact by his own immutability." Because he cannot be affected or vulnerable, he is the perfect object to himself. Keller asks, in the light of the masculine identity of the normative self (whose cultural characteristics of separation and low self-disclosure we have noted in chapter three), "Embarrassed by feeling, could this deity be other than a magnified He?"[5]

A creation myth that predates Genesis portrays the denial of the feminine, the rejection of the Great Mother (symbolic also of earth, nature, embodiment, and feeling). Biblical scholars have noted that the Genesis authors were obviously indebted to this earlier Babylonian epic *Enuma Elish*. In Genesis the primordial oceanic matrix, the "deep" (*tehom*), is a transformation of the First Mother of All, Tiamat from the *Enuma Elish*. In the earlier epic the divine hero Marduk, of the rising warrior class of rulers, annihilates Tiamat in a mighty combat and, by dismembering her carcass, creates his cosmos out of her pieces. Tiamat's tolerance for the creatures of her womb–"Why must we destroy the children we have made? If their ways are troublesome, let us wait a little while"–is contrasted with Marduk's destructive lust for control and his misogynist denigrations of Tiamat. By the time the great combat occurs, Tiamat is represented as a great sea monster, an image of serpentine power (Eve's grandmother?).[6]

There are other ancient myths that echo this fateful contest and suggest that the psychic and spiritual foundation of our civilization is a primordial act of matricide. Indeed it is a world in which heroic masculinity is associated with gynophobia, echoing Mary Daly's premise in *Gyn/Ecology* that 'the universal enemy in all male-sponsored wars is the Self in every woman'. The God vs. world dichotomy is extended to mean self (superior, manlike) vs. other (inferior, femalelike). As Keller notes, the story of Tiamat and Marduk is replete with suggestions of the "separate, autonomous" ethos of the male self over against the "connective, inclusive" ethos of the Great Mother. Monotheism and the abstract laws it would generate required the banishing of the immanent, sensing spirit. And banished it was–to the world of the unconscious, where it would surface again and again in the psyche and in collective symbols. (Jung was perhaps the first to recognize this and name it.)

The disappearance of the mother has left us orphaned from the feminine. Freud, so vehement in his rejection of the traditional Father God as a myth, nevertheless bequeathed to us a father-centered concept of personhood as a "separate self" based, of course, on the notion of male ego-differentiation from the mother. Freud's psychoanalytic principles were not so much a prescription for a patriarchal society as a description of it. Perhaps the most revealing assumption of Freud's paradigm of consciousness for the twentieth century is the implied connection between misogyny and atheism. In *Freud on Femininity and Faith* Judith Van Herik argues that Freud's notion of illusion was applied equivalently to Christianity and femininity. Renunciation of the illusion would also mean redemption from feminine attitudes. Science would save us.[7]

The disappearance of the mother has left us not only abandoned and godless, but also vulnerable to being possessed by false images of God. Ann Ulanov emphasizes the importance of examining those images: "The pictures we have of God, both our individual pictures and our group pictures, will show us unmistakably what we leave out in ourselves and what we must look at. . . . If we do not look at our pictures of God we split off the bad, project it onto our neighbors, force it down their throats and identify ourselves with the good."[8]

Because the God myth has been the legitimating force for so much violence and denial of life, so much tribalism, "nothing novel, kind, or hopeful can be created in the future unless we kill off this God, the idol of the tribe," writes Sam Keen. "The basis of a new social order is a theological revolution."[9]

Across this "night of the fathers" now streaks a comet–the outbreaking of the feminine in the emergence of women's spirituality in our era. What is happening among many women of many cultures is preparing the ground for a new Genesis, a new God myth: the return to God the Mother; the return to earth and embodiment; the revaluation of personal experience, especially when it is not normative; the return to relation and connection; the primacy of caring and of helping life to flourish; the mutual interrelationship and value of all life forms.

It is difficult to represent to the world at large what this means in terms of the return to the real. Many of the dominant symbol systems of the world have already felt the impact of the outbreaking feminine and its purifying excision of the androlatrous, androgenized elements in the traditions. But the power of women's spirituality is chiefly experienced in the rituals that women are creating to free themselves of the patriarchal myth. One that I have experienced comes to mind–the "Ritual of the Apple."

Recalling the story of Eve and the garden of temptation, we gather to read the Genesis account. Then we have readings of related texts in other parts of the Scriptures which reinforce the myth (for example, Genesis 19, 1 Timothy 2). At the end of each reading, all the women gathered resound with vigor, "This is *not* the will or the word of God!" Then an apple is blessed and passed from woman to woman, with the words, "Take and eat, for it is good, and you are good." I cannot describe the powerful, even physical sense of affirmation and exorcism that this communal ritual imparts. Tears, silent awe, a heightened awareness of intimate connection, an incredible sense of something being lifted, wiped away–I still remember the shiver and tremble, the exaltation I felt in my body. Somehow, the image of the apple sums up our common story and suffering, the symbol of our enslavement, our nothingness, now redeemed.

For many years I pursued the God who was imaged and assigned by the dominant culture: the God of my ancestors, the God of my parents and teachers, the God of the priests and chaplains, the God of my theology professors and spiritual directors, the God of my religious community, the quasi-deistic God of the American culture, the mystical Lover of the saints, the cosmic God of the scientists and poets, the elusive Spirit in my own heart. But when I called, no one answered; when I wept for my own pain or that of the world, no God appeared to comfort me. I seemed lost in a forest of abstraction.

One day when I was in my early forties I had a revelation, or rather the beginning of a revelation that still continues. I heard about some women who, in celebrating their feminine reality, had tasted their own menstrual blood. That image, that tableau of a ritual act of "impurity" first shocked me, then shattered my separateness, the armor that shielded me from contact with the feminine in myself. Suddenly what I had always regarded as "the curse"–something to be controlled, transcended, tolerated, but not befriended–became the metaphor for a new intimacy with my own reality as a woman. I had been psychically separated from the oceanic fluids and marrow of my own embodied being. Somehow I knew that my "curse" was a translation of the "curse" of Genesis, a mirror of a God so inscrutable and remote that the sin, evil, and pain in the world seemed inexplicable. I had to discover the "curse" as a gift and sign of our intimacy with Gaia, a planetary-lunar reminder of the womb-travail, and the ebb and flow of creation, of the law written in our inmost being: that to give life, to be fully alive and whole, there must be some pain and dying and leaving.

Gradually I discovered through the medium of other women what I did not know and love in myself. My own experience and that of other women opened me to myself, to my reality as a woman, and to the Holy within me. (Goddess is in many ways too narrow a word.) As I touched my own reality, as I listened to the stories and myths of other women–of their bleeding and birthing, their loving and limning of children, their familiarity with pain and dying, with feeding and caring, their planting and harvesting and baking, their closeness to the rhythms of nature, their connectedness with earth, air, fire and water, with roots and ancestors and kin–I met the Holy in the revelation of my own being and She was Loving, a verb. In that revelation I have been able, oh so slowly and painfully, to shed layer after layer of "clothes"–borrowed or forced upon me–that hide me from myself: From my new nakedness I have moved to grace, to the Presence of the Holy in creation.

I have learned in the company of whole and holy women to exorcise the unreal, to celebrate and ritualize the true and the real, to speak and hear a new language, to feel the spirit through flesh and matter, to see everything–*from within*–as if creation were the Womb of God where, although we experience darkness and obscurity, there is also warmth, nourishment, movement, growth, connection, and delight.

My metaphor for God is much like a moon that has many phases, for it changes as my journey continues. God as Father or Mother is not the question. The question is how do I participate in the divine energy: in the "feminine" energy of opening, receiving, waxing and waning, of relation and connection, of flexibility and fertility; and in the "masculine" energy of ordering, separating, dividing, and naming, of identity and principle, of strength and stamina to create and do. I could not be who I am without both of these kinds of energy. Through the revelation of my own being and the validation of my own experience as a woman I have completed the arc of energy–I am no longer an honorary male or a powerless woman, I no longer have to receive the divine as an alien God.

Our civilization's idolatry of the abstract, omnipotent God has clouded our vision and our capacity for divinization. In the primordial world, this God–and the dominant male culture that he legitimated–rescued us from immanence and unconsciousness. In the world that is coming, God the Feminine will lead us in the way of our lost connections, gently teach us the equilibrium of immanence and transcendence, of vulnerability and power, of consciousness and care that is our reality redeemed from the curse.

The journey for both women and men in modern times may be more like the journey of Ruth than of Abraham. God does not give instructions from afar or from a mountain. Instead, we are confronted with abandonment, nothingness, alienation; we are confronted with the orphan self. Our companion is Naomi, the archetypal wise woman, bereft of male protection and possession. We, like Ruth, engage and attach ourselves fiercely to this outcast feminine. "Your people shall be my people, and your God my God" (Ruth 1:16). Naomi calls upon her God as *El Shaddai,* traditionally translated as "the Almighty." But the literal meaning conveys more, for it means "many-breasted one," conjuring up those wonderful images of ancient goddesses, their multiple breasts heavy with milk, their visages glinting with power and knowing.[10]

We are in the process of recovering these lost images and myths of God, because we are–men and women–discovering and befriending our own protofemininity, the deepest feminine ground of our being. These efforts point the way to the future of religious traditions in our civilization. Because they all share elements of the religion of patriarchy and androlatry, they will in time become alien Gods for everyone. But because they all share elements of wisdom and liberation, we can hope that these traditions will be slowly redeemed.

Questions remain. What have the great traditions preserved of authentic religious experience? Will the present forms of organized religion be the coffins of the great spiritual traditions? Who needs religion anyway? Is what is coming no more like the old spiritualities than the nuclear age is like the paleolithic age?

My intuition is, because the re-emergence of the "Great Mother" marks the threshold of a new spiritual awareness in the evolution of our civilization, she will not be so ruthless as the Father God in destroying all previous gods and rivals. She is the sign of the connectedness of all things, recalling the faithful but fateful tolerance of Tiamat as well as the mediations of other ancient goddesses who mimicked her in human iconology.

Perhaps the fatal flaw in so many great human revolutions is precisely this: the failure to conserve and transform the fundamental myths that are the ground of the people's history. Thus, we seek holonomy, the great principle of growth and completeness: all that has gone before is somehow contained in the new phenomenon. Looked at from this perspective, the emerging forms of feminist spirituality which appear to be iconoclastic turn out to be acts of preservation. Feminists, the great conservators of the tradition!

A case in point is the feminist scholarship which has unearthed the history and prophetic role of women in the Judeo-Christian Scriptures. Moreover, feminist scholarship has also unearthed evidences of the suppression of the feminine in the tradition. Sophia, a goddesslike figure who appears prominently in the Hebrew Scriptures and obliquely in the Christian Scriptures, has been illuminated by these studies. Theologians have suggested on the basis of historical and textual evidence that she is portrayed as a manifestation or hypostasis of God, God's Wisdom – the underlying presence in creation. Her power eclipses Yahweh's at several points and the attributes assigned to her resemble the Great Mother.

The repression of Sophia in the tradition probably began with Philo who substituted a personified masculine "Logos" for the feminine Sophia. In the process of Hellenization the masculine Logos gradually subsumed all of Sophia's attributes and roles, including the image of her as "the firstborn of God." Her divine power and significance was systematically diminished. Although the earliest theological traditions associated Jesus with Sophia (as her messenger), by the time of the last Gospel (John), sophialogy had been transformed into Christology and Jesus associated with the Word (*Logos*) as "God's firstborn." A more definitive repression of Sophia came during the christological disputes of the third and fourth centuries.[11] Perhaps this is part of the explanation for the outbreaking of the feminine in the popular devotion of the third century and the exaltation of Mary of Nazareth as the Mother of God *theotokos* in 431.

Archetypal theory has always associated Sophia with spiritual transformation, as "the goddess of the Whole" who represents our potential for growth as well as our connection with earthbound materiality. Erich Neumann sees this figure as distinct from the other great mother goddesses in her power to wed spirit and matter–"the spirit of the earth"–and to heal the dualisms that have wounded it.[12]

The Catholic tradition of the Virgin Mary has a particular relevance to the significance of Sophia. Clearly, when patriarchal rational theology was most inclined to veil and diminish Mary's goddesslike features, she surfaced powerfully in the popular consciousness. Down through the centuries, many of her epiphanies or appearances – almost always to peasants or children – seemed to occur at those critical historical moments when the populace had lost faith in the prevailing mythos of power that suppressed the feminine.

Women of all faiths are in the process of discovering aspects of the repressed feminine analogous to the Sophia tradition. Feminists, in fact, have become catalysts for the redemption of religious symbols which will undoubtedly characterize the next epoch. Moreover many women, as well as men, are engaged in a search for symbols and wisdom literature that transcends or links the great faith traditions. Women theologians and social historians from the Jewish, Christian, Islamic, Buddhist, and Hindu religions are pursuing the reconstruction of the origins of their faith traditions, lifting up the lost feminine buried under centuries of male hegemony. Others are tracing the vital springs of authentic religious experience that run beneath the formal structures of religion in the testimonies of the mystics and shamans.

There are several pressing reasons for this effort. First of all, it is clear that humanity is experiencing an unprecedented need for connection with a spiritual reality. At the same time, people have never felt so orphaned from traditional sources of spiritual meaning and sustenance as they do today. The wells of organized religion have run dry. It makes sense to turn, as the feminists and base communities have done, to one's personal and collective experience for sources of spiritual enlightenment, symbols, and experience. On the other hand, it is obvious that the God myths of Western and Eastern traditions will persist even if they are not transformed. Indeed, these myths, tacitly or explicitly, continue to be the moving force and shaping consciousness behind the political events and trends of our time. In Northern Ireland, in the Middle East, in Northern India, in Vietnam, so many of the world's conflicts have been influenced and exacerbated by religious motives. Hans Küng has put it very starkly: "These conflicts become bloody and without pity if they are done in the name of God. So we must conclude that without peace among the *religions* there will be no peace among the nations."[13]

This stark and sober reality confirms the call to a "Copernican revolution" that persons of many faith communities are experiencing today. If in the past Christianity, Judaism, or Islam placed itself at the center of the search for truth and unity, there is now a shift away from this kind of tribal centricity to the notion that it is God who is at the center and all the religious traditions of the world must inevitably intersect at this center. One can no longer speak about one's faith outside the ambience of the plurality of religious traditions. How do I understand my belief and my own tradition until I see it through the eyes of strangers?

This is both an exciting and challenging prospect. Thus there is a great effort to return to sources, to strike common ground, to interrupt the monologues of the prophets (Jesus, Muhammad, Buddha) and require that they speak to each other, to inquire what their notions of God and the world really were, to identify their essential truths and meaningful images of God. Arnold Toynbee has argued that the religious system that survives into the future would be the one that proves capable of expanding and evolving in such a way as to embrace the essential truths in other religious systems. Evolution, he argued, always works by growing out of the old into the new, not by picking up and choosing from available options to create a new construct.[14]

If indeed the feminine – the ethos of the Great Mother – manifests the unitive principle of the cosmos, then much of traditional religion must be seen as an elaborate facade and superstructure designed to deny and/or control the feminine, the immanence of the divine in creation. What is so clearly suppressed in the male psyche is visibly acted out in the suppression of women. Fatna Sabbah, an Islamic scholar, has made this connection most dramatically in her book *The Woman in the Muslim Unconscious*. She maintains that in the Islamic sacred universe,

the believer is fashioned in the image of woman, deprived of speech and will and committed to obedience to another (God). The female condition and the male condition are not different in the end to which they are directed, but in the pole around which they orbit. The lives of the male sex revolve around the divine will. The lives of the female sex revolve around the will of believers of the male sex. And in both cases the human element, in terms of multiple, unforeseeable potentialities must be liquidated in order to bring about the triumph of the sacred, the triumph of the divine, the non-human.[15]

This is surely the paradigm of Genesis writ large.

Western Christianity and Judaism, which recognize these human potentialities along with individualism and modernity, therefore represent a demonic threat to the Islamic worldview. Likewise, Christianity is threatened by the nontheistic conceptions of God in the Eastern religions. Asian religions that promote a Stoic personal virtue seem incompatible with Christian and Moslem prophetic and political activism.

Feminism, in exposing the patriarchal structures in all religious traditions can initiate the process of building bridges across cultures, gathering up the complementary elements in the traditions, and diminishing the power of divisive cults. Otherwise each tradition may be doomed to be infected with its own extremes. The antidotes to these extremes often exist in other of the world's great religious faiths. The more inclusive myths, in the spirit of the Great Mother, can become a focus of connection between the Holy One and the many.

Women's spirituality, so fundamentally grounded in women's own experience, is building a kind of chrysalis of the future from which new paradigms will emerge. It is especially in the emerging voices of women that the future is beginning to take shape. Women are the largest single group in history who have a lived experience that is reality-centered and nonnormative for the dominant culture, and women are now beginning to own, name, and articulate that experience. Hazel Henderson is representative of this growing edge when she synthesizes the emerging theories in physics, economics, and social science with ecology and feminism. Her basic principles for a new world order center around interconnectedness, diversity, cooperation, and evolutionary learning.[16] Jonas Salk has described the new paradigm as a shift from "survival behavior" to "evolutionary spirituality." The major shift in human evolution is from behaving like an animal struggling to survive to behaving like an animal choosing to evolve. In fact, in order to survive, humanity has to evolve. And to evolve, we need a new kind of thinking and a new kind of behavior, a new ethic and a new morality.[17]

The survivalist is full of fear, especially fear of losing anything: identity, possessions, nationality. The survivalist reacts to threat; the evolutionary chooses to evolve and to change. Trust and heightened awareness are the key to the new consciousness rather than fear and defensiveness. It is a spirituality that reads the signs and takes its cue from reality rather than from ideology. Evolutionary spirituality renounces self-righteousness and perfectionism. Evolution is an error-making and error-correcting process; therefore the capacity for *forgiveness* is indispensable. The forgiving begins with self-forgiving and becomes a constant process, a way of life – a deep reverence for whatever happens to us, a shedding of past doubts and resentments, and a moving on. Cooperation and caring displace competition and winning as a motive because all things are connected and interdependent.

The evolutionary does not believe God is above us, out ahead of us, or imprisoned only within us, but God is *with* us on the journey. God is present to us as our own experience is present to us, as it calls us from the *past*, in fulfillment of beginnings and acceptance of our limitations; from the *future*, to fulfillment of our possibilities, to change, to things un-dreamed of. What myths, what metaphors will help us bridge the gap between the past and the future? What theologian Sallie McFague calls "a remythologizing of the relationship between God and the world" is crucial to this process.[18]

One traditional image that links the Abrahmic faiths with the women's movement today is the Exodus myth. The biblical story of the Exodus has surely been the most pervasive and dynamic metaphor of social change in the history of the world. Puritans in the 1600s, abolitionists in the 1800s, and civil rights activists in the 1960s; today the base communities in Latin America, Women-Church (a new experience of church, ritual, and community, without clerical presiders, by and for women) – all have used the Exodus myth to energize and solidify political power and social change. It has inspired secular as well as sacred revolutions and revolu-tionaries: John Calvin, Savanarola, John Knox, Benjamin Franklin, the muckrakers, the Zionists, Susan B. Anthony, Mary Daly.

The Exodus myth has a special relevance for us today, caught as we are in the lag between epochs: "Too late for the gods, and too early for God." We are caught between the "no longer" and the "not yet" on so many different levels. We wander in the desert of "the in-between." The way to the promised land is through the wilderness, and there is no way to get from here to there except by joining together, marching, and enduring.

It is important to recall that the Exodus story could not have happened without the rebellion of a few Hebrew women. The great deliverance motif of Western civilization began, not with Moses, but with Hebrew midwives who collectively decided they would not obey Pharaoh's order to kill all newborn male infants. Moses' mother and sister also defied the order; Pharaoh's daughter joined in their subversive action. It all began when women decided to connect and resist, above all, to act in the interests of life and of the future. As Esther Broner puts it, "We owe our survival to disobedient women."[19] Women's awakening in our time is a great sign of the recovery of the feminine in our culture and of our return to reverence for the Great Mother.

Many have voiced the longing of our generation for a God equal to our times. Pierre Teilhard de Chardin wrote in 1919: "The God for whom our century is waiting must be as vast and mysterious as the cosmos, as immediate and all-embracing as life itself, and intimately linked to the human endeavor."[20] We long for a God equal to our aspirations for ourselves, for the universe. These conceptions of the expected, long-awaited God are nevertheless tinged with a bit of our own promethean fallibility. Like the Israelites in the desert, when this God does not appear, we set about making our own—or we drag one out of the cultural attic. Wilderness spirituality will demand that we expect to find God in unexpected places, times, and people. God is surprise.

Perhaps the spiritual journey, the earnest search for a Spiritual Presence, only begins when we feel God has abandoned us and the world. This is the experience of spiritual orphanhood—when we cry out and no one answers, when we are struck down and no one can help us.

What if God, after all, is not the Almighty? What if God is not absolute, unchanging, and infinitely powerful? What if in some way God is becoming, in some mysterious way, is constrained by creation and not in control? Have we been chasing an abstraction of omnipotence? Does God suffer and grow? What if creation is God's Body—The Body of God: not a simplistic pantheism, and not merely a metaphor, but an embodied Spirit extended through the universe of the real, with all of its hidden dimensions? The ultimate Mystery is not how God is in us or for us, but *how we are in God.* Gaia, then, becomes an aspect of the self-revealing energy of the hidden God. Truly we have neglected the primacy of this revelation in trying to understand God's silence, God's impotence.

For some time I have been expressing these intuitions to myself—in a whisper—for fear they would make no sense to most people, much less to orthodox Christians. But my insights have been affirmed by the experience of many others, and recently affirmed by a remarkable theological perspective, *Models of God,* by Sallie McFague. McFague suggests that, if the entire universe is expressive of God's being, of incarnation, then we can speak of the world as God's Body. Moreover, God is at risk, because the world may be poorly cared for, ravaged, and wounded. Our God is a God who cares, but does not—as in the royal, monarchical model—intervene. "Sin," in McFague's view, is "the refusal to be the eyes and consciousness of the cosmos," the refusal to take responsibility for befriending, nurturing, loving this Body and all its parts. The vision that McFague offers is decidedly feminist and includes images that affirm God's loving presence as mother (*agape*), lover (*eros*), and friend (*philia*)—radical, surprising images which derive from woman's experience in a special way.[21]

If indeed these images of God seem more attuned to woman's reality, what can we say of Jesus Christ, the feminine, and our relationship to Gaia? Can a woman be a Christian when her experience—spiritual, emotional, and physical—so often testifies to something other than what the churches have made of Jesus Christ?

I believe so. In Jesus Christ I can discover a paradigm of God's relationship to creation, one that at every turn subverts my expectations of an omnipotent, almighty God as well as many of my expectations of the cultural norm of male dominance. In an era and an ethnic region that despised foreigners, Gentiles, and women, Jesus associated with them intimately. He touched, befriended, and treated women as equals of men. He even risked transgressing the taboos of ritual impurity associated with women. Moreover, his imagery was filled with allusions to the experience of women, of nature, and of human vulnerability.

If the age had no language for feminine realities, nevertheless, Jesus' attachment to *Abba* ("Papa") implied a nurturing, intimate bond and united the masculine principle with the feminine in Jesus' way of being in the world. His death on the cross was an affront to the worship of patriarchal power and a mockery of gods and goddesses who are nothing more than idols of dominance. Jesus was a supreme revelation of the self-communication of God in and through an embodied creation; his life was a God myth that functions as an archetype of our relationship to the past and the future, to the cosmos, and to each other.

For the Christian, Jesus is the Way. All things are measured by his Way: by his healing grace, his call to forgiveness and purity of heart, nonviolence and a concern for justice; by his relinquishment of earthly power and dominance; affirmation of *agape* (friendship and self-giving Love) as a new basis for kinship, of change of heart as the requirement for righteousness, and of the transcendent power of suffering.

There are many profound allusions to the pain of God in Asian theology and spirituality and many answers to the question of our abandonment by God. Choan-Sen Song notes that for Buddhists "the sickness of Buddha's great mercy saves people by absorbing their sickness. Sickness is saved by sickness."[22] For Christians, Jesus, abandoned by his Father on the cross, represents the ultimate *kenosis* or "emptying of God" in and through the human.

Does God suffer? Does God care? It is easy to avoid such questions entirely by claiming that God is the Holy One beyond all images and is impossible to conceive of in human terms. This is an abdication which seems to negate the meaning of our own experience of suffering, abandonment, and meaninglessness. Indeed, the whole motive of our contemporary U.S. culture is directed toward the erasure of pain, suffering, and emptiness, as well as the denial of it even when we are undeniably in pain. We avoid confrontation with the reality of our abandoned, orphaned self.

What kind of God do orphans find when they search? The sense of abandonment – that no one cares or understands – has been experienced most radically by those who have suffered the massive social abuse of political oppression, when that oppression has been publically acknowledged and tolerated. The experience of the *desparadidos* of Latin America, the prisoners of the gulags of Soviet Eastern Europe and South Africa, and, above all, the victims of the holocaust of World War II know this ultimate sense of abandonment. Unfortunately, not many have survived to tell us what kind of God they found as they passed through the tunnels of absolute horror.

One of the few surviving testimonies is the diary of Etty Hillesum, a young Dutch Jewish woman who died in Auschwitz in November 1943 at the age of twenty-nine. Her remarkable journal, which she kept during the last two years of her life, records an incredible journey of the spirit as Etty is transformed by horror from a vibrant, pleasure-loving, agnostic dilettante into an extraordinary spiritual presence whose heart and soul would survive the holocaust even as her body perished. Forty years after her death, her diaries and letters resurrect her voice, and she speaks to the orphan in us all.

Etty's capacity for human love and the creativity she aspired to are gradually transformed by the events of her time into a profound resonance with the shared fate of her people and her world. "Only a few months ago I still believed that politics did not touch me."[23] As the realization of the impending annihilation dawns, her natural optimism, her dreams, her ambitions, wishes, and erotic desires are all melted down into a kind of precious metal that remains at her core. She discovers God by accident, by surprise, at the edges of the unthinkable and incomprehensible events of her time. "My life has become an uninterrupted dialogue with You."[24]

She struggles to keep from being overwhelmed by the sight of her suffering parents, who are confined in the same camp awaiting shipment to Auschwitz. She plunges into the depths of the mystery of suffering as she had once into the pleasures of life and draws out of it the only thing that can be salvaged in the face of annihilation – meaning. She writes, "By 'coming to terms with life' I mean: the reality of death has become a definite part of my life; my life has, so to speak, been extended by death, by my looking death in the eye and accepting it, by accepting destruction as part of life and no longer wasting my energies on fear of death or refusal to acknowledge its inevitability." . . . "Living is not the sole meaning of life."[25]

Etty Hillesum comes finally to an astounding realization of the *powerlessness* of God. "The surface of the earth is gradually turning into one great prison camp and soon there will be nobody left outside. . . . If God does not help me to go on, then I shall have to help God."[26]

Hillesum's experience is echoed by a Christian who suffered and died as a victim of Nazism. Dietrich Bonhoeffer, a man of great faith, never ceased to question God as well as other believers. He, too, came to a vision of God's suffering, weakness, and powerlessness: "We cannot be honest unless we recognize that we have to live in the world *etsi deus non daretur*. . . . The God who is with us is the God who forsakes us. Before God and with God we live without God."[27]

Only the God of pain and powerlessness is adequate to the state of radical orphanhood and abandonment that characterizes so much of the human condition today. Estranged from our own experience and from each other, the image of a powerless God illumines our own forsaken reality. Perhaps creation was, in some way, God's emptying – a *kenosis* so complete that God cannot intervene in the workings of the universe or in the human experiment by force. Is this nonviolence of God, poured out through the suffering of creatures, the meaning of grace? Is this how we are to discover our destiny, the ground of our being? God enters more deeply into that suffering even as we flee it.

Horst Eberhard Richter has addressed our human and cultural condition in what he calls the modern "God complex." A psychoanalyst and social psychologist, Richter views Western civilization, molded by science, technology, and industry, as a flight from the human powerlessness of the Middle Ages to the modern illusion of an egocentric, godlike omnipotence. The modern, anxiety-driven individual has lost God, but appropriated his power. Thus, he says, modern spirituality is in reality a pathology.

In his analysis of our contemporary pathology, Richter shows how we have substituted the schemes of Marx, Freud, or Marcuse, or the satisfactions of a party-going culture, the cult of consumption and sex, addictions and camouflages of all kinds, for the spiritual search. He underscores the relationship between this pathology, the divorce from feeling, the repression of women, and the flight from suffering. The dominant male culture is the carrier of this pathology. Boys and men are indoctrinated to regard themselves as good and worthwhile only when they have repressed the very emotional sensitivity that would give them the strength and capacity to undertake the preservation of our most humanitarian values. Richter claims, "It is essential that we acknowledge and reintegrate into our lives the emotional fragility, weakness and suffering which are repressed, both physically and socially."[28]

Richter sees these repressed feelings of impotence transferred to conscious feelings of omnipotence, godlike powerfulness. The result is the modern disease he calls "a God complex." Our way of imaging "the Almighty" is of course a projection of this complex. The repression of the feminine exacts a severe toll. Richter writes, "The visible suffering of the woman mirrors the invisible sickness of the man."[29] Our social situation reveals the same dynamic, one group acts out in a helpless, confused, pathological, and aggressive way, what is actually the repressed disease of the other.[30]

It is especially in the flight from suffering that our cultural social reality is revealed: the denial of suffering through compulsive hyperactivity and consumption; the removal of death from our everyday world; the concealment of suffering through various social techniques and avoidance mechanisms; the anesthetizing of anxiety and loss.

Surely the "womb theology" of the Great Mother, in labor and agony until creation is reborn, is a timely God myth for us today. Her tolerance of pain, her patience with incalcitrance, her empathy, her inclusiveness, her respect for life and death and natural processes, her embodiment of the unity and connectedness of all creatures speaks to our needs. This Mother God shatters our illusions of omnipotence and separateness, which are fed by a cultural ethos of individualism and ego. She dissolves the false god myths and reveals the hidden face of the one true God, the God of mercy, that mercy which the ancients called "womb-love." In the new myth, God is not "up there," "out there," or "in me." *We are in God.*

Orphans we are, until we return to her.

Pulacchan and
Pacha Mama

eep in the Amazon and high in the Andes of Peru there
are hints of an older tradition in which dominant males
retain their respect for and connectedness with femaleness and fundamental life processes. There are many
forgotten legends of strong men who "mother" the earth, *La Pacha Mama*,
who tenderly nourish and protect her creatures, who make a space for
community and connection. These same men were fierce resisters of the
intruding white male culture and its worship of dominance and
individualism.

Once there was a cacique (chief) named Pulacchan. Pulacchan was a
giant of a man, dark of complexion, but fair haired. He was generous and
compassionate to the poor, but did not give way to his enemies. He
showed his anger or his joy with a storm's thunder and lightning or the
brilliance of a sunny day. He was neither greedy nor selfish but was content to dress and eat and be concerned with the well-being of others.

The colossal strength of Pulacchan was due to the fact that he was born
from the entrails of Pacha Mama, or Mother Earth, and his famous virtue
and intelligence came from her. Pulacchan knew many things; he taught
that Pacha Mama was the supreme goddess, the font from which all human
life and vegetation came. For that reason, humankind must never abandon her—if it does the suffering of the worst kind and death will follow.

Every time Pulacchan needed to increase his knowledge, or when he
faced great difficulties, he would plunge into a deep lagoon called Chimal;
there he would bury himself in the heart of the earth, and have long conversations with Pacha Mama.

In the early days the people roamed about in idle bands and practiced
sorcery, worshiping many gods. Hatred and revenge took root and innocent children often disappeared mysteriously.

Pulacchan went about sowing love for Pacha Mama in the hearts of all. Eventually he gathered the people into one place, which some say is today the town of Cuemal. The people's love for Mother Earth soon made the land fertile. Crops abounded and the people prospered. This evoked the envy of other caciques, who waged war against Pulacchan. The battle was fierce; the enemy rallied gods who launched thunder, lightning, hail, and hurricanes from the heavens to vanquish the Cuemales. But the astute Pulacchan called on the medicine women and the serpent Machacuy to help him save his people. They prepared a huge container filled with clouds which they poured over the Cuemales' enemies while they were celebrating what they supposed was their victory over Pulacchan. In the darkness Machacuy slipped in and killed all the invaders.

After this victory peace and prosperity reigned among the Cuemales until the arrival of the Spanish who tried to convert Pulacchan by baptizing him "Francisco." The wise cacique said he would be baptized only after the Spanish built the church and tower that were to be used for Christian worship. Little did the Spanish know that the church was built on the ruins of the temple where Pulacchan's wife and loved ones were buried. Once the buildings were finished, Pulacchan gathered his people and announced that the church and the tower would not be turned over to the Spanish; neither would he be baptized. Rather the buildings would be reserved for the worship of Pacha Mama as an act of rebellion against the Spanish who had appropriated lands in the river valley by force.

Then one day Pulacchan told his people he was going to leave them in order to renew himself, but that he would return to struggle for Pacha Mama's cause. No one saw him leave. Some say he threw himself into the Chimal lagoon. Others believe he turned himself into a great condor, whose spirit still hovers over the Andes.[1]

In many communities of the Andean mountains Pacha Mama is a living reality, in spite of centuries of Christianity. She is still regarded as the source and end of all things, the one who gives and graces life on earth. Andeans often begin their day's work with an invocation to her, celebrations honor her regularly, and oaths are often taken in her name. Attachment to the land, to tradition, customs, language, and religion are inextricably bound up with her. Many creeds, cults, and religions have attempted to displace her, but she simply gathers them up, in her inclusive way, and remains an integral part of the consciousness of a people.

One of my treasured mementos of my time in Peru is a beautiful *cuadro*—a small patchwork, embroidered fabric mural—depicting Inca women warriors defending a city. The story is told there of women in the Puna who determined to resist the Spanish invasion and to preserve their own native language, traditions, myths, and customs. They founded a secret city which the Spanish never found and which was organized, ruled, and populated almost exclusively by women. To this day, the women of the Andes are the chief preservers of the ancient traditions, and when their granddaughters arrive in the cities, some of that instinct for solidarity still survives. I was amazed to find more grass-roots feminism in the shantytowns of Peru than I have seen anywhere else in this hemisphere.

7.

LEAVING HOME

Losses litter our way through life, as we gradually become – against our will – a mourning and adapting self. Losses are what happens to us, what is taken from us, or perhaps what was never given. Losses shatter our expectations and our trust. Losses can make us fearful of holding on to anything and frightened of letting go.

The first task of the spiritual orphan is to deal with these deprivations and integrate them into a creative self. This means descending into that primal pool of pain that ripples beneath our consciousness, down into the subterranean roots of our behavior in our parental origins and early childhood experiences, our family and gender socialization, our experiences of intimacy and relationship, our self-image and role, our addictions and compulsions, our needs for approval and love. We slough off our refusal to become conscious and aware, and confront the reflection of ourselves mirrored in the deep well of primal pain and anxiety. We sweep away the props, search out the hiding places, and finally achieve some nakedness to ourselves. We shiver at the sight of our vulnerability and weakness. Then we begin the task of letting go and living out of our true self.

In the ancient myths there were two kinds of journeys that summoned the heroes. The first was often a journey into the underworld, a descent into the layers of one's past, an encounter with the spirits of one's ancestry and with the oracles of one's essential being and destiny. For mystics and prophets this journey often took the form of a retreat to the mountain or a flight to a desert place. Today many feminist pilgrims and philosophers bring us to the mouth of a cave and take us on a journey into its depths, a return to the earth and the womb of our being. Whatever the symbolism, it is a centripetal path that we must first follow, the cave that we must first visit. To substitute pseudotranscendental experiences or New Age safaris for this journey is a centrifugal escape – at best, folly, and at worst, a perilous sinking into unawareness.

There is another kind of journey that is often recorded in the ancient tales – the journey of leaving home. Whether it is Abraham called out of the land of Ur or Ulysses called to the Trojan War and many travels, or knights-errant in search of the Grail, each models the second journey we must all make – the encounter with "otherness," the tests and trials that we meet when we plunge into the world, into our social reality. Leaving home means leaving dependency, safety and security, ethnocentrism and tribalism, status and all those things that we make extensions of ourselves.

On the first journey, the descent into the cave, we encounter the orphan within – our orphaned self, bruised and abandoned by the events and exigencies of our own life, by what has happened to us, by what is for the most part beyond our control. The second journey, leaving home, is one that we must *choose* to make. We choose to become a spiritual orphan. Both journeys call us to wholeness, to greater humanity and happiness. All feel the urgings which prompt these journeys. Some make the first journey, but not the second. Others attempt to make the second journey, but find it a dead end because of their own inner unfinished business. Some sit out both invitations. But it is not enough to simply "be," nor is it enough to make the inner journey, to integrate the self and adjust our private, primary world. We must look outward and risk a right relationship with all that is – with people who are not our own and who are not like us, with all creatures, and with the cosmos itself.

I remember my first experience of leaving home. One hot and steamy summer evening a few days after my graduation from high school our urban neighborhood was struck by a tornado. I remember the sudden darkness, the incredible sound as if a dozen freight trains were bearing down on us, the sensation when our house began to lift off its foundation. I glanced up from behind the sofa where we were huddled at the swirling, churning chaos outside the window – it was as if the earth was opening up and engulfiing us. I thought, "This is the end, and I'm only eighteen years old!" Suddenly I had a fleeting image of the cyclone in the movie of *The Wizard of Oz* and hoped that, like Dorothy, I would somehow survive the catastrophe.

Indeed, we did survive. Our house, thanks to the tall trees on our street, settled back on its foundation, with only a piece of the roof blown away. But when we stepped outside a few minutes later, it was like the aftermath of an earthquake. The sky was hidden. The house was buried under the debris of upturned trees, sidewalks, soil, pieces of other homes, twisted automobiles. Power lines crackled over and under the debris, and I will never forget the acrid, nitrous odor of the gouged, gaping earth. Nothing about home or our neighborhood would ever be the same. Like the school I had attended just a few blocks away, it was now marked for death. It would never fully recover from the devastation.

Within a year, as my first months of college unrolled, I made up my mind to leave home—to go off in search of my own Oz. I eventually dropped out of college and went off to a country place with several other young women. I gave up my earthly possessions, access to radio, television, and telephone. I accepted limited mail privileges and separation from my family, except for special occasions when visiting was permitted. I wore a uniform and had my hair cut short. I was often asked to do things that didn't make much sense and was expected to obey. I kept strict rules of silence and was a virtual prisoner for three years in a rural retreat.

My early experience in a religious order was comparable to that of a cult. So was the experience of my old boyfriend who joined the military service and endured several months of training similar to my novitiate. Yet none of us were ever deprogrammed by our parents or social workers—no one ever thought of it, since the cults we had joined were legitimated by patriotic duty or mainline religion. When I look back, I am amazed at the swiftness with which I made that decision to leave home, to begin a new life for myself—even a life that initially required the sacrifice of so many personal freedoms.

Then came the 1960s and a whole generation "left home" psychically, socially, and spiritually. By the 1970s there were many more cults and many more reasons for leaving home—few of which would be acceptable to older generations. A major shift in values had occurred and no one was prepared for it. Norman Rockwell's portraits of American homes, institutions, and relationships suddenly seemed like nostalgic fantasies. Still, there was something familiar in the leaving home that characterized the 1960s.

Leaving home experiences are imprinted in a special way on the American collective consciousness. Leaving home was the dominant cultural experience of those who were destined to build a new nation in the New World, but once was not enough—it was a mode of existence that was demanded over and over again for survival. The forbears of almost all Americans had to leave home in at least one of three ways: as immigrants or refugees, as pioneers who settled the frontier, or as slaves. (The latter, it should be added, left home unwillingly: black people were dragged from their African homes; Native Americans were either decimated, pushed off their land, or put under house arrest.)

Today, it could be said that the so-called free market and upward mobility force Americans to continue the cultural pattern–or at least we rationalize leaving home as necessary for survival or for self-fulfillment. Part of that rationalization is not rational at all, but is the residue of powerful cultural myths that still hypnotize us. The fact that we have the option of self-creation and that our New World history has made us creatures of choice has generated four romantic myths that we have incorporated in our expectations of the pursuit of the American Dream.

The first myth is the expectation that there is a perfect mate for me. (It was the Puritans who popularized marrying for love, abolishing the Old World practice of the arranged marriage.) The second myth is the expectation that if I just work hard enough, sooner or later my opportunity will come–I will suddenly come into "bucks" or get that long-sought job or promotion. (This same myth of success has spawned generations of flim-flam hustlers and get-rich-quick schemes aimed at a hungry, gullible populace). The third myth is the expectation that somewhere there is a piece of land, property, I can acquire for my exclusive possession and use. The fourth myth is the expectation that if I work hard enough and abide by the rules, I can be secure now and in my old age. Today the conditions of contemporary social relations have just about demythologized the first two myths. But the last two will die harder.

To greater or lesser degree, we are still driven psychologically and geographically away from home toward our expectations, hooked on our romantic myths–whether that is the ultimate romance, the "pot o' gold" at the end of the rat race, or a chunk of real estate with a view. Belief in the myth of "mine only"–whether it applies to people, money, food, water, natural resources, or land–generates much of our personal unhappiness and much of the misery in the world.

What a difference enculturation can make. I can never forget the children I have seen in some of the refugee camps in Central America. How different their response was when I offered one of them a small gift, a piece of food, or a small toy. Their immediate, instinctive response was to share it with the other children who were crowded around. I have been in places in the U.S. where small children were together, and their instinctive responses were much more proprietary and selfish. Hoarding is the much more typical cultural reflex here than sharing. But, as the children of the refugee camps demonstrated to me, it is possible to instill a sense of cooperation and distributive justice even in children wasted by deprivation and scarcity. "Mine only" is a theme that programs privileged people from infancy through adolescence and adulthood even to the grave. (Once, when I visited some ancient gravesites in Great Britain and Ireland, I observed how the arrival of the notion of individual ownership coincided with kingship and status, and was reflected in the change from communal grave sites to individual ones.)

Lest the reader fear that I am leading up to a Marxist diatribe against private property, let me say at the outset that I *do* believe in the proposition "mine," but not when it threatens the proposition "ours." Like absolute autonomy, the notion of "mine only" is a narcissistic fiction when applied to many of the social conditions of the contemporary world. But perhaps we need to feel, rather than know, what it is like to "have not" before we can understand how we should "have" things.

Many of the current conflicts on our planet seems to be about land. Some people claim they have been displaced and seek to reclaim their territory by force. Others seem to have less justification in their attempts to expand and expropriate new territory, claiming they need to protect themselves. Still others simply want a share in the 85 percent of the land that belongs to only 5 percent of the people. And elsewhere, there are those who refuse to be moved off their land, braving bulldozers, shovels, and dynamite. In all of these conflicts, the land which is at issue has become a symbol of more than itself. It gathers up all the ethnic, ideological, religious, racial, and tribal animosity that we can feel for an adversary. The land provides the context for our refusal to recognize and accept "otherness" and for our denial of our essential oneness as human beings on a very small planet.

Some years ago I had a friend, a man who had emigrated from Eastern Europe to Israel when he was very young. We loved each other very much and took great delight in our friendship, so unlikely because of our disparate backgrounds. At first the differences were simply complementary; they were certainly catalysts for our mutual attraction and empathy. We were even able to read the Old and New Testaments with each other as precious gifts of mutuality. But as time went on and the prospect of collaboration and sharing became a point of decision, I began to realize how extraordinarily different our worldviews were. For him, everything of value revolved around the land, a sacred place, the ultimate fact in his life. Israel, the very ground on which it stood, was an absolute in his life. My discernment through that particular relationship helped me to realize what were the absolute values in my life. I loved my country, my citizenship, my dual ancestry—indeed I was a professor of American Studies by choice. But my land and my roots did not mean the same things or stir the same passions in me that Israel stirred in him. Nor did it frame every decision in the way the land framed his. For me the absolute value was not the sacred place, the territory possessed as "mine" or even "ours." What was sacred was what happened there: mutuality, community, transcendence.

For many years I was perplexed about this disparity in the midst of so much compatibility and shared values. I began to understand it better when, several years later, I encountered a remarkable memoir of life on the West Bank by a Palestinian, Raja Shehadeh. The author, who had lived his entire life on the land the Israeli interlopers were claiming, was also puzzled by this fanatical attachment to the land. He described his discovery of the "pornography of the land." When you are exiled from your land, he explained, you begin to think about it in symbols. You fantasize love for the land in its absence, and in the process transform it into something else. So, for two thousand years the Jewish diaspora had imagined a Promised Land through these symbols—like a pornographer imagines an erotic fantasy.[1]

Perhaps the second and third-generation Israeli farmers have lost the pornographer's symbolism, but as Shehadeh points out, "The Gush Emunium people who are spilling on to the West Bank have renewed it—ranting and raving over every stick and stone in a land they never knew. It is like falling in love with an image of a woman, and then, when meeting her, being excited not by what is there but by what her image has come to signify for you. . . . The longer the exile, the richer the pornography."[2] But pornography is more than erotic images; it is also the fantasy of possession, of victory, of exclusive ownership, spoils. And in this sense the romance of the land is often a rape of the land, and certainly of the people who occupied it first.

The Palestinian memoir also reveals what is lost in this process—the authentic love of the land as *gift*. Shehadeh says,

There is a difference between the way I used to love the land around me and the way I do now. Sometimes when I am walking in the hills, unselfconsciously enjoying the touch of the hard land under my feet, the smell of thyme and the hills and trees around me—I find myself looking at an olive tree, and as I am looking at it, it transforms itself before my eyes into a symbol of the samidin, of our struggle, of our loss. And at that very moment, I am robbed of the tree; instead, there is a hollow space into which anger and pain flow. . . . This must be the beginning of pornography; the pains of a people have become my own personal, private ones. The olive tree, the land, becomes a symbol of the fury and the grief, of the oppression of a people.[3]

For the Palestinian, every settlement becomes a personal robbery, a violation of the imagination. He begins to think of the hills as "virginal," casting furtive looks over the landscape, wondering which will be the next victim. Then the image changes. Suddenly the hills are treacherous, the landscape is a harlot seducing them all into a war: "a vampire that will suck our blood as we fight for it." The bitter irony of the land possessed haunts him: "All our land which was once state land only in theory, has now been turned into the Jewish state's land in practice – its private property, to settle and build on as it sees fit. All of us samidin have become illegal squatters on the land Israel claims for itself."[4]

The dream of a land that is "mine only" generates the nightmare of violence. Shehadeh's dream of masks fastened to the spokes of a spinning wheel conveys the terrible reality. He tries to find his own face among the masks; he looks behind the masks and he sees not hollow backs but twin masks, "the fragmented faces of our occupiers: riveted to the backs of ours in a way that ensures that we will never see each other, as the wheel spins faster and faster. The Israelis do not know we are glued together on the same spokes of a wheel that is spinning us all to death."[5]

The refrain of "mine only" has echoed down through history, leaving some orphaned from their homes and others from their humanity. The Romans in Gaul, the Spanish in Latin America, the colonists in the land occupied by the first Americans, the British, then the Afrikaners in the land of Africa's native people – the pornography of the land goes on, disguising the orphan's real need for self-esteem, dignity, and a place of belonging. If today in the Middle East, men, women, and children are killing each other over a few feet on the West Bank or the Gaza Strip, we need only remind ourselves that in the U.S. young people have been known to kill each other over a "boom-box" or designer jeans. Material things, like the exile's fantasies of land, and the warrior's dreams of conquest, become the obsessive objects of our distorted desires – the emblems of our own illusion, insecurity, and anxiety, or our own emotional and spiritual deprivation.

The more hollow the inner space, the more we seek to solidify and secure ourselves in outer space, in whatever can be transformed into an extension of our fragile core. The way in which we extend ourselves, absorb and appropriate our surroundings, the way we exert *power*, is the entry point for violence in our world – from stress in our own organism to the threat of catastrophic destruction of our entire planet.

Since ancient times leaving home has been the primary way that human beings have been able to break these cycles of violence and self-destruction. Certainly that was true for the pilgrims who sought refuge in the New World. Leaving home has also been the usual way that young people take up their own power and responsibility and escape dependency— it is a mode of maturation. Leaving home has been a fundamental principle of growth for cultures and cosmos as well as persons.

Perhaps this is why most of the great spiritual traditions originate in a personality that makes a crucial journey out of a settled, secure consciousness and expected lifestyle. Is this not the story of Abraham, of Moses and Miriam, of Jesus, of Muhammad, of Siddhartha Gautama (Buddha), and certainly of many of the great Asian and Indian mystics. Leaving home is a public expression that echoes the interior process of self-transcendence, of shedding the worn-out skins of the self, of being born again. Something must be left, lost. In Western culture, nowhere is this notion articulated better than in the enigmatic words attributed to Jesus: "A man's enemies are those of his own household" (Matt. 10:36); "Call no one your father" (Matt. 23:9); "Unless a man leave father and mother"; "If you would be perfect, go sell what you have, give to the poor, and come follow me" (Mark 10:21); "There is no one who has given up house or brothers or sisters or mother or father or children or lands for my sake and for the sake of the gospel who will not receive a hundred times more now in this present age" (Mark 10:29–30). Leaving home for the sake of the kingdom is the theme of the New Testament.

We must all leave home several times in a lifetime, perhaps not in such radical ways as the great prophets and spiritual pilgrims, but in ways that have the same transformative effect. Culturally we are no longer pioneers and immigrants, no longer slaves, and many of us, at least, are no longer hostages to poverty and famine. How will we, the children of privilege and personal freedom, make the second journey? How will we leave home? For us the journey will be the most difficult of all—the journey out of our own class consciousness and values, our own trajectory of upward mobility, our own ethnocentrism and nationalistic biases. The second journey is, from another perspective, an option. But if we do not choose to risk it, we may pass our lives in a comfortable dis-ease, succumbing eventually to ennui and emptiness, and never know why.

Our culture deludes us with the mirage of choices. The ideal of freedom has been so marketized that we mistake our induced, compulsive needs for authentic freedom to choose. We act habitually and unconsciously out of a self-centered supermarket worldview, assuming that there are options for every possible experience. We are unaware that we have lost the freedom *not* to choose, not to enter the supermarket. Belonging seduces us into a kind of default reflex.

One must experience a kind of separateness, the orphan's sense of abandonment, in order to override the default program. What are some of the experiences that can help us to claim the authentic freedom and grace of the spiritual orphan?

The first is the capacity for *commitment*. Genuine commitment is a journey into the unknown. In a personal relationship, commitment means that my covenant with you transcends changed circumstances, our needs for gratification and novelty, even our love for each other. It means that each time I renew a commitment of love and fidelity, I leave certainties and control behind and enter more deeply into another country— your mystery. It means that I have given you a gift that I will not take back, even when that gift requires letting go and leaving—being apart—so we can grow. In a professional role it means that your right to service and fairness transcends my desire for fame, profit, or comfort. In terms of values it means that integrity, truth, and caring are more important than success or perfection.

The second is *openness to the stranger*. Throughout the span of a lifetime this can have many expressions, ranging from simple hospitality to the deliberate choice of cross-class and cross-cultural experiences— experiences that are more than tokenism or sightseeing, experiences in which we really participate in a different worldview or lifestyle. It means beginning to think of those who are not like us as our teachers, particularly those who are poor, disadvantaged, or stigmatized as outsiders. It means, in the theology of hospitality found in both the Old and New Testament, transforming the stranger into a guest and ultimately into a friend.

The third is the capacity for *relinquishment*. This implies not only the capacity to give up or share wealth, possessions, privilege, and power, but also the commitment to work toward a social order that promotes a more equitable distribution of these earthly advantages. It is not enough to retire to the woods—or the suburbs—"to live deliberately," in the words of Thoreau. The simple life, privatized, could be simply indulgence. The simple life lived in the context of the common good and social change is precisely the call of the spiritual orphan. It means unplugging ourselves from an addictive system of consumption and "mine only" thinking.

In young adulthood, the capacity for openness and relinquishment might mean tithing a few years of service to the disadvantaged in an unfamiliar place; in middle age, it might mean leaving the trappings of careerism and professionalization, giving up one's dependence on status and role, and starting something new. It might mean the adoption of a child of a different race or nationality. In the sunset years it might mean early retirement in order to care for a spouse who has Alzheimer's disease. At any moment in our life, it might mean converting personal profit or advantage to social good. For some, the call to relinquishment might mean the ultimate risk of life for a cause, for others, and the possibility of martyrdom.

The fourth and final is *obedience to Earth*. Our fidelity to Gaia is our fundamental fidelity to ourselves as cells that belong to a larger organism. It means reverence and care for all aspects of creation, not shunning or despising or intending harm to anything earthly. It means putting back in what we take out. It means we make no choices that do not take the equilibrium, the balance of the whole ecosystem into consideration. It means befriending diminishment, suffering, and mortality as part of the meaning and purpose of life. It means joining with those who protect the earth and the cosmos and with those who promote peace.

One of the best descriptions of the goal of earthly life comes from the wisdom literature of the Judaeo-Christian tradition. It is the concept of *shalom*. Often translated as "peace," its meaning encompasses much more. The concept of *shalom* is a vision of harmony and wholeness, of nations and tribes gathered as one, of a unity and balance between nature and the environment and the social economy. It is a vision in which instruments and occasions of violence are consumed in justice and mercy, in which the resources of our cosmos and the joys of the body and the spirit are shared within a "dancing kind of inter-relationship, an ever-shifting equipoise of a life system."[6] What is envisioned is an equilibrium in which all things flourish and nourish each other, none are set over against each other, all things are blessing. It is indeed the original vision of the Gaia, the Earth as Mother, and all creatures – including ourselves – as vital, interdependent and equally important cells of a living organism.

We sigh at the very idea: we are so far from experiencing this in our world – as yet so flawed, so incomplete and in a state of disharmony – that we are tempted to give up hope. We are tempted to ignore our call to spiritual orphanhood, the call to leave this place and struggle through the wilderness. We would rather cherish the attachments and addictions that orphan our souls and psyches; at least our handicaps and habits are familiar and give the illusion of security. The spiritual orphan opts for the challenge of self-transcendence, for becoming a transcultural personality. This means investing ourselves in the long arduous task of curing ourselves of projection (the construction of enemies) and resisting our introjections (the myths, reality frames, worldviews, class biases that motivate us consciously and unconsciously). But a culture sunk in denial of its own losses and deprivations, a culture not listening to its own feedback can be very hostile to spiritual orphans.

There are many today who have sounded a warning signaling the onset of a cultural crisis. Barbara Tuchman believes it is a crisis of "competence," of our unthinking acceptance of image over substance. Norman Lear believes that the root problem is "greed" and the absence of a sense of shared fate. Robert Bellah believes we are experiencing the effects of "the culture of separation." Many others have blamed a general spiritual malaise, a lost sense of meaning and transcendent purpose. Whatever the explanation, all of the symptoms add up to a cultural crisis that is both developmental and ethical.

Some of our most cherished ideas are not working. Some of our myths have become blocks to the development of social and ethical maturity. The ideal of self-reliance and individualism has degenerated into a specious privatism. The idea of national sovereignty and destiny has degenerated into tribalism, chauvinism, and the struggle to maintain political hegemony. Representative democracy has become power hoarding by the elite. Our free market has transformed us from a nation of industrious workers and inventive producers to a horde of locusts that consume everything in sight, yet mount the largest debt in the world. Upward mobility, opportunity and the dream of the New World mostly means that both the rich and the poor are increasing – and flying apart at the speed of light. Every night on our television screens we are programmed with models that adjust to our changing sociology but never challenge our deeper cultural assumptions which include, for example, the notion that we can acquire an exclusive right to almost anything ("mine only") and that "more is better." We still believe, along with Ronald Reagan, that the "good society" is "one where someone can always get rich."

We need new images and models. Many of our cultural myths contain fundamental human values, but they require new translations for a radically changing era. Private ownership – and money, which is a kind of license to hoard whatever can be owned – are the mainsprings of our system; even posing a modified challenge to the myth of private ownership would be a superhuman task in this culture. But, the changing global economy may provide enough of a threat of a major catastrophe that we may be forced into adjusting our runaway consumption, profit, and lust for exclusive ownership.

"Ours" is a possessive pronoun that has not received much use in the English language, primarily because Anglo-Americans have been obsessed with property that is "mine" for centuries. Historians have recorded the barbaric penal code that enforced property rights as late as the eighteenth century. English Common Law has always been reluctant to intervene when violence to a person is at issue; as in instances of child abuse, wife beating, rape, dueling. Mayhem and threats to life and limb, so it has often seemed, were not nearly as blasphemous as threats to property rights. Statesmen once praised the English Constitution, which provided that a man (or woman or child) could be hanged for no less than 160 different violations of the law. Among them were picking a pocket for more than one shilling; purse or goods snatching; shoplifting; stealing a horse or sheep; cutting a hop-bind; snatching gathered fruit; snaring a rabbit on a gentleman's estate. These are the roots of a value system that has enthroned possession.

Cross-cultural perspectives might provide different value models, even if they are not likely to be imitated in the current atmosphere. In a few cultures the notion of "gift" displaces ownership as we know it. For example, the so-called primitive Kula people of the South Pacific have a culture based on the giving of gifts. Among the Kula gifts move continually in a circle around a wide ring of islands; each gift makes the entire circle of islands. Each giver has gift partners in neighboring tribes. The gifts are carried by canoe from island to island in journeys that require great preparation and sometimes cover hundreds of miles. It takes between two and ten years for each gift article to make the full round of islands and complete the circle. Each gift stays with the receiver for awhile, but if he or she keeps it too long they will gain a bad reputation.[7]

The essence of this cultural economy is that there are a limited number of possessions and they must be kept in motion. No one keeps anything for more than a year or two. To possess is to give. Having something brings with it the expectation that one will share it, distribute it, be its trustee and dispenser. It is not barter because the exchange is not reciprocal or bilateral. In circular giving no one ever receives the gift from the same person he gives to. When the gift moves in the circle its motion is beyond the control of the personal ego, beyond the exclusivity of the transacting couple, and so each bearer must be a part of the larger group and each donation is an act of social faith.

In the same spirit, descriptions of cultures like the Balinese suggest that they do not view themselves as possessors of their island, but as guests on property that belongs to the gods. This consciousness of being a guest on the planet is expressed in a continuous atmosphere of gratitude, in sacrifices to all the gifts of life including water, food, and fire. Maintaining a balance, an equilibrium, is the dominant motive of Balinese culture. It is a metaphor that extends to every phase of their lives. Even offenses, "crimes," are not considered to be violations of personal rights, but offenses against the natural order of the universe and the cosmic balance. If quarrels arise, they are registered as "contracts of enmity" but no resolution through force, prosecution, or reconciliation is attempted. Enmity is "plateaued," put on hold. As one commentator observes, "in everything they do, optimization is the issue, not maximization. Balinese economics, for example, cannot be described in terms of the profit motive, nor can the Balinese social structure be seen as a collection of individuals or groups vying for status or privilege."[8] What happens when money, cash payments, and the notion of private ownership are introduced into such a social economy? The history of our intrusion into many of the gift cultures of the South Pacific tells the tragic tale.

Adopting the metaphor of *gift* as the organizing principle of polity in a postindustrial world is a challenge indeed, one that only spiritual orphans might be risk-ful enough to take up. But Western civilization provides at least one approximation of it in the Old Testament tradition of "jubilee." Jubilee implies a sabbath, an amnesty, a cyclic cessation every fiftieth year of the linear, accumulative logic of justice. In the year of jubilee the law proposed that surpluses be distributed, land be returned to the people, debts and mortgages be cancelled, and slaves be freed. Jubilee also extended the gift circle to the realm of relationship: not only did it imply the forgiveness of debts and the transcendence of rights and strict justice with mercy and magnanimity, it also required the letting go of hurts, personal injuries, grudges, hostility, failures, and lack of trust.

Like the law of the sabbatical year to which it is allied, the jubilee tradition in the Old Testament era was more of an ideal than a practical reality. It expressed the ancient belief that Yahweh was the true owner of the land and therefore it must be shared among all of his people as a gift. Thus there was a strong Hebraic conviction that monopoly of land was a social evil—an ironic footnote to contemporary events unfolding in that same land. Jesus, who called his followers to very concrete expressions of the ideals of the Law, seems to have identified his mission with the announcement of a jubilee year: "The Spirit of the Lord is upon me, because he has anointed me to bring glad tidings to the poor. He has sent me to proclaim liberty to the captives and recovery of sight to the blind, to let the oppressed go free, and to proclaim a year acceptable to the Lord" (Luke 4:16–19).

The images of shalom and jubilee, of the gift community, add a cultural and moral context to the covenant which all creatures share with Gaia, the cosmic/earth system. Without this perspective, the pursuit of life, liberty, and opportunity will in time produce a destructive imbalance. Without such a guiding principle we are bereft of a means for the validation of value itself. When abstract values are not connected with reality, the consequences can be as devastating as the tyranny of Nazism or the Inquisition. We cannot transcendentalize value, bypassing the temporal, embodied, material aspect of creation. Without the shalom-Gaia perspective we are vulnerable to the mindless engines of socialization—as in our culture where the economy itself has become the carrier of values and where the media has become a kind of broker for deciding what is right or wrong.

Among the values we cherish one may or may not be any better than another in an abstract context; but value is always validated or invalidated by the way it contributes to shalom. One can conceive of many polarities that might or might not be a value for a particular individual; for example, the choice to:

- be married or unmarried
- be sexually active or celibate
- possess or give up
- keep or share
- have authority or accept authority
- have power or surrender power
- know or not know
- create or not create

These choices reflect four of the dominant pursuits in human culture: *power, property (money), sex,* and *knowledge.* Whether or not they can be pursued as values—legitimate and worthy ends—depends not only on the effect these choices have on us individually, but also the effect on the ultimate value, shalom/Gaia. Whether it is genetic splicing, trade protectionism, or sexual freedom, the choices have consequences that go far beyond the individual. The good of choice is relativized by consequences. For a culture accustomed to the supermarket scheme of personal choice, the onset of a threat like AIDS certainly relativizes individual freedom. Likewise, in certain small villages in India where there is no running water, but where a few sex selection clinics have been set up, the prospect of choice is apocalyptic when promoted in a social context where pregnant women are likely to abort 90 percent of female embryos. Choice in such a context negates the higher value of shalom-Gaia.

Our capacity to achieve openness to the stranger and the planetary sha-lom that we all hope for will no doubt depend on some of the choices we make with respect to power, property (money), sex and knowledge— negative as well as positive choices. The value of celibacy is a case in point. There are many today who would deny that celibacy is a value. Yet its his-torical development reflects this relationship of value to the shalom prin-ciple. The derivation of the word itself means "having no roots" and implies a spiritual leaving home, a letting go of something that is valued in a different way. In the early years of the Christian era virginity acquired a unique sig-nificance. At first when large numbers of men and women went to the des-ert to free themselves for more intimacy with spiritual values and experience—*vacare Deo*—it seemed to have a mystical purpose. In the Roman era, it acquired a distinctive counter-cultural significance and an ascetic purpose, an antidote to the excesses of the period. In the Middle Ages the communal celibates accented another purpose: the value of community.

Indeed the tradition of the three vows of celibate monasticism— poverty, chastity, and obedience—correctly interpreted has always been a translation of the New Testament call to the kingdom, a gift circle. Poverty is a letting go that keeps possessions, resources and money in motion, dis-tributed according to need. Chastity is the freedom for an inclusive love that does not rest in one person as a personal possession or exclusive object of one's affection. Obedience, often incorrectly applied, is the shar-ing of power and responsibility through mutual service and attentiveness to the Spirit speaking in the community. In the ethos of the kingdom there is a gratuitousness in these relinquishments. The person who lets go of the gift is a person who is willing to seem foolish, even playful, a person willing to abandon control, a person who trusts. Where there is no trust and sharing there can be no community, and where there is no gift circle there is scarcity, private hoarding, greed, fear, investment in self-perpetuation, sterility, and stagnation.

The American utopian societies of the nineteenth century (historians estimate there were more than seven hundred) added an economic paradigm to the communal purpose of celibate living. Today the contemporary phenomenon of intentional, nonmonastic communities synthesizes many of these traditional values in a more pluralistic, less separatist conception. Married and unmarried, celibate and noncelibate, straight and gay, parents and singles are seeking unique arrangements in which they can create a gift circle together. The earlier communities drew their raison d'etre primarily from within, from a certain tradition or homogeneity. Today, the seeker of the simple, shared lifestyle consciously or unconsciously makes this choice within the ambience of shalom-Gaia, choosing from a much wider range of possibilities and degrees of commonality. It is no wonder that these experiments are attracting many spiritual orphans. Instinctively they know that our survival as a species, our evolutionary leap forward, and our capacity to receive "otherness" and connect with life-giving sources depends on something much larger than our narrow conceptions of what constitutes "home" and kin.

The contemporary crisis will not be solved unless we can imagine a new relationship to creation and to those with whom we share the earth. We have inherited a consciousness and habits of heart that generate a cultural autism, a disability that leaves us unable to relate authentically to the "other," and leaves us obsessed with things, with what is "mine," and with our own notions of what constitutes right order. Elsewhere we have noted that often our most effective response to an unsolved problem is the invention of a new metaphor. If, for example, the unsolved problem is the "rich get richer and the poor get poorer," where do we look for a new metaphor, or even an old one that can move us into the future?

Poets, artists, philosophers, and scientists have been creative sources of metaphors for interpreting the meaning of the universe and our place in it. The Platonic forms have given way over the centuries to more mechanistic models of reality, and more recently to organic and artistic models—a succession of images that reflects our increasingly more subtle and perceptive understanding of our biosphere and its envelope of consciousness. Ultimate meaning might be said to emerge at that point where the reality and the metaphor coincide. And there is evidence, in the contemporary concern with shifting paradigms that this convergence is in progress. If indeed, our reality is an evolving process, within which human consciousness has an increasingly expanding function, then the metaphor of evolution—of life itself—acquires paramount significance.

Erich Jantsch offers a gloss on this metaphor with his image of the flowing stream. The relationship of human consciousness to this stream or process represents three stages in the development of our relationship to the world and the cosmos. Standing on dry land on one bank and watching the stream go by corresponds to a *rational* attitude. Most of the institutions our civilization have been established to preserve this world view and vantage point of control. If, on the other hand, we enter the stream in a canoe and try to steer the canoe *in* the stream, interacting with its currents, we have assumed a *mythological* attitude. We enter into direct relationship with the forces around us, we become involved with and influence the overall process to some degree. On the other hand, if we imagine that we *are* the stream, just as a group of water molecules is the stream, and at the same time only one of its aspects, we have adopted an *evolutionary* attitude. In Western civilization, such an evolutionary view is difficult to achieve, as Jantsch notes.[9]

A society that maximizes the *rational perspective* will place great emphasis on control and will require managers, administrators, engineers, and hierarchy. Setting goals and reaching them will have priority. A society that maximizes the *mythological perspective* will require sages, therapists, guides, and a great deal of interaction and coordination. Achieving structured relations within the system will have a priority. A society that seeks to maximize the *evolutionary perspective* will require catalysts and people skilled in facilitating feedback, structuring new learning, and imagining alternatives. The priority here will emphasize leadership that has openness to innovation and sensitivity to creative processes in subsystems. The evolutionary leader would not be afraid to abort the corporate plan from one era and replace it with another. Process planning in an evolutionary spirit ends the dualism between planner and planned, organization and environment, corporation and society, culture and nature. We become enhancers of the process within and around ourselves, knowing that our purpose and meaning does not wait for us at the end of our path to the future – in a Land of Oz – but is immanent in the process itself.

Evolutionary leaders, like survivors and orphans, are more skilled in imagining the future because they have learned to "travel light" and live by their wits. The most discouraging aspect of our social systems is undoubtedly the lack of imagination that is applied to incremental change. Our cultural malaise is often the result of our failure to face up to the painful process of change – our institutions as well as our leaders stagnate in self-perpetuation. Our political, judicial, economic, information, and social service systems are adversarial and given to imagining change as the opposite of what we have now. (The opposite so easily becomes more of the same.) Evolutionary, imaginative thinking exploits a second-order response: one that rethinks the solution previously tried and suggests something altogether unexpected. Paradox and surprise – the power of the imagination – is at the heart of evolutionary thinking. It requires a radical breaking out of the conceptual frameworks that limit our response to problems, dilemmas, and impasse.[10]

The spiritual orphan is not threatened by the instability of our times because it represents opportunity for new thinking to break through. The more uncertainty, the more unfulfilled expectations in the social order, and the more disorder and waste, the more we are compelled to question, to listen to the feedback, to learn, and to adapt and invent. Indeed this is the lesson of so many of our evolutionary forebears. Perhaps the greatest threat to evolutionary thinking is complacency. In this respect the conservatism of institutions like the Church can be a positive force for social evolution recalling us to be faithful to successful evolutionary learning from our past, or it can be a serious obstacle to movement toward the future and social maturity.

Ilya Prigogine, the Nobel prize winning theorist of the science of dissipative structures, has shown how, in the natural order, the evolution of the universe depends upon fluctuations and instability that are induced by positive feedback in a system that has been stressed or pushed beyond its limits. The ensuing chaos is the necessary precursor of a higher level of organization. He observes that most of the crucial phenomena of the universe are open rather than closed, machinelike systems; they exchange matter, energy, and information with their environment. Human systems – biological, political, economic, and social – are also open, which means that attempts to understand and control them in mechanistic terms are doomed to failure. Prigogine notes that all of the previous metaphors for the universe – the clock, the engine running down, the finished masterpiece of creation – are inadequate symbols for our reality. He sees in the dancing Shiva, the Hindu god of destruction and reproduction, a more appropriate symbol for our times, for the discovery of our oneness with the evolutionary process as Gaia's children, as sisters and brothers.[11] In Hindu mythology it was Shiva was led the other gods and creation itself back into the good graces of the Great Mother after they had offended her.

For the spiritual orphan this perspective offers a worldview that complements and parallels the inner reality that one is always in the process of discovering. The acceptance of inner chaos in the form of losses, anxiety, or suffering—being fully in touch with that reality—creates the positive feedback that spins off a new integration, an evolutionary leap in our own development.

Jean Houston has described this "loss of linkage" to mother, father, family, or ideology as the deep wound that thrusts us finally out into the world where we "really begin to grow, often bleeding and grieving all the way."[12] But the orphan is seeking a deeper bond, a wider linkage: the rediscovery of our connections with it all, with everything in creation, with birth and death, reproduction and destruction, dissipation and waste, reintegration and preservation—the return to Gaia. This is the key to the orphan's finding his or her true home. Our true home is in the structures of kinship and sharing, the gift circles, that we create to honor our bond with Gaia.

Oz is a projection of wish fulfillments and worn-out myths. Kansas is real. It can be dreary and grim, but somehow it looks different after you've made the journey of leaving the familiarity, safety, and security of the place you once called home.

Gaia's Tale

nce upon a time a poor man and his wife and three children lived near a great forest. A great famine came over the land and then a long deep winter. The man and his wife anguished, wondering how they would feed their children even when they no longer had anything for themselves. They decided, since the children were almost grown and very resourceful, that the children would have to be sent away into forest to fend for themselves – for indeed, the poor couple believed that they would soon starve if they remained at home.

When the children were told of their parents' decision, they were sad. The eldest son, Frederick, was angry and asked why. He felt that life owed him something better than this, for he had planned to inherit his parents' small plot of land. The second son, Martin, grumbled, for he was a little more used to getting second best; he was more concerned about how they would survive in the forest. The third child, Gaia, was a daughter. Gaia began to weep, wondering how her parents would survive alone, with no food and no help. She wished her parents would come with them into the forest; unlike her brothers, she accepted more easily what she did not understand, but her sadness was most of all for the loss of her parents.

The day of departure came. Tearfully, the poor man and his wife gave the eldest son the horse and a bag of meal and sent him on his way. The second son got the cow and a bag of meal and was off. For Gaia they had only the beautiful swan from the pond and a little bag of meal, for they assumed that she would most likely find a man and prosper sooner than her brothers. Gaia took her beloved swan, her small portion of meal, and she carved a small piece of wood from her parents' cottage.

Off they went, each in a different direction, thinking that it might be easier to find food and support themselves if they did not travel together. Gaia sat for a long time on the hill overlooking the cottage where she had been born, crying bitterly. Soon night was coming and she set off with the swan into the forest. It wasn't long before she ran out of food, for she shared the bag of meal with Swan. One night while she was gathering

firewood, shivering, weeping, and feeling very lost, a clever Raven heard
Gaia, and alighted on a branch near her. Now Raven was a trickster and
often played jokes on people; sometimes she outsmarted herself. But she
was clever with her wits and had magic when it was needed for difficult
times. She was always a helpful companion, but sometimes she could be
sneaky and full of mischief. Raven played many tricks on Gaia, but it
sharpened Gaia's wits and she became wise in the ways of surviving in the
great forest.

Soon all three of them became companions. What a strange threesome
they made: the girl, the beautiful but mute Swan, and the chattering
Raven! They had many adventures in the forest and, with the help of the
Raven, learned how to keep going. Gaia began to be more cheerful, Swan's
feathers took on a healthier gloss, and Raven felt appreciated, as indeed
she was.

As the winter deepened, Gaia grew cold as she had no warm clothing.
Raven offered to teach her how to trap a fox or two so she could make a
warm winter cape. But Gaia, who by this time regarded the animals of the
forest as her friends and helpers, said no. She did not want to harm any
of them. That night, as she lay down to sleep she clutched her wooden
piece of home and said a prayer. The next morning she was roughly awak-
ened by a huge bear. Frightened, she screamed for Raven, who soon learned
from the bear (in a language Gaia could not yet understand) that the bear
had brought Gaia a fur cape, made from his grandmother's bearskin, for
she had passed away a fortnight ago. Gaia thanked the bear warmly and
invited him to share some of the honey they had gathered.

As they came to the edge of the forest, they began to see other people
now and then. At first strangers avoided this curious trio, but one day
someone with a friendly face approached. After introducing himself, he
admired Swan and began to stroke her beautiful feathers. Much to everyone's surprise and shock, the man stuck to Swan's feathers, and try what
they would, not even Raven could free him. Soon the man resigned himself to their companionship and off they went, now a foursome. (Raven
assured him that beyond the great River there was a Sorceress that could
free him from Swan.)

But this was not the first time that a friendly person became stuck.
They noticed that Swan's mysterious energy seemed to pass from the man
to whoever touched him, and so on, with each person whom they
chanced to meet on their way. Soon Gaia and her attached companions
numbered a dozen! After a while Gaia ceased to worry about the Swan's

magic and enjoyed the people who had joined them. They learned more of the ways of the forest and the mountains, played games, helped with food gathering, and even, on occasion, danced and sang songs around the fire.

One day they came over the mountains into a country where it was very cold. They learned of a legend that the land would grow colder and colder, and the cold would spread to other lands until the Queen was released from a spell. The sleeping queen's castle was surrounded by a huge river, which was really a moat. Many warriors and clever princes had tried to reach the Queen and had fallen through the ice into the frigid water. Others had denuded the local forests and depleted the village resources in trying to construct bridges or boats to reach the castle – all had mysteriously failed. A few of the brave warriors who survived the icy waters and made it to the castle had kissed her (as all legends require) thinking she would awake from the spell, but nothing happened. The Queen's own magician despaired, for none of his magic potions or chants had any effect. The Queen slept on as if in a coma, while the land around grew exceedingly cold, and nothing could grow or move.

One night Gaia had a dream, and the next day she packed a bag of wet leaves and herbs and her stick of wood from home. After her companions had eaten, she announced they were going to reach the castle and release the Queen from her spell. Even Raven, who usually saw things coming, was surprised. All expressed grave doubts, but since they were all stuck together, they screwed up their trust and off they went. When they reached the banks of the great frozen river, Gaia instructed Swan to position herself to the right, while she and Raven took the left. They all held onto each other for dear life, as Gaia instructed Swan and Raven to fly them up over the river to the castle! What a strange sight it was – Swan and Raven dangling Gaia and her companions like links on a chain between them.

When they reached the Queen's chamber Gaia instructed them to come as close as possible to the sleeping Queen, whom they could see was not only asleep, but frigid and cold as if she were in hibernation. Gaia covered her with the wet leaves and herbs from her sack, touched her with her stick of wood, and then asked everyone to hold her and hug her as close as they could. The warmth from Gaia and her companions soon began to have an effect, for the Queen's cheeks suddenly began to grow pink. They rubbed her blue hands and feet and they too began to grow soft and warm. Suddenly the Queen opened her eyes and said, "At last, you've come!" At that same moment, Gaia's companions came unstuck and Swan honked for the first time since Gaia had known her!

Afterward, there was much rejoicing in the land. The icy river warmed, the fields grew fertile, sunny days and soft nightly rains came. Animals, fish, birds, and trees flourished again. The village prospered and shared their huge surpluses with the starving people on the other side of the mountains.

Gaia and her companions remained with the Queen, and the Queen was so fond of Gaia that she adopted her as her daughter. It was thus, that when the Queen passed away, Gaia became the Great Mother of a new civilization called Earth. And she gave herself a new name, "Sister of All the Living and the Dead."[1]

GETTING BACK TO KANSAS

Kansas is where we have come from. It is also where we are going. The way home – the way out of the past and the way into the future – is empowerment through the myth of the orphan and the recovery of our connection with the feminine.

This urgency is most felt and most visible today on a planetary scale. Women are the largest single group of human beings who are coming to a consciousness of their reality, becoming acutely aware of their orphan state. Significant numbers of women are exiting stereotyped roles and cultural expectations. New challenges are thrusting them into unprecedented personal situations, and there are few role models to follow. As the old rules and roles blur, and new ones emerge, women learn by going where they have to go. Out of their experience, humanity is discovering its hermeneutic of the future, and reinventing its capacity to give and sustain life. Everywhere, in different ways, from different perspectives, women are casting out the curse of Genesis: "I will put enmity between thee and the woman" (3:15).

Across the globe all relationships are undergoing realignment: the dynamics of power are changing between husbands and wives, parents and children, management and employees, governing officials and the governed, teachers and students, doctors and patients, priests and people, the oppressed and their oppressors. Why? Because, like the shifting plates of Earth's crust in an earthquake, the most fundamental model of power – masculine dominance and feminine dependence – is in the process of a massive shift. A profound revolution has begun and the old models of relationship are breaking down.

Woman's experience has become a newly rediscovered mine, a precious lode of human potential that we turn to now in our bankrupt, depleted state. Women have endured exclusion, rejection, divorce, battering, discrimination, male competitiveness, loneliness; have always been active participators in the development of others; have for aeons known how to surrender to pain in the process of birthing; have understood the arts of healing and harmony with the rhythms of nature and have had to invent nonviolent strategies for change (because they were not dominant). Women, probing and sharing their evolving wisdom, have something to teach the world.

I remember well one such group of women who gathered one summer for a retreat. A disparate group it was, of married and unmarried women, mothers and grandmothers, divorced women, celibate women, hetrosexual women and lesbian women, women who lived alone and women who lived in community, women from various faith traditions, and women of little faith. Out of our experience together came this covenant:

A WOMAN'S COVENANT WITH HER WORLD

As women, we love ourselves and each other. Thus, the process of composing this covenant began in anger, thinly masked with humor. We would, we thought, rewrite the Ten Commandments, for they represent the patriarchy and are not whole.

But we found that the Ten Commandments are not really a set of rules imposed from above to enslave us. Rather, they are the foundation – the basic design – of a sane and just society, of which we are a living part. However, because they do not include a woman's perspective, they are incomplete.

So the task became to answer the question: What are the requirements of a whole society? We felt that, at present, the answer lies in acting on our experience, in each of us pledging ourselves to behave in such a way as to assist in the creation of a more humane and just society.

This Covenant, then, is written from women's knowledge and women's experience, and represents a woman's response to the need for Shalom.

THE COVENANT

To the very limits of my ability, I shall:

1. honor those who have gone before me, for truly it is on their shoulders that I stand.
2. make every day a holy sabbath in my heart and with my hands.
3. affirm and support life in all its aspects.
4. seek truth in my own experience, and name it.
5. acknowledge and explore the many aspects of divine power in the universe.
6. treat every person in my world as a neighbor.
7. strive to create conditions in which the individual and community may flourish together.
8. cultivate a community which honors and nutures all children.

9. make of my relationships holy expressions of thought, feeling, and spirit.
10. honor the divine contribution of all people.[1]

There are other such covenants (the Shakertown Pledge is one) to which men have also brought their own experience of the feminine to bear on the social order. But I have found among women the most radical (meaning "touching the roots") way of seeing through to the inner structure and essential dynamic of being, in a way that distinguishes their vision from some of the most prophetic male visionaries.[2] The difference is precisely the ability to see what culturally induced male consciousness obscures: the illumination of the anima, the soul of the universe, the Gaia.

The challenge to both men and women is to invent new myths. *People are changed, not by intellectual convictions or ethical urgings, but by transformed imaginations.* We must begin to live out of new myths. For men, the relinquishment of the old myths, the models of masculinity, will be painful because the culture has enthroned these myths as images of empowerment. The man who acknowledges the orphan in himself must leave some of these behind when he goes in pursuit of the lost caretaker, the lost sister, the frozen feminine in himself.

A recent study tracks the increasing focus of advertising and segmented marketing on the independent male. The myth of the self-indulgent, privatized good life is doing to men what has been done for years to women – transforming them into compulsive consumers, prime objects of artificially stimulated needs. The myth of the male as the provider and familial anchor has been replaced by the hustler; the occasional voyeur by the unapologetic narcissist.

One study in the early 1970s revealed that only 7 percent of university men were willing to modify their own roles to facilitate their future wives career expectations. Today surveys indicate that somewhere between 12 and 19 percent could be considered "new men," willing – at least at the cognitive level – to experiment with new roles and new arrangements. One study shows that 10 to 12 percent of fathers are substantially more involved with their children today than ever before. Slowly, at an almost glacial pace, American manhood is trying out new roles, new myths: caretaker, helpmate, homemaker, teacher, and nurse of the young. But the old myths die hard.

The strength of those stereotypes was shown in tests of college students in Utah and of rural men in North Carolina. Both groups were shown a nurturing father who hugged his child, rubbed his back, and sang to him, and a father who refused to do these things. They rated the first more feminine, less active, less potent, and less likely to succeed than the second.[3]

If individual men find it difficult if not impossible to change, the urgency of social catastrophe may accelerate behavior modification. A crisis – especially in an open society – can generate a new sense of responsibility, new breakthroughs and imaginative solutions, as we have seen in the case of AIDS. Men and women cannot solve their problems of power, responsibility, and relationship alone. We are, whether as individuals, couples, or nuclear families, dwarfed by the task. We cannot evolve new roles and new familial arrangements without support, without a caring and intervening community, and most certainly not without a social order and social policy that promotes these ends. The accelerating urgency of problems like child care, literacy, education, health care, domestic and social violence, homelessness, and drug traffic are overwhelming us.

But out of our failure and inadequacy, out of our desperation and impasse, comes the spark of hope. Honestly facing the abandonment and absence of caring social environment that is our real situation can create the energy for imaginative restructuring of the shape of our lives. Hurt is hope's home – if we truly acknowledge that we are hurt and broken.

In spite of its predisposition to self-creation, individualism and taking things by force, the American character has shown remarkable resources of fellow-feeling and cooperation in moments of crisis. From the Plymouth Plantation on, the ideal of the commonweal has been a tacit although often supressed myth in our culture. The growing sensitivity to human rights, hunger, and poverty in our own era suggests that the recognition of pain, brokenness, and social wounds may call forth some of our better qualities. One social analyst has remarked: "This expansion of consciousness to the pain of others is an American phenomenon as impressive as the phenomena of greed and fantasy-violence, and America cannot be understood if either trend is slighted. And the wave of fellow-feeling, though spoken of less, is the stronger of the two, the wave that will get to shore."[4]

Perhaps it is not altruism so much as a sense of shared fate that will finally free us from our fetish for individualism and release the indigenous pragmatism and cooperation that are also part of our national ate new myths. Rambo can be replaced by the lovers of Gaia; religious hustlers by the friends of a suffering God.

Feminists—women and men—are potters of the future, and they are slowly, patiently shaping new models on their wheel, many of which are flawed and have to be discarded. But some will provide the models for the future: new models for a world order;[5] new models for human development and learning;[6] new models for redistributing power and resources in organizations;[7] new models for cross-class and cross-cultural cooperation;[8] new models for reconstructing and revisioning religious traditions;[9] new models for the reconstruction of the social environment;[10] new models for conflict management, domestic and social peace.[11]

In the past we have drawn our models for society from the dominant culture. *Patriarchy* was the earliest: Aristotle, among others, advised us that the model for a perfect society could be found in the patriarchal family. Then, with the birth of democracy and individual conscience, we were mesmerized by a new model: *fraternity*, a concept that had its roots in male bonding and the equality of peers. Much that characterizes the North American culture was founded on this latter concept. But neither patriarchy nor fraternity provides an adequate model for the survival of the wounded, broken, and ravaged planetary people we are today. Male supremacy is not enough, male bonding is not enough—neither patriarchy nor fraternity is inclusive enough, intimate enough, cooperative enough, dialogic enough, mutual enough, supportive enough, nurturing enough to be a model for the future of the human community. Today a new model is emerging at the horizon of history, a model based on a relationship the world has never before taken seriously—sisterhood and sistering. The solidarity of women, the solidarity of the devalued, may be the hope of the future. Out of women's experience as outsiders, as the most impoverished of the poor, as the most excluded of the marginal comes an understanding of powerlessness and its only alternative, solidarity—a united effort to effect social change. Women's evolutionary inheritance is a familiarity and experience with the human skills of nurturing and participating in the development of others, of cooperation, of coresponsibility, and of negotiation in resolving conflict. Moreover, women have never been able to create change by force, so they have mastered other arts of instigating change.

The paradigm of women's interpersonal relations has always been intimate and familial; hence, women can imagine new models of bonded and inclusive relationships in the social order. Women can bring a sense of belonging, kinship, and connectedness to a world driven by abstract dogmatism and ideologies, permeated with self-interest. They can bring a sense of the organic and the spiritual to a social order too often governed by default, by the ethic of technology or expediency. What we are seeing is the emergence of something Michel Foucault described several years ago as the key to evolutionary development: "an insurrection of subjugated knowledges."

But lest we fall once again into the fallacy of femininity, we must recognize that there are many disturbing evidences of the fact that women have squandered their privileged relationship to Gaia. Some women have been co-opted by the male-modeled, acquisitive, competitive ethos of our culture: "whatever I want I must take by force." We don't have to look very far for examples: ruthless female entrepreneurs, insensitive corporate lawyers, or juvenile females in the schools, taunting their male peers to "flash the cash," goading their adolescent peers into the drug trade to find status and esteem in their eyes. How *do* we model and transmit the values of shalom-Gaia to the generations to come? This may be the most critical question of all.

Let us hope that in rearranging the basic dynamic of power in our social relations we can invent successful experiments in changing behavior. The media presents both the greatest threat and one of the most powerful instruments available for this social transformation. Nor can we emphasize too much the crucial role that the workplace can play in modeling human behavior.

We are the children of the Enlightenment: our world is circumscribed by our notions of ego, personal consciousness, and autonomy. This worldview is now being radically altered. A perception of our radical inseparability and connectedness is emerging as the next threshold of social evolution. Indeed, the depth of our interdependence with the whole earth-cosmic system is now becoming a much more primary reality than our own autonomy or survival or salvation.

We are, as a species, on the verge of becoming a transcultural person actively planning and compelled to plan our future. Breakdown, chaos, disorder and impasse will provide the feedback, stimulating the self-correcting process—but it will no longer be a totally unconscious process. We now have a chance to consciously invent and imagine our evolution. The consequences of not doing so will be far more cosmic and catastrophic. Our universe is neither random, nor finished, nor progressive—

it is groping. We are like a fetal organism, connected to and suspended in Gaia, waiting in darkness for the advent of a new birth.

So now you're back in Kansas. By comparison with Oz, it seems a bit drab, grey, and dull. Sometimes it's downright grim. But at least it is *real*. Oz, after all, was something people invented to fend off the real, to avoid seeing, feeling, and hurting. You are conscious of having left your three companions behind; it was a tearful good-bye, and it will be a permanent loss. (They will not reappear, reincarnated in three farmhands; life is not a Hollywood version!) What now? Everything is less than it should be, but now you have a better idea of why. You have a better idea of what has been missing in your self, in your work and living situation, in your relationships, in your nation, and in your world. At long last you are grieving your losses. At long last you are befriending your inner orphan.

Now that you've been there you can map the journey. You will need the map because the journey sometimes goes in circles. If you've been there before, you will probably find yourself there again – but with a difference: you will see the way ahead more clearly through the mist; you will recognize your own footprints leading back from Oz.

THE FIRST JOURNEY

The first journey begins with a kind of *exorcism*: the purging of the internal father, the one that not only monitors your sense of yourself and your relationships, but the one that nods approval when you measure up to societal, religious, or cultural expectations. The internal father is the master pedagogue who has set all the norms and instilled your reward and punishment reflexes.

Then move on to reconciliation with your *real* mother, not the ghost you imagined all these years but the real one, whose energy and power were buried beneath the cut-out costumes and parts she had to play in order to mother. This woman gave birth to you but may be still unborn herself, or she may mimic the internal father.

Recognize the father worship, father abuse, the absence of mothering, the still unuttered cry that lies buried deep in your suffocated heart. Acknowledge the waltzing steps, the push and pull of this dancing couple that you learned so well, and practiced over and over on everyone you have ever loved. Rerun the old movies of your sibling bonds. What was the part alloted to you? Are you still playing the role? Take the costumes out of the attic. Try them all on – in the light.

Mourn the lost child in your self. Grieve all your losses – this is the reservoir of your growth and creative potential.

Now you are ready for the *recovery of the authentic feminine*. The first place to look is the unconscious, that reservoir of images, desires, and experience that has been conveniently "deep-sixed" by our culture. Make it your companion. Seek out your shadow; it will be your guide. Whatever you have repressed of feminine energy has probably gone into hiding in your unconscious. You need to go deep into the cave and revalue all those things you tried to deny or ignore: your feelings, your weaknesses, your preferences, your passion, your fragility and vulnerability, your power and creativity, your anger and aggression, your intuition and imagination, your dreams and rainbows. Whatever you have devalued, whatever you have dwarfed has probably been "feminized" in your consciousness. It might even be yourself. You need to turn yourself inside out. Befriend what you find there.

Another place to look is your relationships with women. Have they been mannequins, bric-a-brac of your own illusions? Or have they been real women? Have you taken them seriously as friends, companions, sisters, lovers, mentors, mothers, doctors, presidents, coal miners, cops, bricklayers, truck drivers? Are there spaces in your life, overcrowded with things or business or causes, that women, children, outsiders – the carriers of the feminine – should fill? Who are your "lost sisters"? Find them and connect.

In our culture we learn early how to pamper and indulge the body, how to package our sexuality. But did anyone teach you how to love your body and befriend your sexuality? Your own earthliness may be the most neglected and repressed part of yourself because it has been identified with what is feminine, with what we have to be afraid of, ashamed of, in control of. You have probably used your body and your sexuality as a support system for the primary pursuits of your life. You have probably been so distracted by cultural noise that you have failed to listen to its wisdom. Listen for a change.

THE SECOND JOURNEY

The second journey begins with *leaving home*. But you have spent a good deal of your life trying to get home – to get to that point of security and comfort with your roles, commitments, and ambitions fulfilled, when you can at last have the luxury to sit back and enjoy yourself and life. You've had to work hard at keeping yourself in a position not to lose anything. In many ways, you're still on automatic pilot, running efficiently on the class biases, professional cloning, gender socialization, and self-fulfilling cliches that came with your original program and upbringing. Yet you often experience a lost feeling, as if the projects, systems, and institutions that you have poured yourself into did not after all give you that inner sense of being home, of living a life that has meaning.

To find home means leaving home. Leaving home means shedding your mollusk shell of defenses – the safety nets and status that you have secreted around yourself. It means getting to the space where your narcissism starves, your lifestyle withers down to the essential, where getting and spending are interrupted by risk and gift – above all the risk of community, of sharing yourself. Stand naked in nothing but your integrity and your passionate belief in something.

Leaving home means risking the encounter with the one who is not like you, "the other" – the one who is the face behind your mask. Begin by learning to listen to what you say about "them" – you will learn the truth about yourself that you have repressed. Look for the ones who have been invisible, the ones your blind spots or deafness has erased from your experience. Discover what it means to live in their reality. It could be someone next door; it could be someone half a world away.

Can you get up tomorrow and look at your lifestyle, your job, your role, your friends, your plans and goals with and through different eyes? Step outside of everything you've ever invested yourself in for awhile. Can you look at the corporation, the office, the school, the factory, the hospital, or the prison and see how different logic might transform it? When was the last time something or someone rearranged the furniture there or in your head?

Leaving home means engaging in the struggle to shape community in a fragmented society. It means finding something that lots of folks care about, or should care about, and forging a web of solidarity. It means finding a group of people who care about each other in a special way and putting up a tent (something "lightweight," movable, that stretches easily) where they can gather. It means a table fellowship that reaches around the world.

Leaving home means taking up the challenge of reimagining the separate self in a whole world, of stretching, transforming, creating social structures that promote human flourishing. It means overcoming our fear of survival in a changed world. Anthony Wilden puts it very starkly: "The fear of survival in a truly humanistic world – and thus the fear of radical change – has become a greater fear in our society than the fear of death itself."[12]

The second journey leads finally to the *reconnection with Gaia* and the *rediscovery of the feminine in God*. You have always thought of the earth, the cosmos as a kind of stage prepared for the achievements of humankind. It was easy to think such thoughts until that day when we first saw the earth from the astronaut's eye: "It is so small and so fragile.... [Y]ou can block it out with your thumb, and you realize that on that small spot, that little blue and white thing, is everything that means anything to you.... And you realize from that perspective that you've changed, that there's something new there, that the relationship is no longer what it was."[13]

What the poets and mystics always knew, the scientists discovered a few years ago: that humans are involved as partners in the planet's extraordinary production of life and atmosphere in a way that defies ordinary laws of chemistry and thermodynamics.[14] You who have known the planet partially, in a fragmented and dispersed way, now you are coming to *know* Gaia in the biblical, holistic sense. You are experiencing Gaia – the cosmic/earth system – as being totally alive, pulsating, and sensuous. Your inseparability from the Great Mother: so symbiotic that every breath you take or pour out, affects her, affects everything that is a part of her. The merging of object and subject in the divinization of matter takes place in Gaia.

Up to now you have accepted the notion of the fragmentation and separateness of matter, of a material universe atomized, a visible, apparent order of everything outside everything else – and if you believe that, you accept the necessity of violence, destruction and wars and little hope of humankind becoming one. But now you know that notion of reality is an abstraction. There is in fact an invisible, implicate order in which all is one. Gaia is the embodied visible aspect of that order, of Being itself. Gaia is God's Body, a self-conscious universe realizing itself to be whole and interconnected, in which knower and known are one.

This is unquestionably a feminine God. Her masculine predecessor ruled the consciousness with "Thou shalt" and "Thou shalt not." Gaia the Mother, the feminine face of God, "smiles as she utters the new word, 'You may.' We may indeed, but as we sow, we shall reap. In Gaia's unfathomable eyes we read the cautionary afterword, 'But be careful.'"[15] The patriarchal principle was either/or, a fiat. The Gaian principle is an invitation, with a warning about the oneness and the equipoise of all things: "Play with me. Discover me. Dance with me. But do not violate me."

Your belief in God, in Gaia, will require that you give up your need for a Cosmic Parent who keeps you forever a child. Orphans form extraordinary, empowering attachments to each other in the absence of all-knowing, all-powerful parents. The Gaia is more than your Mother – she is your Sister, and all living creatures are your kin, your siblings. This is the kinship of profound, transcendent mutuality, beyond dependency, more than fraternity. Once again women are leading us into the chrysalis of the future. They have explored the mystery, the grace and the power of sisterhood in our times. They have even learned how to become sisters to their mothers and grandmothers, to their daughters and granddaughters, sons and spouses – sisters to all living things, to all that has been and will be. It is a special relationship, unlike any that the world has ever taken seriously before.

Finally, your belief in God, in Gaia, will require affirmation of death, acceptance of pain, mortality, limits, vulnerability, forgiveness, change, and rebirth: the theology of the womb.

THE THIRD JOURNEY

There is a third journey that you must make, one that is not optional. Those of us who are middle-aged or younger do not know very much about this journey. The third journey is the journey into aging and death. This is the path to the final wisdom of your being through emptiness, powerlessness, loneliness, loss of identity and purpose, vulnerability and perhaps prolonged physical suffering or diminished human capacity. It is the twilight we all fear, but it is a way of profound light and intensified connection with the earth-womb from which we have come.

You have always believed that death, your death, would be a final expression of your orphan self, your separateness. The voices of our culture, even of the great spiritual traditions have spoken of the ultimate aloneness of death. But I am skeptical of this commonly accepted view. Death has struck so often, so close, so unexpectedly in my life that it has had a profound influence on who I am, how I am in the world and in time, how I am present to myself and to others. Death has been the uninvited companion of my life. In seeking to understand the mystery of death's intrusive presence and surprise in my life I have come to believe it will not be a private experience. What if death is not the ultimate solo but our initiation into the greatest communal adventure of all? What if in that transitory moment, our orphan self falls away, all the barriers of separation—of time and space, of flesh and spirit—are dissolved, and we are present to all the living and the dead at once in an epiphany of mutuality? Then we are home.

Our lives are intertwined and enveloped in these three journeys. If we are faithful to them, they are ongoing, overlapping, spiraling on through time—they are never finished until we are home.

Perhaps you have lived a good portion of your life as a scavenger, collecting scraps of power, roles, possessions, affection, self-worth, celebrity wherever you could and pasting them on yourself like fig leaves to hide your fear of meaninglessness, abandonment, your sense of being lost. Now you are ready to enter into a process of stripping and emptying because you understand that's what life is really about. Now you are ready for a real adventure.

The Christian mystics called it "the dark night" or "the way through the desert." Hindu philosophy describes it as a liberation to "the forest life." Buddhists seek out the path of "enlightenment" and "emptiness." The Jewish Kabbalah has a parallel to the "orphan self" in the concept of "galut" or "exile," and in the one who exists in "painful alienation," a fundamental reality of human existence. This tradition teaches that one of the causes of this alienation is the estrangement between God and the Shekinah, the feminine divine principle. Each of us helps to bring about a healing of creation when the masculine and feminine aspects of God are reunited and the female half of humanity is returned from exile.[16]

So you have been invited to design, build, and take passage on the next Ark, riding out the flood and the waves of chaos that threaten the entire Gaia system. You are ready to carry the seeds of a shalom covenant, a gift to the future.

My book is unfinished. Indeed, it seems a bit disheveled and disrupted in its form, very much a product of my orphan self. But it is a faithful record of a journey; it is a survivor. I have no doubt that you will return to it more than once to ponder its meaning for your life. So I fear not to abandon it here, knowing it will find many other spiritual orphans on its way.

Notes

DEDICATION

1. Susan Griffin, *Women and Nature, the Roaring Inside Her* (New York: Harper Colophon Books, 1980), 219.

THE CHILDREN OF MACHA

1. Adapted from Marie Louise Sjoestedt and Myles Dillon, trans., *Gods and Heroes of the Celts* (Berkeley, CA: Turtle Island Foundation, 1982), 37–51. See also Merlin Stone, *Ancient Mirrors of Womanhood*, vol. 1, (New York: New Sibylline Books, 1979), 1:53–57.

CHAPTER ONE: THE ABANDONED SELF

1. Robert Jay Lifton, *Boundaries: Psychological Man in Revolution* (New York: Random House, 1969), 37–63.
2. Nelle Morton, *The Journey Is Home* (Boston: Beacon Press, 1985), 210–15.
3. George Lakoff and Mark Johnson, *Metaphors We Live By* (Chicago: Univ. Chicago Press, 1980), 139–46.
4. Edward Edinger, *Ego and Archetype* (Baltimore: Penguin Books, 1974), 110.
5. Rose-Emily Rothenberg, "The Orphan Archetype," *Psychological Perspectives* 14 (Fall 1983): 181–94.
6. In his *Memories, Dreams, and Reflections*, Carl Jung tells of a mistake made in the dimensions of the cornerstone for his tower in Bollingen. The mason wanted to replace the misfit stone with another one but Jung insisted on keeping it. Jung had this inscription, translated from Latin alchemical texts, carved on the stone: "I am an orphan, alone; nevertheless I am found everywhere. I am one, but opposed to myself. I am youth and old man at one and the same time. I have known neither father or mother, because I have had to be fetched out of the deep like a fish, or fell like a white stone from heaven. In woods and mountains I roam, but I am hidden in the innermost soul of man. I am moral for everyone, yet I am not touched by the cycle of aeons."
7. Judith Viorst, *Necessary Losses* (New York: Simon & Schuster, 1986), 326.
8. Robert Kegan, *The Evolving Self* (Cambridge, MA: Harvard Univ. Press, 1982), 257.
9. Alice Miller, *The Drama of the Gifted Child* (originally published as *Prisoners of Childhood*), trans. Ruth Ward (New York: Basic Books, 1981), 11.
10. Rothenberg, "Orphan Archetype," 187.
11. Ibid.
12. Alice Koller, *An Unknown Woman* (New York: Bantam Books, 1981), 181.
13. Miller, *Gifted Child*, 63.
14. Andre Haynal, quoted in Paul Tournier, *Creative Suffering* (San Francisco: Harper & Row, 1982), 13.

15. Donald Dale Jackson, "It Took Trains to Put Street Kids on the Right Track," *Smithsonian Magazine*, August 1986, 94–103.
16. Tournier, *Creative Suffering*, 34.
17. Gail Sheehy, *Spirit of Survival* (New York: William Morrow & Co., 1986), 356.
18. Ibid., 361.
19. L. Frank Baum, *The Wizard of Oz*. Reprint, 1900. Originally published in 1900 as *The Wonderful Wizard of Oz* (New York: Holt, Rinehart & Winston, 1982), 2.
20. Carol Pearson and Katherine Pope, *The Female Hero* (New York: R. R. Bowker Co. 1981), 68–71. In her recent book, *The Hero Within* (San Francisco: Harper & Row, 1986), Carol Pearson describes the "orphan" archetype as an initiatory phase of human development marked by narcissism, anxiety, and denial. Although her description captures a partial aspect of developmental reality, my analysis of the archetype explores what is precious as well as worthless and transcendent as well as limiting in the power of the "orphan" archetype. It is not so much a phase that we pass through as a self that we decipher, reveal, redeem, and embrace.
21. Rosemary Haughton, "The Economics of the Dispossessed," *Religion and Intellectual Life* (Fall 1986): 23–33.
22. Fritz Kunkel, *Selected Writings*, ed. John Sanford (New York: Paulist Press, 1984), 267.

THE SNOW QUEEN

1. Condensed from Hans Christian Andersen, "The Snow Queen" in *Hans Andersen's Fairy Tales* (London: Children's Press, 1972) 71–102.
2. See Wolfgang Lederer, *The Kiss of the Snow Queen: Hans Christian Andersen and Man's Redemption by Woman* (Berkeley: Univ. of California Press, 1986). Lederer develops this theme at length.

CHAPTER TWO: A NATION OF ORPHANS

1. Henry Littlefield, "The Wizard of Oz: Parable on Populism," in *The Wizard of Oz*, ed. Michael P. Hearn (New York: Schocken Books, 1983), 221–33.
2. Th. P. Van Baaren, "The Flexibility of Myth," and Lauri Honko, "The Problem of Defining Myth," in *Sacred Narrative: Readings in the Theory of Myth*, ed. Alan Dundes (Berkeley and Los Angeles: Univ. of California Press, 1984), 217–24; 41–52. Culture has been described as a constellation of compelling metaphors. These metaphor-myths are the means by which knowledge and experience are transformed into power. Myth is the "supernatural charter on which a society is based." Myth is the source of the cyclic scenarios for action that create the history of a people. Finally, myth is a kind of shorthand for the process by which meaning and motivation are structured in our consciousness by a culture.
3. F. Scott Fitzgerald, *The Great Gatsby*. Reprint. 1925. (New York: Charles Scribner's Sons, 1953), 159.
4. Richard Slotkin, *Regeneration Through Violence: The Mythology of the American Frontier 1600–1860* (Middletown, CT: Wesleyan Univ. Press, 1973), 47.
5. Ibid., 18.
6. James Glass, *Delusion: Internal Dimensions of Political Life* (Chicago: Univ. of Chicago Press, 1985), 69.
7. Slotkin, *Regeneration*, 241, 269.
8. Timothy Flint, quoted in Henry Nash Smith, *Virgin Land: The American West as Symbol and Myth* (New York: Random House, 1950), 89.
9. Kenelm Burridge, *Someone, No One: An Essay on Individuality* (Princeton, NJ: Princeton Univ. Press, 1979), Quoted in L. Tiger, *The Manufacture of Evil*, p. 109.

10. Frederick Pike, "Latin America and the Inversion of U.S. Stereotypes in the 1920s and 1930s," *Americas (Md.)* 42 (October 1985): 131–62.
11. Ibid., 145–46.
12. David Bakan, *The Duality of Human Existence* (Chicago: Rand McNally & Co., 1966), 53–88.
13. David Shapiro, *Neurotic Styles* (New York: Basic Books, 1965), 86.
14. Glass, *Delusion*, 101.
15. Maurice Friedman, *The Confirmation of Otherness in Family, Community and Society* (New York: Pilgrim Press, 1983), 15.
16. Carter Heyward, *The Redemption of God: A Theology of Mutual Relation* (Washington, DC: Univ. Press of America, 1982), 154, 158.
17. Robert Bellah, Richard Madsen, William Sullivan, Ann Swidler, Steven Tipton, *Habits of the Heart: Individualism and Commitment in American Life* (Berkeley: Univ. of California Press, 1985), 75.
18. Ibid., 76.
19. Anne Wilson Schaef, *When Society Becomes an Addict* (San Francisco: Harper & Row, 1987).
20. Roland Delattre, "The Culture of Procurement: Reflections on Addiction and the Dynamics of American Culture," *Soundings* 69, (Spring/Summer 1986): 127–44.
21. Ibid., 128.
22. Frances Fitzgerald, cited in Delattre, 141.
23. Lionel Tiger, *The Manufacture of Evil: Ethics, Evolution and the Industrial Sytem* (New York: Harper & Row, 1987), 137.
24. Lee Iacocca, *Iacocca: An Autobiography* (New York: Bantam Books, 1986).
25. Ibid., 356.
26. Emma Lazarus, "The New Colossus," in *Emma Lazarus: Selections from Her Poetry and Prose*, ed. Morris U. Schappes, 3rd revised and enlarged edition. (Emma Lazarus Federation of Jewish Women's Clubs, 1967), 48.

THE FROG PRINCESS

1. See my discussion of "The Frog Prince" in *Kiss Sleeping Beauty Good-Bye*. 2d ed. (San Francisco: Harper & Row, 1988), 205–208.
2. "The Frog Princess," in *Russian Fairy Tales*, ed. Aleksandr Afanas'ev. Reprint, 1945 (New York: Random House, Pantheon Books, 1973), 119–23.

CHAPTER THREE: THE MYTH OF MAN-KIND

1. L. Frank Baum, *The Land of Oz*. Reprint, 1904 (New York: Ballantine Books, 1979).
2. Ibid., 257–59, 263.
3. Ibid., 159. It may be of some interest to note that Baum's mother-in-law was Matilda J. Gage, author of the radical feminist classic *Woman, Church and State*, and coeditor with Susan B. Anthony and Elizabeth Cady Stanton of *The History of Women's Suffrage*.
4. Osmond Beckwith, "The Oddness of Oz," in Hearn (ed.), *The Wizard*, 244.
5. Compiled from several sources, including: Sidney Jourard, *The Transparent Self*, rev. ed. (New York: D. Van Nostrand Co., 1971; Herb Goldberg, *The Hazards of Being Male* (New York: Signet Books, 1977); Joseph Pleck and Jack Sawyer, eds., *Men and Masculinity* (Englewood Cliffs, NJ: Prentice-Hall, 1974); Joseph Pleck and Robert Brannon, eds. Special issue on "Male Roles and Male Experience," *Journal of Social Issues* 34 (Winter, 1978); Michael Kaufman, ed., *Beyond Patriarchy: Essays by Men on Pleasure, Power and Change* (Toronto: Oxford Univ. Press, 1987); Joseph Pleck, *The Myth of Masculinity* (Cambridge, MA: MIT Press, 1981).

6. Jourard, *Transparent Self*, 35.

7. Lillian Rubin, *Intimate Strangers: Men and Women Together* (New York: Harper & Row, 1983), 140.

8. Nancy Chodorow, *The Reproduction of Mothering* (Berkeley: Univ. of California Press, 1978), 92-130.

9. L. J. Kaplan, quoted in Samuel Osherson, *Finding Our Fathers: The Unfinished Business of Manhood* (New York: Macmillan Free Press, 1986), 152-53.

10. Robert Stoller, M.D. *Presentations of Gender* (New Haven, CT: Yale Univ. Press, 1985), 183.

11. Dorothy Dinnerstein, *The Mermaid and the Minotaur: Sexual Arrangements and Human Malaise* (New York: Harper & Row, 1976), 186-87, 202.

12. Ibid., 205.

13. Charles Ferguson, *The Male Attitude* (Boston: Little, Brown & Co., 1966), 274, 278.

14. Robert May, *Sex and Fantasy: Patterns of Male and Female Development* (New York: W. W. Norton, 1980), 20-ff.

15. Klaus Theweleit, *Male Fantasies* (Minneapolis: Univ. of Minnesota Press, 1987). (Vol. 1.)

16. Demaris Wehr, "Religious and Social Dimensions of Jung's Concept of Archetype: A Feminist Perspective," in *Feminist Archetypal Theory*, ed. E. Lauter and C. Rupprecht (Knoxville, TN: Univ. of Tennessee Press, 1985), 33.

17. Ibid., 37.

18. Luce Irigaray, cited in Theweleit, 432.

19. Barbara Ehrenreich in Theweleit, *Male Fantasies*, xvi.

20. Ibid., 403.

21. See my reference to Jung and discussion of this phenomenon in my book, *Kiss Sleeping Beauty Good-Bye*, 2d ed. (San Francisco: Harper & Row, 1988), 201.

22. See M. Scott Peck, M.D., *People of the Lie, the Hope for Healing Human Evil* (New York: Simon and Schuster, 1983).

23. David Mantell, *Family and Aggression* (Frankfurt, 1972), quoted in Theweleit, 151.

24. Donald Morlan quoted in "The Battered Wife," *Joint Strategy and Action Committee Grapevine* (newsletter) (June 1977): 3.

25. Joseph Pleck, "Men's Power with Women, Other Men, and Society," in *The American Man*, ed. Elizabeth Pleck and Joseph Pleck (Englewood Cliffs, NJ: Prentice-Hall, 1980), 420-23.

26. Joseph Pleck, "Prisoners of Manliness," *Psychology Today*, September 1981, 77.

27. Ibid.

28. William Goode, cited in Anthony Astrachan, *How Men Feel* (Garden City, NY: Anchor Press/Doubleday, 1986), 150.

29. Ibid., 150.

30. Ibid.

31. Joseph Pleck, in Pleck & Pleck, *American Man*, 431.

32. Barbara Ehrenreich, *The Hearts of Men* (New York: Anchor Press/Doubleday, 1983), 121.

33. Astrachan, *How Men Feel*, 376-77.

34. Seymour Kleinberg, in *How Men Feel*, 376-377.

35. Ibid.

36. John Shelby Spong, *Into the Whirlwind: The Future of the Church* (Minneapolis: Seabury Press, 1983), 117.

37. Osherson, *Finding Our Fathers*, 196.

38. Phyllis Chesler, *About Men* (New York: Bantam Books, 1980), 23.

THE HUNTER MAIDEN

1. Condensed from "The Hunter Maiden," a Zuni tale from the North American Southwest, in *The Maid of the North*, ed. Ethel Johnston Phelps (New York: Holt, Rinehart and Winston, 1981), 79–84.

CHAPTER FOUR: WOMEN – OUT OF THE CAVE, INTO THE DESERT

1. L. Frank Baum, *Ozma of Oz*. Reprint, 1907 (New York: Ballantine Books, 1979).
2. See Jean Baker Miller, *Toward a New Psychology of Women*, 2d ed. (Boston: Beacon Press, 1986); Carol Gilligan, *In a Different Voice: Psychological Theory and Women's Development* (Cambridge, MA: Harvard Univ. Press, 1982). Also, M. Belenky, N. Goldberger, et al., *Women's Ways of Knowing: The Development of Self, Voice and Mind* (New York: Basic Books, 1986).
3. Louise Bernikow, *Alone in America: The Search for Companionship* (New York: Harper & Row, 1986), 60.
4. Shere Hite, *Women and Love: A Cultural Revolution in Progress* (New York: Alfred A. Knopf, 1987).
5. Bernikow, *Alone*, 81.
6. Morton, *Journey*, 153.
7. Luise Eichenbaum and Susie Orbach, *Understanding Women, A Feminist Psychoanalytic Approach* (New York: Basic Books, 1983), 96.
8. Cited in Sylvia Brinton Perera, "The Descent of Inanna: Myth and Therapy," in Lauter and Rupprecht, *Archetypal Theory*, 137–86.
9. Miriam Greenspan, *A New Approach to Women and Therapy* (New York: McGraw-Hill Book Co., 1983), 298.
10. Ibid., 294.
11. Judith Bardwick, "The Seasons of a Woman's Life," in *Women's Lives: New Theory, Research and Policy*, ed. Dorothy McGuigan (Ann Arbor, MI: Univ. of Michigan, 1980), 37.
12. Madonna Kolbenschlag, *Kiss Sleeping Beauty Good-Bye*. 2d ed. (San Francisco: Harper & Row, 1988).
13. Cited in Arthur Janov, *The Primal Scream* (New York: Dell Publishing Co., 1970), 171.
14. The work of the Wellesley College Center for Research on Women, Wellesley, MA has pioneered the exploration of new models of women's development. Among their outstanding working papers are Jean Baker Miller's "The Development of Women's Sense of Self," No. 84-01 and Janet Surrey's "The Relational Self in Women: Clinical Implications." No. 84-02 Wellesley, MA: Stone Center Working Papers Series, 1984.
15. Surrey, "Relational Self," 10.
16. Sara Maitland, "Two for the Price of One," in *Fathers, Reflections by Daughters* ed. Ursula Owen (New York: Pantheon Books, 1983), 26.
17. Ibid.
18. Greenspan, *Women and Therapy*, 311.
19. Toni Wolff, "Structural Forms of the Feminine Psyche" (Zurich: C. G. Jung Institute, 1956).
20. Charlene Spretnak, "Introduction," in *The Politics of Women's Spirituality*, ed. Charlene Spretnak (Garden City, NY: Anchor Press/Doubleday, 1982), xviii.
21. See Sylvia Brinton Perera's discussion of "The Descent of Inanna: Myth and Therapy" in Lauter and Rupprecht, *Archetypal Theory*, 137–86.
22. Sylvia Marcos, "Toward Permanent Rebellion," in *Speaking of Faith: Global Perspectives on Women, Religion and Social Change*, ed. Diana Eck and Devaki Jain (Philadelphia: New Society Publishers, 1987), 260–61.

A DREAM IN THE DESERT

1. From "Three Dreams in a Desert," in *A Track to the Water's Edge, The Olive Schreiner Reader*, 1st ed., ed. Howard Thurman (New York: Harper & Row, 1973).

CHAPTER FIVE: SYSTEMS AS FAILED PARENTS

1. Text by W. Sargant and E. Slater (1972), cited in *Women, Violence and Social Control*, ed. Jalna Hanmer and Mary Maynard (Atlantic Highlands, NJ: Humanities Press, 1987), 118.
2. Liz Kelly, "The Continuum of Sexual Violence," in Hanmer and Maynard, 50.
3. James Prescott, "Somatosensory Affectional Deprivation (SAD) Theory of Drug and Alcoholic Behaviors," in *Neuropharmacology: Clinical Applications*, eds. W. Essman and L. Valzelli (Jamaica, NY: Spectrum Publications, 1982), 19–39.
4. "Interview," in *Omni Magazine* March 1987, 81; and Alice Miller, *Thou Shalt Not Be Aware: Society's Betrayal of the Child*, trans. Hildegard and Hunter Hannum (New York: Farrar, Straus, Giroux, 1984), 220, 319.
5. Miller, *Gifted Child*, 103.
6. Batya Weinbaum, *Pictures of Patriarchy* (Boston: South End Press, 1983), 23–63.
7. See Kathy Ferguson, *The Feminist Case Against Bureaucracy* (Philadelphia: Temple Univ. Press, 1984); Michel Foucault, *Power/Knowledge: Selected Interviews and Other Writings* (New York: Pantheon Books, 1972); Alan Sheridan, *Foucault: The Will to Truth* (London: Tavistock Publishers, 1980).
8. Documented in Ann Crouter's "Participative Work as an Influence on Human Development" and "Corporate Self-Reliance and the Sustainable Society," unpublished studies, 1982. Since Crouter's research, additional studies have reinforced her thesis.
9. Gregory Bateson, cited in Morris Berman, *The Reenchantment of the World* (Ithaca, NY: Cornell Univ. Press, 1983), 243.
10. Harry Braverman, *Labor and Monopoly Capital* (New York: Monthly Review Press, 1975), 276.
11. George Gerbner, "Television: Modern Mythmaker," *Media and Values* (Summer/Fall 1987): 9.
12. Berman, *Reenchantment*, 243.
13. Lifton, *Boundaries*, 21–27.

THE LEGEND OF HIAWATHA

1. Condensed from "Hiawatha the Unifier," in *American Indian Myths and Legends*, ed. Richard Erdoes and Alfonso Ortiz (New York: Pantheon Books, 1984), 193–199.
2. Judith Brown, "Iroquois Women: An Ethnohistoric Note," in *Toward an Anthropology of Women*, ed. Rayna Reiter, (New York: Monthly Review Press, 1975), 235–51.

CHAPTER SIX: SPIRITUAL ORPHANS IN SEARCH OF A GOD

1. Sigmund Freud, *Civilization and Its Discontents*, trans. and ed. James Strachey (New York: W. W. Norton & Co., Inc. 1962), 38.
2. Hans Küng, "Religion: The Final Taboo?" (Address to the American Psychiatric Association, Washington, D.C., 12 May 1986).
3. Alice Walker, *The Color Purple* (New York: Harcourt Brace Jovanovich, 1982), 164–68.
4. Gerda Lerner, *The Creation of Patriarchy.* (New York: Oxford Univ. Press, 1986), 180–98.
5. Catherine Keller, *From a Broken Web, Separation, Sexism and Self* (Boston: Beacon Press, 1986), 38.

6. Ibid., 70–85.

7. Judith Van Herik, cited in Keller, 151.

8. Ann Belford Ulanov, *Picturing God* (Cambridge, MA: Cowley Publications, 1986), 171, 176.

9. Sam Keen, *Faces of the Enemy: The Psychology of Enmity* (San Francisco: Harper & Row, 1986), 172.

10. Virginia Ramey Mollenkott, *The Divine Feminine: The Biblical Imagery of God as Female* (New York: Crossroad, 1983), 57.

11. Susan Cady, Marian Ronan, and Hal Taussig, *Sophia: The Future of Feminist Spirituality* (San Francisco: Harper & Row, 1986), 10–15. Elisabeth Schüssler-Fiorenza, in her book *In Memory of Her* (New York: Crossroad, 1983), explores the "sophialogy" of the New Testament in respect to Jesus.

12. Erich Neumann, cited in Cady, Ronan, and Taussig, *Sophia*, 62.

13. Hans Küng, cited in Dave Toolan, "Religions of the One God," *Commonweal*, 13 March 1987, 146.

14. Arnold Toynbee, cited in Spong, *Whirlwind*, 188.

15. Fatna Sabbah, cited in Fatima Mernissi, "Femininity as Subversion: Reflections on the Muslim Concept of *Nushūz*" in *Speaking of Faith*, ed. D. Eck and D. Jain, 95–96.

16. Hazel Henderson, "The Warp and Weft: The Coming Synthesis of Eco-Philosophy and Eco-Feminism," in *Reclaim the Earth*, ed. L. Caldecott and S. Leland (London: Women's Press, 1983).

17. Jonas Salk, "Courage, Love, Forgiveness," *Parade Magazine*, 4 November 1984, 9–10.

18. Sallie McFague, *Models of God: Theology for an Ecological, Nuclear Age* (Philadelphia: Fortress Press, 1987).

19. Esther Broner, quoted in Letty Cottin Pogrebin, "Hers," *New York Times*, August 25, 1983, C-2.

20. Pierre Teilhard de Chardin, *The Heart of Matter* (New York: Harcourt Brace Jovanovich, 1978), 212.

21. McFague, *Models of God*, 77, 91–125.

22. Choan-Seng Song, *Third-Eye Theology: Theology in Formation in Asian Settings* (Maryknoll: Orbis Books, 1979), 60.

23. Etty Hillesum, *An Interrupted Life: The Diaries of Etty Hillesum 1941–43* (New York: Washington Square Press, 1985), 131.

24. Etty Hillesum, *Letters from Westerbrook* (New York: Pantheon Books, 1986), 116.

25. Hillesum, *Interrupted Life*, 162.

26. Hillesum, *Interrupted Life*, 181.

27. Dietrich Bonhoeffer, cited in C. S. Song, *The Compassionate God* (Maryknoll, NY: Orbis Books, 1982), 9.

28. Horst Eberhard Richter, *All Mighty: A Study of the God Complex in Western Man*, trans. Jan van Haurck (Claremont, CA: Hunter House, 1984), xvii.

29. Ibid., 98.

30. Ibid., 180.

PULACCHAN AND PACHA MAMA

1. Adapted from the oral legends of Peru by Isaias Grandes Huaman, published in *Latinamerica Press*, May 8, 1986.

CHAPTER SEVEN: LEAVING HOME

1. Raja Shehadeh, *The Third Way, A Journal of Life in the West Bank* (London: Quartet Books, 1982).

2. Ibid., 86–87.

3. Ibid., 87.

4. Ibid., 125–25.

5. Ibid., 138.

6. Richard J. Foster, *The Freedom of Simplicity*, (San Francisco: Harper & Row, 1981), 31. See also Walter Brueggeman, *Living Toward a Vision: Biblical Reflections on Shalom*, (Philadelphia: United Church Press, 1982).

7. Lewis Hyde, *The Gift: Imagination and the Erotic Life of Property*, (New York: Random House Vintage Books, 1983 [1979]), 11.

8. Morris Berman, *The Reenchantment of the World*, 213–15.

9. Erich Jantsch, *The Self-Organizing Universe*, (New York: Pergamon Press, 1980), 266–67.

10. For a discussion of "First and Second-Order Change" theory, see Belden C. Lane, "Spirituality and Political Commitment: Notes on a Liberation Theology of Nonviolence," *America*, March 14, 1981.

   W. Edwards Deming, a man who has been called an unconscious feminist, has been preaching a gospel of evolutionary thinking in business for many years. His best converts, however, seem to be Japanese rather than American businessmen. See video productions, *The New Economic Age, vol.I, Management's New Job, vol.II,* and *Corporate Leadership, vol.III.* Produced by Clare Crawford Mason, available from Films Inc., Chicago, Ill.

11. Ilya Prigogine, *From Being to Becoming.* (San Francisco: W. H. Freeman Co., 1980).

12. Jean Houston, "On Therapeia," interview in *Dromenon*, 3(3): 37–41.

GAIA'S TALE

1. This tale was written one night while I was listening to Paul Winter's *Missa Gaia*. The hour was late, the conscious brain relaxing its hold on reality; the door to the unconscious opened a crack and the tale poured out as in a dream. Pondering it some days later, I wondered where the Swan and the Raven had come from. I remembered a wonderful story from the Green Fairy Book, "The Magic Swan," and the many other swans that appear in fairy tales. In Jungian analysis dreams about swans often represent the anima or the unconscious. But the Raven? That mystified me until I recently ran across a comment by Jung linking the Raven to the shadow or the encounter with the shadow self. And then I remembered how often the Raven appears as a guide or catalytic presence in Northwest Indian mythology.

CONCLUSION: GETTING BACK TO KANSAS

1. "A Woman's Covenant" was created by Averil McClelland, Sally Tatnall, Sandra Parker, Phyllis Balcerzak, Patrice McCarthy, Theresa Conroy, Linda DeYoung, Kierste Carlson, and Mary Christensen at Woman's Way Retreat, Villa Maria, PA, 16–21 July 1987.

2. Margaret Brennan faults Thomas Berry for overlooking the relevance of the feminist critique of patriarchy and normative male standards in his vision of the cosmic economy. See her essay, "Patriarchy: The Root of Alienation from the Earth?" in *Thomas Berry and the New Cosmology*, ed. Anne Lonergan and Caroline Richards (Mystic, CT: Twenty-Third Publications, 1987), 57–63.

3. Astrachan, *How Men Feel*, 231–32.

4. Henry Mitchell, "Reflections on the American Crosscurrents," *Washington Post*, 19 February, 1988.

5. For example, see Hazel Henderson, *Politics of the Solar Age* (Garden City: Anchor Press/Doubleday, 1981) and *Creating Alternative Futures* (New York: Perigee, G. P. Putnam's Sons 1980). Henderson also has numerous pertinent essays and lectures, including "The Warp and Weft: The Coming Synthesis of Eco-Philosophy and Eco-Feminism," in *Reclaim the Earth*, ed. L. Caldecott and S. Leland (London: Women's Press, 1983).

6. For example, see Jean Baker Miller, *Toward a New Psychology of Women* and Carol Gilligan, *In a Different Voice* (cited above); Mary Belenky, Blythe M. Clinchy, Nancy Goldberger, Jill M. Tarule, *Women's Ways of Knowing* (New York: Basic Books, 1986).

7. For example, see the work that many feminists have done on consensus (Caroline Estes, "Consensus," *In Context*, special issue on "Governance: Power, Process & New Options," Autumn, 1984, 19–22); on feminist process in organizations (Charlene E. Wheeler and Peggy Chinn's *Peace and Power Handbook* [Buffalo, NY: Margaretdaughters, Inc., 1984]); on women's and workers' cooperatives (Carol Coston); on grass roots political reconstruction (Nancy Sylvester and NETWORK).

8. For example, see Charlotte Bunch, Nancy Hartsock, and others in *Building Feminist Theory* (New York: Longman's, 1981). Bunch has written and lectured widely on international feminism and strategies for change. See her recent book, *Passionate Politics*, (St. Martin's Press, 1987.)

9. For example, see Elisabeth Schüssler Fiorenza, *In Memory of Her*, and Sallie McFague, *Models of God* (citied above). See also Rosemary Ruether, *Women-Church* (San Francisco: Harper & Row, 1985), as well as her many other works.

10. For example, see Joanna Macy, *Dharma and Development* (Kumarian Press, 1984), which describes the principles of the Sarvodaya movement.

11. For example, consider the Benedictine Sisters and Pax Christi; numerous organizations like the Women's Institute for Freedom and Peace; others like Marie Fortune's Center for the Prevention of Sexual and Domestic Violence in Seattle, WA.

12. Anthony Wilden, *System and Structure: Essays in Communication and Exchange* (London: Tavistock Publications, 1972), 349.

13. Russell Schweickart, astronaut, in "Earth's Answer, Exploration of Planetary Culture at the Lindesfarne Conferences," Harper & Row.

14. James Lovelock, *Gaia: A New Look at Life on Earth* (Oxford and New York: Oxford Univ. Press, 1987), *The Ages of Gaia* (New York: Norton, 1988).

15. Edward Whitmont, *Return of the Goddess* (New York: Crossroad, 1982), 97.

16. Rita Gross, "Female God Language in a Jewish Context," in *Womanspirit Rising*, ed. Carol Christ and Judith Plaskow (New York: Harper & Row, 1979), 167.

Index

God, 13, 15, 127–49; and authentic identity, 128; the Body of, 144, 145; in Bonhoeffer, 147; in de Chardin, 144; experience of, and orphanhood, 146–47; the feminine in, 185, 186, 188; in Freud, 129, 135; in Hillesum, 146–47; in Keller, 134; Mother, return to, 136–37; omnipotence of, 130–31, 144; powerlessness of, 147; in Richter, 147–48; and the spiritual journey, 144; suffering of, 146, 147; in Ulanov, 135; and the universe, 145
Goddesses, 46, 63, 92, 93, 133
Goddess, the, 95, 137
Goldberg, Herb, 56
Goode, William, 68
Grail, search for the, 5, 155
Great Mother, the, 136–39, 141–42, 148–49
Greenspan, Miriam, 85
Guilt, 12, 82, 85, 86, 87; in children, 109; and the internal Father, 91
Gunkel, Herman B., 29

Hanna, Mark, 30
"Hansel and Gretel," story of, 17–18
Haynal, Andre, 14
Hemingway, Ernest, 53
Henderson, Hazel, 142
Henry, Patrick, 112
Herik, Judith Van, 135
Hero, the, 23, 35, 36–39, 115–16; as an ego archetype, 5; as a model for behavior, 7; in the New World, self of, 35; as an orphan, 5–6; on television, 70; Western, 6, 56
Heterosexuality, 67, 109
Heyward, Carter, 41
Hiawatha, the legend of, 123–26
Hillesum, Etty, 146–47
Hitler, Adolf, 8–9
Holding environments, 11, 23, 46
Holocaust, the, 7, 146
Holonomy, 118–19, 139
Homeostasis, 118–19
Homosexuality, 53, 67, 71–72
Houston, Jean, 172
Hugo, Victor, 9
"Hunter Maiden, The," 75–77

Iacocca, Lee, 5, 44, 45, 46
Identity, 6, 120, 128; female, 20, 53, 57,

78–97; male, 53–74, 134, 179–80; and the mother-child bond, 11, 84. See also Self, the; Self-creation, myth of; Selfhood
Imagination, and transformation, 179, 180
Immortality, 122
Incest, 106
Indians, Native American, 34–35, 36, 37, 40
Individualism, 6, 7, 38, 82, 117, 180–81
Individuation, 10, 16, 62
Innocence, 80, 81; assumed, of parents, 109
Intimacy, 11, 50, 57, 85
Iran arms scandal, 3, 31, 44, 116
Irigaray, Luce, 61

Jantsch, Erich, 169–70
Jesus Christ. See Christ
Jourard, Sidney, 56
Journey: into the cave. See Cave, symbolism of the; the first, second, and third, 183–88; of leaving home, 155–72, 184–85; spiritual, and God, 144
Jubilee, 166, 167
Jung, C. G., 27, 61, 63, 92, 135

Kaplan, L. J., 58
Keen, Sam, 136
Keller, Catherine, 134, 135
Kleinberg, Seymour, 71
Knowledge, 167, 168
Ku Klux Klan, 112
Küng, Hans, 130, 141

Land of Oz, The (Baum), 51–53. See also Oz, myth of
Langer, Susanne, 8
Lasch, Christopher, 38
Lazarus, Emma, 46–47
Leadership, 56, 170
Lerner, Gerda, 133
Lifton, Robert Jay, 6, 7, 122
Limits, acceptance of, 119
Littlefield, Henry, 30
Logos, 139
Loneliness, 9, 43, 82–85
Losses, grieving of, 11, 154
Love, 11, 15; ability to, 56; a definition of, 50; and the internal Father, 91; need for, 89

Virgin Mary, 63, 140
Virgin, stereotype of the, 93
Vulnerability, 54, 74, 86, 111, 119

Walker, Alice, 132
Wall Street, 43, 44, 103
Wehr, Demaris, 61
White, William Allen, 30
Wholeness, 95, 155, 163
Winfrey, Oprah, 80–81
Wizard of Oz, The (Baum), 127–28; the
  character of Dorothy in, 18–20, 29,
  30–31, 51; the image of the cyclone in,
  155; political analogies in, 30–31, 103,
  104. *See also* Oz, myth of

Wolfe, Tom, 38
Wolff, Toni, 92
Women, 53, 62–63; and orphanhood,
  81, 85–88, 90, 177; as other, 93, 112;
  and the possession of power, 65, 67;
  and public policy, 86; socialization
  of, 86; theologians, 140. *See also*
  Female; Femaleness; Feminine, the;
  Femininity
Women's spirituality, 140, 142–43,
  178–79
Workplace, the, as a primary system,
  106, 111–17, 182

Yahweh, 139, 166

ABOUT THE AUTHOR

Madonna Kolbenschlag was born in Cleveland, Ohio, and lives in Morgantown, W. V. She studied for her doctorate at the University of Notre Dame, South Bend, Indiana. Later she was a professor of American Studies and Women's Studies at Notre Dame and lectured at Loyola University of Chicago. She is a member of a Catholic community of religious women, the Sisters of the Humility of Mary of Villa Maria, Pa.

From 1980 to 1985 she held a position as legislative aide and research analyst in the U.S. House of Representatives. From 1983 to 1987 she was a senior fellow at the Woodstock Theological Center, a Jesuit-sponsored research institute at Georgetown University, Washington, D.C.

Dr. Kolbenschlag has gained a national and international reputation as a writer and lecturer on women's development and spirituality, and on public policy and religious affairs. She was a 1988 visiting ecumenical fellow at the Washington Cathedral and is a member of the board of directors of the Churches Center for Theology and Public Policy.

Dr. Kolbenschlag is the author of five books and is currently pursuing further studies and research in the field of clinical psychology.